PLAYBACK:

a marriage in jeopardy

compiled by

DAVID FANSHEL

with the collaboration of

FREDA MOSS

Columbia University Press 1971

NEW YORK AND LONDON

David Fanshel is Professor of Social Work, Columbia University School of Social Work. Freda Moss is a therapist at the Park East Counseling Group in New York City.

Copyright © 1971 Columbia University Press
Library of Congress Catalog Card Number: 72-170925
Cloth-bound Edition ISBN: 0-231-03573-X
Paper-bound Edition ISBN: 0-231-03574-8
Printed in the United States of America

Playback: a marriage
in jeopardy

This book is dedicated to

Mrs. Arthur Lehman

whose gentleness,
and warmth, whose wish
to ameliorate the lot
of troubled people
is hopefully reflected
in this volume

SOCIAL WORK with its origins in assistance to the disadvantaged has as yet to be accepted as a profession whose knowledge and skills can be of value to persons in all walks of life. In fact, social work is often regarded as "the poor man's psychiatry." The implication is that if a person in need of help with matters of personal adjustment can afford the cost, he will elect help from psychiatry or psychology rather than from social work. Even some social workers believe this. However, most are agreed that each of these professions, by virtue of its origin and history, brings attributes to the therapeutic treatment of individuals and families that the other professions so engaged do not. They are believed to account for their greater effectiveness and appropriateness in certain situations. The problem, however, is that to date no great agreement exists within or among these professions as to their characteristics and attributes.

Social workers have tried to identify what components of knowledge and skill they have been able to distill from their training and their experience in social agencies. Some believe it is a greater willingness and experience in dealing with problems of the social environment as they interact with intrapsychic difficulties, thus providing a broader basis for diagnostic appraisal and of the type of help offered. However, before one can clearly identify these differences, much research is required.

By virtue of its goals and associated staffing patterns, the Arthur Lehman Counseling Service provided an excellent place in which the treatment offered under social work auspices could be studied. The agency was established in 1954 as a specialized service organization unlike other social agencies in that it was designed to reach and serve an economically advantaged group. It was to serve as a pilot program in the field of social work and as such to encourage social agencies to extend their services to all persons in their communities, regardless of their economic status, as well as color, race, and creed. The hope behind this objective was to assist in shifting the public's image of social work as a resource for and champion of the underprivileged only, to that of social work as a profession obligated to serve advantaged and underprivileged alike as are all professions. With such a shift, the founders of the agency believed that the quality of service for all clients would be improved.

To assure that the results of the pilot program would be sound, the Arthur Lehman Counseling Service selected only experienced practitioners whose competence in casework therapy had been established and recognized. Thus the agency offered as a milieu for the study of social casework in its therapeutic role a setting where experienced practitioners offered help to a noncaptive clientele, that is, to a group who could by-pass the help of social agencies and buy their services from any resource or profession they desired.

For some time I searched for a researcher interested in the study of treatment. Thus when Dr. Fanshel commented in passing one day of his own wish to study what went into treatment, I rejoiced in our good fortune and he suddenly found himself with an opportunity. This was first made possible through a grant from the Adele and Arthur Lehman Foundation. Their seed money made it possible for Dr. Fanshel to undertake the task of preparing a project proposal to the National Institute of Mental Health designed to study the working styles of experienced caseworkers. A grant was received for this purpose. In addition, funds were made available by the John L. Loeb Foundation to cover costs that had not been anticipated and therefore were not included in the original requests.

This book and the companion volume and tapes are only one part of a larger research enterprise. They reflect the work of one skilled practitioner, illuminating what she believes entered into her therapeutic work with one family and her retrospective evaluation of her own treatment decisions. Other publications will follow and will deal with findings based on the work of several experienced caseworkers.

In presenting this volume and the companion materials, it

is our hope that they will offer both content and stimulus useful for training of persons entering into the various fields of psychotherapy. If this aspiration is fulfilled, we will all then be indebted to the Adele and Arthur Lehman and the John L. Loeb foundations, representing families who have long believed in the social work profession and its potential role in enhancing the human condition. They have given stalwart support to the profession's search for greater knowledge, skill, and effectiveness. We will also be indebted to the National Institute of Mental Health for its generous financial support and for its continued encouragement of a searching examination of professional practice. As Dr. Fanshel indicates in his preface, I am also most mindful of the contributions of Freda Moss for her willingness to expose her own practice and her own evaluation to the study of others and, most of all, Mr. and Mrs. Porter. With full understanding of the difficulty of guaranteeing anonymity to them despite our serious efforts in this direction, this couple has been able to rise above personal concern and anxiety to make available for future students an opportunity to study closely the problems of a troubled marriage and the treatment it involved.

Ruth Fizdale
Executive Director
Arthur Lehman Counseling Service

New York, New York
January 12, 1971

WITH THE AID of a research grant from the National Institute of Mental Health (R01 MH 14980–04), four case-worker-therapists employed at the Arthur Lehman Counseling Service in New York City agreed to cooperate in an investigation of the working styles of advanced casework practitioners. The research began in 1965 with the identification by the therapists of patients from whom consent could be secured to have their therapy sessions tape recorded for research purposes. In this research investigation, I collaborated with Dr. Herbert Aptekar, then Professor of Social Welfare at Brandeis University and now Dean of the School of Social Work at the University of Hawaii. We developed a procedure we called the *playback*. At a two-hour weekly conference, a therapist and Dr. Aptekar or I listened to the latest recorded clinical session of a patient of that therapist. The arrangement permitted the researcher to inquire about events happening during the session and provided the therapist an opportunity to volunteer his own appraisal of the phenomena being revealed on tape. A stereo recording was created at the playback session containing the original clinical transactions and the interchange between researcher and therapist. This created a permanent record of each playback session. Eight cases were monitored in the three-year period in which this review procedure was carried out. Close to 300 treatment sessions were thus recorded and analyzed.

This volume represents a spin-off from the original research conception, much more modest in scope and yet representing a potentially important innovation for teaching and scholarship in clinical work, whether it be social casework or therapeutic work carried out by psychologists or psychiatrists. We present case material from the experience of one married couple whose treatment extended over a two-year period and where some 50 playback sessions were conducted. The decision to publish six of these sessions stemmed from my conviction that the teaching of practice would be considerably enhanced and scholarly work encouraged if the student and scholar had access to live material in which the real-life drama of psychotherapy was made available and where the interchange between the therapist and the researcher in the playback sessions could be utilized to identify the choice facing the practitioner in the conduct of therapy. The decision to venture into this realm of teaching materials was finalized by my experience in finding that I had become deeply absorbed in two aspects of the research: the human problems faced by the patients and the extraordinarily demanding tasks faced by the therapist. Over time, I found myself particularly struck with the sense that the phenomenological reality of the therapy sessions took on a kind of theater experience for me. It was as if the transactions taking place had been created by a gifted playwright. Surprised by my own personal reaction, I began to test out the experiences of students in some of my classes with disguised typescripts and found a very similar response on their part. Their enthusiasm was explained by the fact that a good deal of the teaching of casework has depended upon summarized narratives which tend to be devoid of many of the elements that constitute the drama of the real encounter.

This publication coincides with the release of the six tapes upon which this volume of typescripts is based, as well as a volume containing the typescripts supplemented by the comments and interpretations of therapist Freda Moss on what took place in each session and my own commentary on significant features of the transactions. We have represented here the unusual circumstance wherein the married couple who are the object of scrutiny of this volume gave permission for the release of the tapes of their therapy sessions for educational purposes to appear concurrently with the printed transcriptions. Aside from the deletion of identifying information (i.e., the names of persons, places, and organizations which would identify the couple or their associates), the tapes are exact replicas of the originals. Thus the reader and/or listener has access to the original therapy sessions as recorded

on a tape as a basis for reflecting upon the nature of therapeutic work as revealed in the conjoint treatment of this
marital pair.

Teachers who wish to employ these materials in their classes
will find that the availability of the therapeutic transactions in
three forms affords a versatility in teaching strategies. One
approach would call for the students to read the clinical
transactions in the version presented here prior to hearing the
tapes in the classroom. The review of the raw clinical material
affords the student an opportunity to develop a critical
orientation to the interventions of the therapist prior to being
exposed to her own self-criticisms in the course of the playbacks. Thus, either in the classroom situation or subsequently,
the student can compare his or her own reactions with those
expressed by Freda Moss in the companion volume. In this
way, an inquiring posture can be developed toward the clinical enterprise as reflected in Freda Moss's work.

The publication of this volume and the materials described
above required the cooperation of a number of important
people. I feel a very special debt to Ruth Fizdale, who encouraged and supported my efforts at the Arthur Lehman
Counseling Service. As the agency's executive director, she
facilitated the research because of her strong commitment to
scholarship. My many talks with her helped me to clarify
my goals in working with these materials. I am indebted also
to the therapists who, like Freda Moss, exposed their practice
to me in playback sessions. Alice Fine, Milan Stoeger, and
Ruth Baker broadened my perspective and deepened my
understanding of the complexity of clinical work. Exposure to
their self-critiques of their own work was invaluable in my
own growth. I look forward to further development in the
future of the materials we jointly produced.

I am deeply indebted to Dr. Herbert Aptekar, with whom
I collaborated in the larger research enterprise. A sensitive
and thoughtful critic, his observations on the nature of advanced casework practice will hopefully yet be displayed in
the continued mining of the vast materials that we have
jointly collected.

Obviously, the most important debt I and the reader share

is to the couple, "Jack and Sally Porter," who generously and courageously gave up their right to total privacy about the trying experiences revealed in their treatment sessions. To share their experiences with students and scholars who seek to develop increased effectiveness in the treatment of troubled marriages must command respect and deep admiration.

The help of Ann Gerlock in typing the many drafts of this manuscript was invaluable. Her splendid skills and high order of intelligence enormously reduced the burdens I faced in the production of this volume. I am very thankful to her.

Nina Kimche created several rough drafts of typescripts and this proved very helpful. I also wish to thank Barbara Frank who, as secretary at the Arthur Lehman Counseling Service, provided gracious assistance on many occasions.

Sumner Glimcher and Edward Cosgrove of the Center for Mass Communication of Columbia University Press early recognized the value of the tapes and their potential use in the education of clinicians. Their experience in film and radio work brought a perspective to the development of this enterprise which was of a high professional order. I also wish to acknowledge with thanks the professional editing assistance of John D. Moore, Associate Executive Editor of Columbia University Press.

I wish to acknowledge the help of Dr. Lotte Marcus of McGill University in formulating the questions posed at the end of each session in this volume.

Last but not least, comment is in order about the relationship between myself and Freda Moss, whose work is fully displayed in tape and printed word. I know of no other social worker whose professional practice has been made so openly available for scrutiny by peers. This was an act of great courage on her part as well as a reflection of her strong sense of professional responsibility for contributing to the development of a better knowledge base for clinical practice. I should make clear that the choice of the particular sessions to be displayed in the volumes and through tape recordings was my own. There were many sessions to choose from and I selected those that appeared to offer the most promising possibilities for enhancing our perspectives about the nature of treatment. Aside from this, however, it will be amply clear to anyone who inspects these materials that Freda Moss's role has been paramount in this entire endeavor. It is her work that is on display.

David Fanshel

New York, New York
January 6, 1971

Contents

Playback: a marriage in jeopardy

Introduction: Orientation
and scope

MARITAL DISORDER is widespread in the United States. At the time of the 1960 census, over two million people were reported as separated and over three million were divorced.[1] These are dismaying figures. The consequences for the children of such ruptured marriages may be even more ruinous than for the adults. Yet the legally separated or divorced may be exceeded in number by partners of marriages where the family unit is ostensibly intact but where daily bickering and antagonism erode the basic structure of family life.

Efforts to treat marital disorders achieve plentiful justification when one considers the prevalence of the condition and its potential consequence for society in the aggravation of other problems, for example, mental illness, alcoholism, juvenile delinquency, school failure, and so forth. Yet the treatment of marital disorder is neither well understood nor firmly supported in the United States. There is suspicion as to the purpose of such treatment and considerable skepticism about the efficacy of current methods.[2]

There is confusion about the sources of help for marital disorders because of the various professionals engaged in its treatment: psychiatrists, social workers, psychologists, and ministers. Even laymen are not precluded from giving advice on a myriad of family problems in newspaper columns and on radio and television.

For those involved in the direct treatment of marital disorders, there are many possible sources of knowledge and treatment. Traditional Freudian psychoanalytic concepts, the more modern ego psychology, and the recently revived interest

[1] Hugh Carter and Paul C. Glick, *Marriage and Divorce: A Social and Economic Study* (Cambridge, Harvard University Press, 1970) p. 222.
[2] See article by Earl Ubell, Science Editor of the New York *Herald Tribune* reviewing *Girls at Vocational High*, by Henry J. Meyer, Edgar F. Borgatta, and Wyatt Jones (New York, Russell Sage Foundation, 1965) in the New York *Herald Tribune*, February 28, 1965.

in behavioral modification are but some of the intellectual centers from which those engaged in treating disturbed marriages derive their basic approaches and formulate their diagnostic and treatment procedures.

Most professionals treating marital disorders, be they social workers, psychologists, or psychiatrists, have experience in clinical practice with individuals. While in recent years the treatment of families in groups has become common and increased daring is displayed in the procedures employed, the underlying clinical orientations of the treating persons can still be identified in their work.

This volume is concerned with one form of marital treatment—the conjoint psychotherapeutic treatment of a man and wife by a social worker. By displaying what actually transpired in six treatment sessions we hope to aid graduate schools of social work and departments of psychiatry and of psychology in the training of those who will engage in direct clinical practice. A secondary aim is to make the raw material of the treatment experience available to a variety of researchers, for example, scholars evaluating the effectiveness of psychotherapy, investigators of the modern family, and students of communication processes in small groups.

The material made available here is unusual if not unique. Six full sessions of the treatment of a couple pseudonymously called "Jack and Sally Porter" are displayed in transcriptions of tape recordings. The recording of each session was replayed. In the presence of a researcher-interviewer (David Fanshel), the therapist (Freda Moss) then commented upon many aspects of the transactions taking place. The playback, with comment, was also recorded and is available in a companion publication.[3] We believe this is the maximum presentation of treatment of a case thus far made available in the published literature of psychology, social work, and psychiatry.[4]

---

[3] In a companion volume, *Playback: A Marriage in Jeopardy Examined,* transcriptions of the session are presented interspersed with dialogue between the researcher and therapist which took place when they listened back to the sessions. The tape recordings of the sessions, *Playback: A Marriage in Jeopardy,* are available through the Center for Mass Communication of Columbia University Press.

[4] Among publications directly displaying practice are: Merton Gill, Richard Newman, and Frederick C. Redlich, *The Initial Interview in*

Teaching possibilities in the material are enhanced by the concurrent availability of the full tape recordings of the six sessions.[5] Only identifying names of persons, places, and organizations have been deleted and there has been slight modification of the sound to remove intrusive noises. The set of tapes and the two books combined represents a contribution to the literature that: 1) gives the full verbal picture of marital treatment as captured by a tape recorder and rendered in typescripts, the full details of *what* was said; 2) provides the original tape recordings so that one can hear *how* statements were said; 3) gives the therapist's interpretation of what was going on in the sessions; and 4) provides six full sessions scattered over a twenty-month period, thus providing a quite broad display of the treatment process.

STUDY OF ADVANCED PRACTICE

The tapes come out of a larger research enterprise supported by the National Institute of Mental Health. The research explores the cognitive processes and working styles of advanced caseworkers through the device of the playback procedure, that is, by offering the therapist the opportunity to reflect upon his treatment performance as he hears it taking place. The research involved monitoring eight treatment cases known to four staff members with an average of about twenty years of clinical experience. Some cases involved individuals while others included couples in conjoint therapy.[6] The playback sessions involved two researcher-interviewers, Dr. Herbert Aptekar and myself; we participated in an average of three playback sessions on alternate weeks over a three-year period. An unusual feature of the research was that the

Psychiatric Practice (New York, International Universities Press, 1954); Robert E. Pittenger, Charles F. Hockett, and John J. Danehy, *The First Five Minutes* (Ithaca, Martineau, 1960); Louis A. Gottschalk, ed., *Comparative Linguistic Analysis of Two Psychotherapeutic Interviews* (New York, International Universities Press, 1961); and Jay Haley and Lynn Hoffman, *Techniques of Family Therapy* (New York, Basic Books, 1967).
[5] The tape recordings that constitute the companion material to this volume may be purchased from the Center for Mass Communication, Columbia University Press, New York.
[6] At the time the eight cases were selected for inclusion in the research, there were close to 350 cases in active treatment at the Arthur Lehman Counseling Service.

therapists were paid for time spent in the playbacks on the same basis as if they were conducting clinical sessions.

The Porter case, the focus of this volume, is one of the eight cases included in the larger study.

BACKGROUND

The training of clinicians—whether social caseworkers, psychologists, or psychiatrists—has, in the past, heavily relied upon the use of narrative case records as the basic source material for illuminating issues of diagnosis and treatment. Even now, despite the widespread availability of audio and video recorders, narrative case accounts are the major vehicle for teaching clinical material. For example, in many schools of social work in the United States, this represents the almost exclusive source material for displaying practice. While use of tape recordings, video tapes, films, and public interviewing of clients and patients is not uncommon, the heavy reliance for ongoing exemplars of practice is still upon the summarized, narrative accounts provided by clinicians who have, from memory, written up their encounters with patients. This is a practice which was heavily emphasized over the years by Freud and the leading writers in the psychoanalytic and other clinical traditions.

Obviously narrative case accounts have been and continue to be extremely useful in the development of a frame of reference for many issues of clinical practice. Through written narration, the clinician can focus upon the phenomena that seem most relevant to his or her interests and can separate the wheat from the chaff to spare the reader many details that are not of concern. It is through the narrative account that the clinician-scholar most often has molded the materials into the form desired to display his intellectual wares to one's colleagues. It is not my aim to dismiss the narrative case account as outmoded. Still we should reduce the overly heavy reliance upon narrative procedures which now characterizes clinical scholarly work and move to develop investigations which deal with clinical practice through the medium of "live" materials in which the details of the transactions are retrievable through audio or video recording.

The use of "live" clinical materials has many obvious advantages for both scholarship and teaching:

1. Greater verisimilitude of the events that transpired is achieved through taping. The clinician can only write what he or she remembers. The account is subject to deterioration or forgetting if there are delays writing it—he or she will have seen other patients and may not be able to recapture the impressions collected at the time of the clinical session. Further, the clinician can report only those aspects of the encounter which have made an impression. One's theoretical or ideological viewpoint, concerns at the moment, and ability to view oneself objectively all affect the clinician's account of what transpired. After many playback sessions I can attest that the clinicians often hear themselves performing on tape in a manner which they had evidently forgotten. Instances were frequent in playbacks where the therapist exclaimed, "I am fascinated with the concern I was able to show in my voice there." Or, with obvious chagrin, "How could I say something that stupid!" The therapists who participated in the playback procedures agreed that listening to themselves in scheduled playback sessions exposed them to aspects of their own performance they could not otherwise perceive. For example, they were able to discern behaviors they had engaged in of a countertransferential nature that helped explain sessions which they regarded as less productive than usual. Listening to themselves on tape in the presence of the researcher made it less likely that they would avoid confronting modes of work at odds with their own convictions about the nature of good clinical practice.

2. Summaries of clinical sessions or full narrative process recording, while useful for some purposes, fail to capture the subtlety and nuance of the interaction between participants in the therapeutic session. There is much "face work," to use Goffman's term,[7] that characterizes the behavior of patients. Emotional turmoil is often covered for fear of alienating or provoking the therapist. Much of the anger and other raw feelings are only alluded to or hinted at and a rich variety of mitigating devices are used to avoid upsetting the

[7] Erving Goffman, *Interaction Ritual* (Chicago, Aldine, 1967) pp. 5–45.

5

relationship. Feelings are often expressed through varieties of laughter, silence, intonation, hesitation, glottalization, and other paralinguistic phenomena. These cues tend to be lost in the narrative accounts. It is as if a musical composition were presented only in terms of its melodic line, and elements of harmony and counterpoint were excluded.

3. Narrative case records, particularly as developed in social work education, often fail to stimulate interest in students because the cases they portray have been robbed of much of their human interest. What are essentially fascinating life dramas are too often transformed into tepid, dull accounts. When carefully selected, live materials can evoke considerable interest in students as human documents. When their interest is whetted by the inherent dramaticism of the material, learning can be enhanced and the clinical encounter can appear "relevant" and meaningful to the human condition.

ABSENCE OF MODELS IN THE TRAINING OF CLINICIANS

In the training of medical students, the clinical professor displays a medical treatment procedure under conditions which enable the students to see exactly what is done. Through exposure to the students in clinical rounds, in the clinic or operating room, and the display of treatment of patients in the classroom, the clinical professor becomes a model for the student or young professional. The professor not only talks about the skills required but also demonstrates them. Such a model is rare in the training of clinicians in social work, psychology, and psychiatry. The tendency is widespread in social-work education for teachers of the method of casework to spend little or no time in direct clinical encounters with clients or patients. Often their workloads do not permit direct practice even when they desire such experience. Their knowledge of treatment skills is thus often secondhand, based upon reading or their recall of past experience—sometimes very distant—or their examination of the practice experience of their students through reading case records.[8] Thus, students in

---

[8] See, Florence Hollis, *A Psychosocial Therapy* (New York, Random House, 1964) p. 270; Arthur Leader, "The Clinical Professorship in Social Work Education," *Social Casework*, XLIV, No. 6 (June 1965), 339–44; Burt Schachter, "Relevance of Direct Practice for Today's Social Work

graduate schools of social work often remark that they are well trained in psychosocial diagnostic procedures but the whole realm of treatment tends to be sparsely portrayed. Even in agency settings, the most seasoned clinical personnel withdraw from direct practice experience to become supervisors and administrators. The over-all condition is one in which the divorce between theory and practice is very pronounced, and in my view this is the Achilles' heel of social work.

The counterpart of the educational problem is the fact that seasoned practitioners while sharpening their skills over the years are somehow outside of the educational establishment. While they relish direct involvement in practice and are capable of a high level of theoretical discussion of their own and others' cases in seminars and other contexts, writing for professional journals or pursuing other scholarly activities seems to have little appeal.

These circumstances leave the student clinicians at a decided disadvantage. They rarely see displayed what might be considered skillful clinical practice. The work of their professors and supervisors and consultants in their agency is hidden from them. Further, the student's own work is essentially hidden from the professors and supervisors since they are only privy to the distillation of his or her clinical encounters via the narrative accounts he or she provides, written or oral. This privacy about clinical work—the failure to display the skills the student is supposed to learn—may be the source of two attitudes I have encountered in many students completing graduate social-work education: 1) they are not quite sure whether they have acquired a minimal degree of professional skill; 2) they tend to downgrade the intellectual competence required to do good clinical work.

One aim here is to bridge the gap between the seasoned nonteaching clinician and the classroom. Even though the clinician chooses not to teach or to write and does not engage in research *per se,* it is still possible for students to examine a clinician's on-the-spot skills. The availability of both the live tape recordings of the sessions presented here

Educator," *Journal of Education for Social Work,* Vol. V, No. 1 (Fall, 1969).

and the playback discussions with the therapist in the companion volume constitute one approach to achieving this aim.

The "live" materials presented here and the accompanying tapes are available only because of unusual circumstances. The Arthur Lehman Counseling Service opened its treatment procedures to research scrutiny through the audio taping of counseling sessions and their subsequent review and evaluation by playback. While many agencies have taping facilities for their staffs, the tapes are seldom examined systematically. Typically, tapes accumulate in file cabinets and are infrequently consulted. In the research at the Arthur Lehman Counseling Service, tape recordings of clinical and playback sessions were made over a three-year period. A content analysis was completed by the two participating researchers for each playback session, covering major themes brought in by the patients and the salient treatment issues.

Four therapists associated with the Arthur Lehman Counseling Service participated in the research. While some individual taping had been done earlier, it was never played for others. The other staff members declined to participate; they opposed taping therapy sessions, regarding this as intrusive and counterproductive to their therapeutic aims. They expected taping would create undesirable self-consciousness in them and their patients. The four who did participate were aware that errors in their modes of work would be revealed as well as apparent successful interventions. On a number of occasions their work, as they heard it, did gravely displease them. Yet, the feeling prevailing among them after the experience was that the playback procedure offered valuable opportunities for enhancing self-awareness.

THE THERAPIST

The therapist, Mrs. Freda Moss, had some twenty-five years of experience as a practicing caseworker at the time the Porters entered treatment. Before receiving a graduate degree from a school of social work, she had earned a Master's degree in psychology. She also sought training in psychotherapy at an advanced institute. Always having an interest in treatment, she eschewed the path taken by many seasoned caseworkers, that is, becoming a supervisor or an administrator. She joined the staff of the Arthur Lehman Counseling Service after many years of experience as a caseworker and associate supervisor in the family agency field to concentrate on psychotherapeutic treatment with individuals where the economic base of family life was not in itself the major source of difficulty. Having herself experienced psychoanalysis, she has had a strong interest in keeping up with the psychoanalytic and relevant social work literature, a practice supported by weekly seminars at the agency. While the Freudian underpinnings of her practice orientation are manifest, there is an eclectic cast to her intellectual commitments with considerable awareness of current developments in ego psychological concepts and sensitivity to the understanding of human problems contributed by sociology and social psychology.

If you anticipate that the Freudian commitment presages stiff, formal encounters with patients in which minimal verbal responsiveness characterizes the style of the therapist, you will soon find you are mistaken. The therapist comes across in very live fashion in the sessions. While a professional demeanor is maintained throughout, she enters into dynamic interaction with the Porters and shows a broad range of response. Her language can be colorful and reflect the patient's use of vernacular and slang. She also reveals a gift for apt phrasing to portray a mood or behavior in its most graphic form.

ORIENTATION TO THE MATERIAL

Sessions 1 through 6 display the clinical sessions as they have been transcribed from tapes. While many listenings were required to render verbal speech into transcribed form, there are occasions in the tapes where external noise or the overlapping of speakers makes the rendering somewhat hazardous. On the whole, an effort has been made to portray faithfully the actual clinical encounter as heard on the tapes. I have found that listening to the tapes and following the transcription at the same time enhances the listening experience.

To protect the confidentiality of the Porters, it had been agreed that all references to them by name would be removed from the tapes as well as references to other identifying material such as places, other persons, and employers mentioned by them in the clinical session. A procedure was developed to replace all personal references by a standard silence of two-thirds of a second to serve as a signal to the listener that a deletion has been made. This seems to have minimal impact upon the comprehensibility of utterances. Aside from deletions of names and removal of some extraneous noise, the tapes are thus faithful renditions of the originals.

TIME PERSPECTIVES

The full course of treatment experienced by the Porters is not contained herein. While changes take place in the lives and orientations of the couple over the six sessions presented —changes that might be considered progressive—it is obvious that much of the difficulty in their relationship remains to be resolved. The display of the six sessions—a fragment of the treatment experience—is oriented toward disclosing treatment procedures as they were experienced by the Porters and viewed by the therapist. The aim is not to evaluate treatment or to convince the skeptical or the undecided about the efficacy of face-to-face therapeutic encounters in resolving personal difficulties.

Presenting the fragment of a case rather than a whole calls up the difficulty encountered by researchers in psychotherapy who face the excessively large corpus of data in a case that has lasted several years. The conceptual underpinning and the methodological procedures for tracing the evolution of a case over long periods is still scant. The transcriptions of all such sessions would make an impressively high pile on the investigator's floor! Even six sessions of treatment give us six hours of dialogue to examine and digest—a formidable volume of material.

Playback and commentary upon most of the sessions was done several months after the session; more than eighteen months elapsed between the last session and its playback. Although the playback of the tape helped recreate for Mrs. Moss the aura of the original session, a partial substitution of current treatment perspectives for some she used earlier is, no doubt, possible. Mrs. Moss sought to recall her earlier thinking but, as the reader of the companion volume will observe, she occasionally expressed uncertainty about this.

CRITERIA FOR SELECTING SESSIONS

The sessions displayed here were chosen from more than fifty which had been subjected to playbacks. Major criteria for selecting the six sessions included:

1. Only playback sessions in which commentary by the therapist and the researcher interspersed were selected. Some sessions, in contrast, had been played without comment until the end.

2. By and large, the sessions selected are focused upon defined life-space areas, so as to provide a fairly full display of the problem besetting the Porters in a given aspect of their lives. Some important areas such as the difficulties experienced by the Porters as parents and their relationships with their extended families are not shown here. Thus Session One points up the problem of Jack Porter's drinking and Sally Porter's reaction to it. Session Three deals with the strains the Porters feel about entertaining dinner guests. Session Four reveals the issue of race and how it is handled in their marriage. Session Five deals almost exclusively with the stress of Mr. Porter's work responsibility on him and his wife, whereas Session Six is focused upon the couple's sexual difficulties.

3. The sessions were selected to cover passage of time in the treatment process. The average interval between sessions is four months, the minimum interval being two months and the maximum six.

4. An important requirement for selection was that a session be interesting simply as human drama, as well as for its clinical relevance.

5. Each clinical session presented gives ample opportunity for the therapist to display in the playback session her orientation to the treatment of marital disorder. The complexity of the demands made upon the therapist—in terms of both long-term treatment strategies and more immediate intervention tactics—is well displayed throughout.

SEQUENCE OF SESSIONS

The Porters were seen jointly in their first two sessions on September 1 and September 7, 1965. From September 8 until November 18, there were eight individual sessions with Sally Porter, seven such sessions with her husband, and one joint session. They then asked to be seen jointly; the therapist in a later playback session noted her reasons for going along with their request:

They wished to be seen together and I thought it extremely important on several grounds. One, since they were ready to be seen together, it would help me to understand the interaction. Two, as is very possible in many joint treatment situations, it is possible to help each of the spouses become aware of the unconscious problems in himself which, through miscommunication, gets misinterpreted by the other. This kind of awareness is certainly possible in individual therapy; it goes on all the time. However, I found the joint particularly useful for helping them communicate more directly and of becoming more conscious of what their eruptions were about . . . They were occasionally seen individually, but the predominant mode was the joint interview.

From November 22, 1965, until November 16, 1967, the Porters experienced eighty joint sessions of treatment. During these two years only four individual sessions were held with Mrs. Porter and two with Mr. Porter. In mid-November, 1967, Mr. Porter said he felt they had made as much progress as they could and, after two individual sessions, he withdrew from treatment. Sally Porter decided to remain in treatment and had thirty-six individual sessions until October 16, 1968, when she felt she had her problems sufficiently in hand to withdraw from treatment. There were four especially arranged joint sessions from March 14 to April 10, 1968. Jack Porter was not seen again by the therapist until the summer of 1969 when he came in with his wife to discuss the publication of the materials contained in this volume. Since then both Sally and Jack Porter have said they might want to resume treatment on an individual basis to complete some unfinished business in therapy.

To summarize, the Porters were seen for eighty-five joint sessions; Sally Porter was seen for fifty individual sessions and Jack Porter for twelve sessions. Table 1 shows the date and sequence of the six sessions set forth in this volume.

INTRODUCING THE PORTERS

"The Porters" came into treatment after having been separated for about six months. Their marriage was obviously in deep trouble and they were seeking a basis for reestablishing their home around limited goals, that is, for the sake of their three children if for nothing else. The nature of their request for help was diagnostically significant for the therapist: even if they would not be completely happy with each other and if the sexual difficulty continued which had long troubled their marriage, they wanted to get together. They asked for help in order to reestablish their home without the immediate explosion one might predict from their past incompatibility. After about three months in treatment, Mr. Porter moved back into the home and they continued in treatment for about two years.

TABLE 1

	As a joint session	As a session, either joint or individual
2/8/66	13th	32d
5/16/66	27th	46th
10/13/66	39th	59th
2/6/67	51st	71st
4/14/67	59th	80th
10/26/67	79th	100th

Sally Porter, an attractive, vivacious woman, was in her mid-thirties and Jack, her husband, was about forty when they entered treatment. They had been married about four-teen years at the time of the separation. She was white, of Catholic background from a middle-sized community in the northeastern United States. Her mother had been seriously ill when she was young and had died well before her adolescence. Her father was a white collar worker whom she described as a sensitive, cultured person who loved poetry and reading. During the mother's illness, the father's tendency to drink became exacerbated and after her death he rapidly became disabled by severe alcoholism, drastically reducing his capacity to be a stable wage earner and responsible parent to Mrs. Porter and her younger sister. When their circumstances became very extreme, the family moved into the house owned by Mrs. Porter's grandmother and also occupied by her aunt and uncle. Her adolescence was full of

13

emotional turmoil because of the abject failure of her father to maintain normal responsibilities as the head of a household and the carping of the maternal relatives, who were strait-laced and resented and condemned Sally's father. In this home Sally keenly felt herself to be a second-class citizen. Upon graduation from high school, she was glad to take a clerical job in a different city. Her father's death was both a sorrow and a relief to her. It is of interest that she married Jack Porter within a year after moving to New York City when she was about twenty-two years old.

Jack Porter, a light-complexioned, heavy-set, black male grew up in an environment strikingly different from that of his wife. His father was a professional man of high status in the black community of a small Southern city. His family was important in the community and his parents were extremely strict, taking care to sustain the family's good reputation by being ever watchful of the behavior of their children and taking strong measures if a child seemed to be "cutting up." In a family of five children, Jack Porter was the least conforming and aroused the greatest parental concern. When he showed behavioral difficulty in high school, his parents took the extreme measure of sending him to live with relatives in another city. In the new school community, Mr. Porter was one of only a handful of black children. While he managed to graduate from high school with average grades, his experience in college was a distinct failure and a disappointment to his parents. In a sense, he confirmed their worry about him over the years. Unable to concentrate upon academic work and something of a playboy, Mr. Porter was forced to leave college in his sophomore year. His lack of achievement contrasted with the performance of his siblings, each of whom staked out a successful professional career line.

Over the years, Mr. Porter's sense of having failed to exploit the educational opportunities made available to him and his lack of success compared to his siblings constituted one of the sources of his deep self-deprecation and doubt. He had frequent bouts of depression before he met his wife and had been hospitalized once after an almost fatal suicide attempt. He had about a year of psychotherapeutic treatment after

14

the episode, but tended to downgrade the benefits achieved from this effort to get at his basic personality difficulties.

The reader or listener will quickly discern that both Jack and Sally Porter are highly intelligent and have many attractive elements in their personalities. Each has the capacity to speak eloquently when passions are aroused. In the course of treatment, Sally Porter shows a greater ability than her husband does to capture feelings that originate in the earlier trauma she has experienced. For Jack Porter, this kind of recall and association has been difficult to achieve, since his pattern has been to push his feelings underground and to present a veneer of affability and good feeling as an overlay to the inner turmoil.

The life-style of the couple has reflected their middle-class backgrounds. For many years, they lived in an apartment in New York City. After their third child was born, they bought a home in a suburb where they were able to develop a number of friendships among white and black residents who shared their liberal outlook on civil rights and other social issues.

For Jack Porter, the world of work has been a challenge and the source of considerable anxiety. While intelligent and well-organized, with an apparent talent for administrative leadership, he has always had a nagging doubt about his own worth and a fear that he will "muff" his opportunities in work, just as he did in college. There has been a pervasive doubt about being able to compete in the work world as a black man without a college degree.

His employment at the time the couple entered treatment was in the commercial business world where he had a sub-administrative job in a factory engaged in packaging and printing on plastic products. While he had gained good experience in this field in several prior work settings and was showing increasing capability in administrative tasks, the factory was beset by confused administrative lines and other organizational problems which often created considerable emotional turmoil for Mr. Porter. Part of the stressfulness of the situation stemmed from his emotional involvement with a female employee on the same level in the organization—an attachment that preceded the Porters' separation and was

15

quite intense for a time afterwards. During treatment, work pressures were frequently brought in by Mr. Porter as matters of concern, and he, on occasion, made plans to change jobs. After about a year in treatment, however, he achieved gratifying promotional opportunities with his firm, but with these came inner stirrings of uncertainty about his capacity to fulfill his new responsibilities.

The couple had found it necessary for Sally Porter to work throughout most of the marriage, because of Jack Porter's limited income. She worked on a clerical and office managerial level for quite a few years before taking on semiprofessional work in an organization concerned with human relations. While she enjoyed going to work, finding contact with adults to be more stimulating than the full-time role of homemaker, Mrs. Porter was beset by misgivings about leaving her children in the care of a full-time housekeeper and being unable to put in the time required to create a well-run, attractive household.

A GUIDE TO THE SESSIONS

There are a variety of ways in which the reader may wish to approach the materials that follow. One can read the clinical sessions in this volume without benefit of the playback discussions between myself and Freda Moss presented in the companion playback version. This affords the reader the opportunity to develop his own critical perspectives prior to learning how the therapist evaluated her own efforts. If the reader has access to the tapes issued simultaneously with this volume, he or she may wish to experiment with various procedures, for example, first reading the typescript and then listening to the tape with typescript in hand; following the tapes with this volume and stopping the tape recorder at points where one can read the critical evaluation that takes place in the playback, and so forth. With three variations of case presentation available—1) typescript in clinical version, 2) typescript in playback version, and 3) audio tape—the reader can choose whichever approach seems most calculated to promote independent thinking and learning about the treatment process.

This volume has been prepared for the student of clinical practice. It can be used as supplementary to classroom lectures allowing reference back to the transcript after hearing the tapes in class, as well as for preparation beforehand. It can also be used within agencies and clinics for purposes of staff self-development. At the end of each session there is posed for the reader and/or listener a series of questions which focus upon treatment issues confronting the therapist. The student is asked to take the position of the therapist and to consider the treatment alternatives available. Comparison can then be made with the self-criticisms of the therapist available in the companion volume.

SESSION ONE *The impact of Mr. Porter's
drinking upon his wife*

THIS SESSION * *took place about three months after the Porters had commenced treatment. It was the 13th session in which they had been seen jointly. They were still separated, but coming closer to the point when they would attempt to live together again. Mrs. Porter raises the issue of her husband's drinking and her very low tolerance for it—even when it does not take place in excess. The drinking is connected with Mr. Porter's anxiety on his job and brings out a candor and openness in him which arouses deep anxiety in his wife. She cuts off his attempt to spell out his feelings thus frustrating him and creating considerable anger in him. He feels this leaves him with nobody to talk to, a problem which he feels existed earlier in their marriage. She even cuts off his talking when they are having sexual relations. The session highlights features in the unique life histories of the Porters which make it difficult for them to understand, or cathect sympathetically, each other's anxieties. Of particular significance is the specter of Mr. Porter's apparent attempt at suicide before his marriage. As with almost all of their sessions, the Porters interact in a highly labile manner exposing dramatically the depth of their feelings about the issues being raised.*

* Session of February 8, 1966

19

(Couple comes in and there are a few preliminary remarks of greeting which are not too clear.)

1 MRS. P:	There's something I'd like to talk about. If you want to . . . uh. . . .
2 THERAPIST:	Are you asking me or Jack?
3 MRS. P:	Well, both of you. It's been bothering me . . . and . . . maybe we'd better talk about it and get it out. Uh . . . I think we're both here because, you know, we want to cooperate with each other in trying to work something out. Uh . . . and I realize this meant that we both, you know, in order to live together, we both may have to compromise and ignore a lot of things about the other that we haven't been willing to do before (takes breath). But there's one thing that really upsets me (expels breath), and I think part of the problem is with me and part of it is with Jack. And . . . (hesitatingly) it's something in which I don't feel that I am able to compromise. And this is . . . Jack's drinking. And I say it's me, *too*, because the . . . the feelings I have about it are as strong when he has two drinks as when he, you know, drinks excessively. Uh . . . I think we should just talk (voice choked with emotion) . . . it's something that upsets me to the point where I can't ignore it. My feelings are just too strong in this. And . . . uh. . . .
4 THERAPIST:	What are some of these feelings? Because you say that they're strong even when he takes two drinks.
5 MRS. P:	Jack changes! He's a . . . he's really like two people for me. Uh . . . this past weekend, we had a very good weekend, we had nothing to drink, I don't think. Maybe Jack had one drink during the day on Saturday with a couple of friends. And, it was a *wonderful weekend!* Um . . . but other times— Jack. . . .

	Jack is different when he has had—like Wednesday! When Jack came out Wednesday . . . and he wanted to talk and relax and be with me . . . and . . . the children were there. He's just different when he drinks.
6 THERAPIST:	In what way is he different?
7 MRS. P:	He's more open, perhaps. He wants to talk intimately and . . . he's *weak* when he drinks.
8 THERAPIST:	Weak? Wait a minute . . . he's. . . .
9 MRS. P:	He's . . . he's . . . he's very vulnerable when he drinks. He's more honest with me and admits to all kinds of things I don't want him to admit to . . . to me.
10 THERAPIST:	(soft-spoken) What happens when he admits weakness to you . . . what happens for you?
11 MRS. P:	It just makes me feel . . . (self-interruption) I looked to . . . I want him to be strong! And when he isn't, I don't know . . . I don't know what to do.
12 THERAPIST:	Is it that you then feel you can't lean on him? Depend on him? (Mrs. P.: Yes!) Takes some of the feeling of strength away so you need him to be strong so that otherwise you feel weak yourself.
13 MRS. P:	I probably feel weak anyway. (Therapist: Hmm.) You know when I see him. . . .
14 THERAPIST:	In what way do you feel weak, Sally? Weak in what sense?
15 MRS. P:	(at first tearfully silent) I don't know. I know that I'm capable in . . . in certain areas but I'm not often as capable as I think I need to be for any situation whether it's the children, or anything else. I can do whatever I have to do but . . . Uhm . . . there are times when I just want to be weak.
16 THERAPIST:	Well what do you call "weakness"? You know, I—I don't think I know. . . .
17 MRS. P:	I just want to depend on somebody else . . . once in a while.
18 THERAPIST:	And that you call "weak."
19 MRS. P:	Ya, because it (. . . unclear) with me.
20 THERAPIST:	And when he's opening up it feels to you as if he's leaning on you?
21 MRS. P:	Yeh! And I don't know how to handle it . . . I don't want him ever to be that way.
22 THERAPIST:	You don't want him ever to be which way?
23 MRS. P:	No . . . to . . . to lean on me . . . I'm not the type.

24	THERAPIST:	That makes it pretty tough for both of you. (to Mr. P.) What sort of things do you open up about, Jack?
25	MR. P:	I (laughs uncomfortably) I wish she'd be more specific because (Therapist: You mean you're not aware of this.) . . . I don't know—I'm not quite sure, you know.
26	MRS. P:	Well, he talks about work in such a weak way! A. . . .
27	MR. P:	. . . All right . . . yeah . . . that's (voices overlap)
28	MRS. P:	(voice quivers with emotion) I hate to keep using that word . . . and you let people beat you *down!* And you reveal all the things that you're anxious about!
29	MR. P:	To you.
30	MRS. P:	Yes . . . and you . . . you show me that you think in a certain way about yourself. I don't want you to think that way about yourself. And I don't think, in addition, that you need to think that way about yourself. But you do! And I don't know what to do about that! I feel like I'm . . . I'm a doctor or something listening to him. (dissolves into tears) And I don't know how to handle it!
31	MR. P:	Now I know what you're talking about . . . I know . . . I've forgotten really specifically what I was talking about. Uh. . . .
32	MRS. P:	Well the time you called me, like—what night was that? (Mr. P.: Last Thursday night?) Tuesday night or something . . . (Mr. P.: Thursday.) . . . Then he called me—he was in the apartment and he had been drinking because his boss had said something to him. And his reaction was to go home and blame himself . . . and be—he was very frightened (Mr. P.: Are you talking about Thursday?) and he was drinking . . . it was two weeks ago.
33	MR. P:	Oh, you're talking about two weeks ago. All right, but last Wednesday night, uh, when I was there and we were talking . . . and we were talk—I was talking something about work . . . I think I had two drinks at that point and I was very well aware of what I was doing and what I was saying. Uh, I found you . . . and maybe this was because of, you know, my sitting there and having two drinks in me.
		Uh . . . that you suddenly became very impatient. And . . . and . . . and . . . and, when I was . . . whatever the point I was making—I really don't think it's immaterial—uh, but I was trying to, to the best of my ability, to spell it all out. You know, detail. And . . . Sally at this point really becomes impatient and. . . .

34 THERAPIST:	(interjects) She gets frightened and *then* gets impatient.
35 MRS. P:	Well, when Jack tells it he's got (Therapist: Or gets anxious.) to tell it way down to the last little dotted i and I get impatient with that.
36 THERAPIST:	Yeh . . but maybe you get impatient with it because you expect that this is some *demand* of you to—. Two things seem to be happening as I gather, maybe more, but two things seem to be emerging. One, that he is leaning on you—and leaning on you means what?—that you have to right something, you have to offer him a solution. And the other is that it frightens you because you then see in him—you interpret that as: the weak man, instead of the man who has the Rock of Gibralter front. And it seems to accentuate your own sense of what you feel is weakness in you.
37 MRS. P:	Yeh. (quietly)
38 THERAPIST:	(to Mr. P.) So then she communicates impatience to you.
39 MRS. P:	The other thing that was aggravating that was that the children were still up. And instead of . . . you know, the children go to bed at eight o'clock or eight-thirty. . . . Instead of, you know, coasting and . . . and—Jack just wanted to sit and talk. And I know we both wanted to be with each other. But the kids are there! And I'm more resigned to them than he is. He didn't want anything to do with them. He didn't want to, you know, talk to them. He just wanted them to go away and let Mommy and Daddy talk. Well this is fine, but we could have easily, you know, done this after they were in bed. But that's not as important.
40 THERAPIST:	No.
41 MRS. P:	But that irritated me, too.
42 THERAPIST:	(overlaps) That's another issue.
	But I wonder whether even if they weren't around if some of the same feeling wouldn't obtain . . .
43 MRS. P:	(overlaps) Ya. Yes, you're right. (pause)
44 THERAPIST:	(to Mr. P.) How do you feel when Sally gets impatient?
45 MR. P:	Well, at this point I (voice breaks, in high pitch) . . . I . . . I . . . well in the . . . in the past . . . let me put it to you this way: (to Sally) I've said, "You're not interested," and I don't say any more. . . . and I shut up. (Therapist: Uhm.) And you know this is *perhaps*, you know (nervous laugh), the underlying reason . . . and I think this is real—one reason why I used to not go home! (Therapist: Hm-hm.) Because I

knew if I sat down and tried to talk about things the way *I* talk about them . . . and I . . . you know, it may sound laborious but it . . . it also helps me with my thinking. (Therapist: Hm-hm.) If I hear it, you know, hear myself saying it, you know, instead of just thinking it. You know, and yeh, in a sense I'm using you as a sounding board. (voice quivers) But, I mean, you know, what, what is communication between people but *this*. I . . . eh . . . or this is certainly a part of it . . . let's put it that way. Uh . . . I didn't get angry. I backed off, I think (to Sally) didn't I? Huh? (Mrs. P. makes inaudible comment) Well I think I did . . . (to Therapist) I mean, you know . . . I was very much aware of it. Uh . . . well, you know, this . . . this impatience does come through from Sally. You know if I'm telling her about an incident in order to help me in my thinking and to really know what went on—and I want to try to remember every detail (Therapist: Uh-hm.) so that something doesn't become distorted or I'm . . . I'm seeing it wrong. (Therapist: Uh-m-m.) And . . . how can . . . if . . . if . . . in reality, what I'm sure I'm doing is saying: "What do you think about this?" Uh . . . it seems to me, in order for someone to make a judgment, that he's got to have as much factual information about the incident as possible.

46 THERAPIST: Are you asking her for a judgment?

47 MR. P.: (voice squeezed in high pitch) Well, I . . . I . . . I think this is part of it. Part of it is myself trying to (Therapist: Hm-hm), you know, come up with an answer. The other is, you know, certainly Sally if she has a judgment on the thing, I'd . . . I would be interested in it.

48 MRS. P.: And the other thing was that I didn't a-agree with what you were saying. I felt what you were saying was really . . . (Mr. P.: Really what?) unrealistic.

49 THERAPIST: I'm a little in the dark here because I don't know what went on between you. (voices overlap)

50 MRS. P.: What he was talking about was his plans for himself in the future and he was going to spend the next two months in looking over (mockingly exaggerated) you know, the situation, seeing what his potential is. And. . . .

51 THERAPIST: (voices overlap, unclear) You mean . . . the offers are in his field or. . . .

52 MR. P.: Right, right . . . We talked about that once before.

53 MRS. P:	And . . . this goes back to my feelings about money and things like this. I was irritated because—for Jack to sit and talk in terms of this—he talks as if he were a free man! And he's *not*. And I tried to tell him that. First, he owes money at the office—he owes money to the job. And he owes, you know, he has a lot of bills.
54 THERAPIST:	You owe money to the job, too?
55 MR. P:	Ya. . . . About a hundred dollars.
56 MRS. P:	(overlaps) He borrowed money.
57 THERAPIST:	Hm-m?
58 MR. P:	A hundred dollars I think, but. . . .
59 MRS. P:	And . . . and I thought that if he was going to be making any kind of plans, he should say, "Well, I think in terms of a year, I stick out this job no matter what and get myself financially straight and pay them off and *then* I can tell them to go to hell if I want, or whatever I want, and start looking." But to just work on one level of fishing around for a job or asking people where they think he would fit in or what his potential is, when he can't do anything anyway! It seems so foolish.
60 MR. P:	(high pitch) Well, why can't I improve myself?
61 MRS. P:	You can't! You owe them money! You can't quit your job! (voices overlap)
62 MR. P:	Sally . . . it's less than a week's salary. . . . It's less than a week's salary.
63 MRS. P:	I thought it was like five hundred dollars you owed to them.
64 MR. P:	No . . . no.
65 THERAPIST:	Where did you get that from?
66 MRS. P:	He had borrowed that from them.
67 MR. P:	That was a long time ago, Sally, that's. . . .
68 MRS. P:	Well, I didn't know whether you paid it off or not. (voices overlap)
69 MR. P:	That's been paid off a long time. . . . That's been paid off a long time.
70 THERAPIST:	So that the thought of his looking for a job makes you in addit-additionally very uneasy.
71 MR. P:	(speaks with defensive ring to voice) And I'm not saying . . . I'm not saying in any of this that I am quitting! In the sense that I'm quitting and I'm gonna be out of work. What I'm saying is that if I come up with something it will be, you know, leaving here on . . . on Mon . . . on Friday and going

	here on Monday! So that. . . . There's no break in terms of money coming in—I'm certainly not saying this.
72 MRS. P:	Maybe I just resent the fact that you give attention to that part of it when you *don't* give any attention to the, the problem that you have and that is making a plan for paying off the bills that you have. . . . Maybe you can do both at once. I didn't know that you didn't owe them all that money. . . . (fades out)
73 MR. P:	No.
74 THERAPIST:	But maybe you can't ask these for clarification because you get so anxious.
75 MRS. P:	Ya. I wasn't, you know. . . .
76 THERAPIST:	So you don't count to ten. (Mrs. P.: Ya.) And this comes through. . . . (to Mr. P.) And I can understand the way it comes through *to you* as disapproval and impatience.
77 MRS. P:	Yeh. I didn't even want to hear anything (Therapist: Hm-m.) he was saying about going to see this man and talking and about his . . . 'cause I . . . I . . .
78 MR. P:	(voice rising in high squeal) Well, Sally, who do I talk to? You know—here we go again. You know one of the problems that you say—claim about me—is that I don't talk and this is true. Uh . . . ya know, if I can't talk to *you* . . . I certainly can't sit down and talk to the children about this kind of thing. Now, whom am I going to talk to?
79 THERAPIST:	Are you saying then that you have to go find somebody?
80 MR. P:	Well, you know, if I want to talk to someone, if Sally is not interested. . . .
81 THERAPIST:	(pause) What came out to you as "weakness," Sally, in what Jack was telling you?
82 MRS. P:	Just . . . I think the fact that he wasn't giving any attention to the things that bothered *me*, that I think are a mutual problem—and that is the money as of—you know, the prob-the bills that . . . as they exist now.
83 MR. P:	My God, ya know, the . . . the purpose of all of this—at least my purpose in all of this—and you know maybe I haven't made myself clear. That, you know, if I can earn another three thousand dollars a year more than I'm making . . . these problems don't disappear but it certainly helps with them.
84 THERAPIST:	But I think maybe what happens for you, Sally, is that first, it's very real that you're in financial debt. And that's one thing.

27

		And the other part that might have also been real is that it felt to you as if *you* had to find ways and means of paying these debts and scrounging. And I think that this must call up the past in a way which is most painful and most humiliating for you, too. And I'm talking about the past of your childhood.
85	MRS. P:	(expels air)
86	THERAPIST:	And I think this has, you know, this has another dimension that in your everyday talking together isn't very clear to you.
87	MR. P:	(somewhat hesitatingly) I mean, this . . . this carried over into the evening, you know, if I may. Uh . . . after we had supper, we watched TV. We went to bed. . . . And . . . uh . . . we were entering into a sexual relationship and, you know, I began to talk to Sally and say things to her, and uh . . . even there (to Mrs. P.) you were telling me "shut up . . . just do." And yet there have been other times when perhaps I have just acted and not talked and so forth . . . uh, that she will say to me, "For God's sake, say something to me." Ya know. "Just don't treat me as a piece of meat," I think has been your expression. Uh. . . .
88	MRS. P:	(softly) You see, Jack, when people talk at other times, it isn't necessary to (soft laugh) talk, to say, to say . . . even say, "I love you," if you . . . if you communicate it in some *other* way. But when we lived together, before, we had no communication of *any* kind. . . . (voices in strident overlap)
89	MR. P:	(tries to defend self) Well, all right, I'm just say- I'm just saying that. . . .
90	MRS. P:	(does not give way) And, satisfied I didn't need you to say anything to me. . . .
91	MR. P:	(tries unsuccessfully to break in) Ya . . . ya know.
92	MRS. P:	I didn't want you to say anything. (angrily) I didn't want to *talk* about it!
93	MR. P:	Ya know . . . this. . . .
94	THERAPIST:	You didn't want to talk about what . . . Sally?
95	MRS. P:	(angry, strident tone) Anything—what he was doing, what I was feeling. Anything. I just wanted to feel and to be with him and *do* it! And that's all! And not sit and talk about it!
96	THERAPIST:	But weren't you already upset before you went to bed? Upset with Jack? (voices overlap)
97	MRS. P:	No. I wasn't upset when I was in bed or I wouldn't have got

	into bed with him. I wasn't upset anymore. I'd . . . I had . . . had called him during the day because I wanted to sleep with him.
98 THERAPIST:	But this was the even . . . night (Mrs. P.: Yes.) of the evening that you were feeling so . . . rootless and so without the Rock of Gibralter in Jack.
99 MRS. P:	Uh-hum.
100 THERAPIST:	I wonder whether some of this in the past hasn't occurred, too, to make the marriage break down and communication between you get so charged?
101 MRS. P:	(long silence and sigh) I don't know. Maybe. (sighs)
102 THERAPIST:	What is it that's happening on the job for you, Jack, at this point; that you're so. . . .
103 MR. P:	I don't really know, what it was . . . really what it was. I mean I know I talked to Sally . . . about seeing the guy at ——— Corporation and talking to him.
104 THERAPIST:	No, I mean what are the additional. . . .
105 MR. P:	Oh-h . . . business is not good. I don't really know what it is.
106 THERAPIST:	Are you being criticized a good deal these days?
107 MR. P:	There's a lot of criticism coming my way, ya. And I don't think necessarily justly so but, I mean, this is my opinion. . . . And . . . uh . . . it's not something, quite frankly that I . . . I am prepared to ride out and I think I can ride out . . . and, you know, come out on top, ya know, (stammers) in-in the controversy, if there's controversy.
108 THERAPIST:	What are they accusing you of? Was it carelessness? Loss of business or what?
109 MR. P:	Well, this is part of it. This has been part of the accusation. That, uh, I'm not running a tight ship suddenly after five years. (voice lowers and is almost inaudible) And that, you know I've been left to operate on my own too much and so forth. I must have more direction from the top than I've been receiving.
110 THERAPIST:	This is what they're saying?
111 MR. P:	Hm-m.
112 THERAPIST:	This is what your boss, your immediate boss (Mr. P.: Yeah.), that woman is saying?
113 MR. P:	Yeh . . . (almost inaudible) After a conference with the other . . . other two, I suppose (fades out). . . .
114 THERAPIST:	After she had a conference or after you had a conference?

115 MR. P:	They-she had a conference. Apparently the three of them got together. There was a mistake on a job and . . . uh . . . un . . . it was an unfortunate mistake. It was one that occurred after I had left there, you know, in the evening and . . . working late, and of course they blamed me for not staying around and checking this out.
116 THERAPIST:	What sort of mistake was this?
117 MR. P:	(gives details of error) This was with a new account.
118 THERAPIST:	And one of your men did this?
119 MR. P:	(voice is low, sounds depressed) Yeh. A supervisor who was there did it wrong, that's all. All of the orders were cleared and so forth. And . . . uh, they felt I should have hung around since it was a new account and very peculiar and so forth . . . I should have hung around and made sure that it was right, and so forth and so on.
120 THERAPIST:	You needed to check each detail.
121 MR. P:	Yeah—no not each detail, but to check the job.
122 THERAPIST:	I mean on this job.
123 MR. P:	Yeh! Yeh . . . yeh. As it was being set up. I didn't. I was there till eight o'clock that particular evening, you know, they had worked till about eleven.
124 THERAPIST:	So on the strength of this one error they are making this state . . . this, uh, assessment of you? Because, you know. . . .
125 MR. P:	(interrupts) There have been others. I mean, you know, over the years, there have been others. And so finally they've just started in saying, you know, that all of these mistakes are basically at my lap and that . . . uh . . . you know, it's my fault . . . you know. I don't know, it may be my fault. I don't know but . . . I don't! . . .
126 THERAPIST:	Do you really not know or are you saying now maybe you think they are?
127 MR. P:	Well, let me put it to you this way—in each case, I'm sure they could have been prevented. But (laughs lightly) I think there were also circumstances in, you know, around it. And uh . . . whether these circumstances are valid—I mean at least as I see them they're valid. Uh . . . and, uh . . . in each case I'm quite willing to, you know, discuss it, and I have discussed it, with them very openly.
128 THERAPIST:	With "them" meaning the other two bosses, too?
129 MR. P:	Yeh . . . yeh—all three of them. And, uh, but you know, suddenly —— (specific job) had

fiasco. And we ended up taking about a four-thousand-dollar licking. This goes back four years ago . . . uh . . . so that, uh . . . you know, all of these—you know, suddenly this is all being laid at my feet—and saying that, ya know, it's because I've operated "inefficiently . . . blah-blah, blah . . . blah, blah, blah," you know. Quite frankly, you know, I think there may be some . . . some validity in it. I think, on the other hand, in each case there have been some extenuating circumstances, ones which, ya know, maybe they'll accept, maybe they'll accept, maybe they don't accept.

130 THERAPIST: Well, the question is not only what they accept but what you feel is justifiable. Do you feel that in this instance where the over . . . where the mistake was made, that. . . . Do you feel you should have stayed around?

131 MR. P: No. This was what we're paying a supervisor out there for.

132 THERAPIST: And in your judgment, this was a responsible, careful supervisor?

133 MR. P: No . . . but I have said this and I get nowhere with it. This was a nice kid who we've raised up through the ranks (Therapist: Hm.) . . . ah . . . had been with the firm ten years . . . he has very decided weaknesses which I had pointed out . . . to my boss. Uh. . . .

134 THERAPIST: You mean she insists on keeping him in that position?

135 MR. P: She insists on keeping him. Or as I used to have . . . I had two people out there. Uh . . . and she won't, you know, replace the other one that left. I had two people out there which offered a balance . . . Bill has technical know-how but the person who should be supervising the department should have technical know-how and also judgment. And when I say "judgment," I, uh . . . someone who I . . . I call it "thinking clearly." And I'm not—that Bill doesn't think clearly but I think he gets very flustered at times and, uh, I try to . . . I am supportive of him in this area. But, you know, I . . . I think actively running the operation as we have it . . . there should be two people who are on that floor at all times . . . with all that we've got going on. They don't see it. (Therapist: Uh-hm.) Uh . . . and I have said . . . I have said to them that I have no intention of—and this may be wrong on my part—yes, if something important is being done, you know, I want to see it started. I want to check it out . . . and so forth. But I have no intention of spending the kind of hours I used

to spend there. Uh . . . and, uh, you know, if they're looking for me to be there at eleven o'clock at night—then they, you know—I'm not going to be there. Ya know, I'm just not.

136 THERAPIST: Uh-hm . . . and the —— job thing was a similar situation where. . . .

137 MR. P: No . . . the —— job, no. A totally different situation. See, when they gave me the job manager, there were two of us there. And the fellow who used to be my boss moved over into sales. They didn't give me an assistant as such. And I was excited about it. When I talked about it, they said *no.* I let it ride, simply because it was a way of me really getting into it myself, and getting my hands on everything so that I knew what was going on. (Therapist: Uh-hm.) I now know that this was very foolish on my part. I should have insisted that they give me someone. Because, uh, there was just, again, too much to do. And one person couldn't do it.

138 THERAPIST: And the boss . . . your boss had done the job? You replaced him?

139 MR. P: Yeh. The fellow that I replaced, and I came there as his assistant. And then I got moved up and he moved on over into sales.

140 THERAPIST: But he had you as an assistant (Mr. P.: Yes . . . yes.), and now this time you had no assistant.

141 MR. P: Yeh . . . no assistant.

142 THERAPIST: But you felt you wanted to prove yourself?

143 MR. P: Yeh. Yeh. And uh . . . this was foolish. This was very foolish on my part . . . because, uh . . . and foolish on the firm's part if I might say. Because the four-thousand mistake—the four-thousand-dollar mistake on the —— job would have paid half of somebody's salary, you know.

144 THERAPIST: So how was the mistake . . . ?

145 MR. P: Well, it was a job that was, uh . . . (explains information was not on the order and the job was done in the wrong fashion). It was an unfortunate mistake. Very, very unfortunate.

146 THERAPIST: But part of it was because you wanted to prove yourself.

147 MR. P: Yeh. I, you know—I think if I'd a had someone else there and, you know, I had an opportunity to really stop and think about what I was doing or really stop and examine the job, or something like this, I would have really picked it up. . . .

148 THERAPIST: But what about this element of needing to prove yourself? You know, it's as if you need to prove yourself in your own eyes, too. So, what were your questions about *you?* Apparently you had arrived at a point four years ago—this was about four years ago? (Mr. P.: Yeah.) . . . when you were feeling some questions about yourself.

149 MR. P: I had no questions about myself. It was the first real break-through. Let me put it to you this way for myself . . . you know, being given a whole plant to run, and, uh, I had a lot of obstacles to overcome in terms of . . . you know, the kind of personnel and things of this nature.

150 THERAPIST: Was this a question of people who were there a long time? (Mr. P.: Oh yeh. Oh yeh.) Who would now be working under you?

151 MR. P: That's right! Uh, this is part of it.

152 THERAPIST: Were there any other factors?

153 MR. P: No, other than my desire to just do (laughs nervously) as good a job as I could . . . and to . . . you know . . . continue to grow. (pause)

154 THERAPIST: You had been with that firm how much before that?

155 MR. P: Just a year.

156 THERAPIST: Just a year. What had you done before, Jack?

157 MR. P: I had been with other similar firms. I had been in this line about fifteen years—about sixteen years in various capacities. . . . (inaudible)

158 THERAPIST: Not in managerial capacities before. . . .

159 MR. P: (overlaps) Hm hm. Always—always in supervisory cap-capacities, let us put it this. . . . You know, never as a, just a worker although I have always, up until this poin—up until the job prior to this, really have always liked to do some of the work just to get the technical knowledge that I don't necessarily have. And I'll do it now. You know, get a new piece of equipment and I'll go down and run it this minute to know what the heck it's all about. . . . (becomes inaudible)

160 THERAPIST: And did the supervisory jobs run smoothly for you?

161 MR. P: Basically, I have not had any, uh, real problems . . . no . . . not really. I would say that they have. . . .

162 THERAPIST: You seemed to look to Sally at this moment.

163 MR. P: I was just trying to think maybe she thought of something, that you know. . . . (fades out)

164 THERAPIST: You're looking very sad, Sally . . . as Jack is talking. . . . Can you share with us what you were thinking?

165 MRS. P: (softly) No . . . I was just listening.

166 THERAPIST: Oh. Are you feeling very sad at this moment?

167 MRS. P: (sigh) No. Not really. I'm not feeling anything. (Mr. P.: Uh?) I said I'm not feeling anything.

168 THERAPIST: Nothing?

169 MRS. P: No . . . my feelings are in abeyance until . . . (fades out laughing). I'm not feeling anything right now, I'm just listening.

170 THERAPIST: Well, we've gotten away from a plea that you made. . . . (pause)

171 MRS. P: See, there are a lot of things that Jack does and feels and says, like he was talking about his attitude when he first got this job and his need to prove himself, and Jack thinks he can't make a mistake—even he is not allowed to make a mistake that this . . . he-he just can't do it . . . (Mr. P. tries unsuccessfully to interrupt)—anybody else can mis- make a mistake, but he can't. And if a mistake happens, he's got to take the whole blame for it . . . (Mr. P.: Now Sally . . .)—all of these things, I don't know . . . I don't agree with him. I don't think he's sensible . . . and I don't know how to handle (sounds tearful) . . . and I know I'm supposed to be a wife and I'm supposed to be understanding and sympathetic and supporting . . . but I . . . I don't feel I'm capable of it! I feel I should be a trained psychologist or something.

172 THERAPIST: Now wait a moment. What are you not capable of?

173 MRS. P: (almost tearful) Of being tolerant of the way he feels . . . (fades out in tears).

174 MR. P: Well, Sally . . . there is no question . . . and . . . uh . . . you know . . . let's forget the circumstances . . . and I, you know . . . I think this is real whether, you know, you understand it or not . . . the ultimate responsibility for whatever happens at my plant is mine!

175 MRS. P: Right! And live with it! And don't labor it and blame yourself for it. (voices overlap)

176 MR. P: Now, if something *happens,* if something happens (Mrs. P.: Yeah.) that is not right, it is my responsibility.

177 MRS. P: Sure! And accept it. And know you're gonna make mistakes (voices overlap) some of the time . . . they're paying you to

		make decisions, and some of those decisions are going to be wrong.
178	MR. P:	But the point is to get it down so that mistakes are at a very, very minimum.
179	MRS. P:	Sure! Anyone wants to do that. But someday, somewhere it's going to go wrong. (voices overlap and clash) And you're gonna do what? Slit your wrists because of something went wrong?
180	MR. P:	No. I'm not slitting my wrists. I'm not slitting my wrists.
181	THERAPIST:	Well, wait a moment. You're using terms like "slitting the wrists."
182	MRS. P:	(animatedly) He goes home and he drinks! You know. 'Cause. . . .
183	THERAPIST:	You mean when things go wrong, then he gets—you're not . . . not talking now about two drinks—but now he goes into the real doldrums about it.
184	MRS. P:	Yes. Yes! . . . The woman told you about a mistake that you had made, and they used that as an excuse to, you know, haul out the whole history, which people are, are liable to do and and instead of reacting one way, you. . . .
185	MR. P:	What way would you have had me react?
186	MRS. P:	All right. So you're paid to make mistakes.
187	MR. P:	I'm not paid to make mistakes.
188	MRS. P:	(laughs) I mean you're paid to make decisions. Excuse me. And if they trust you enough to run that place, they've got to realize that sometimes things are going to go wrong. You know this went out wrong. (Mr. P. attempts to interrupt) But you don't go home and drink about it and blame yourself!
189	MR. P:	Sally, if you . . . if you . . . if you had a business position; if you owned a company, and you're in the danger of losing a fifty- or a hundred-thousand-dollar a year account, because of a mistake—irregardless of the circumstances—it was a mistake (Mrs. P.: Uh hm.), would you take that attitude?
190	MRS. P:	I am talking about. . . .
191	MR. P:	(interrupting) No . . . would you take that—would you take that attitude that you just said?
192	MRS. P:	I would, I would say to you, "What are you doing? Messing up . . . this account?"
193	MR. P:	(vehemently) Well, this is *exactly* what they're saying! All right now. . . .

35

194 MRS. P:	(overlaps) Yes, but what do you say (in mocking intonation): "Oh, I'm so sorry." And you come home and drink it off.
195 MR. P:	(voice in high squeal) Well, hell, I am sorry! (voices in strident overlap)
196 THERAPIST:	(to Mrs. P.) But they are also demoting him in a sense. . . .
197 MRS P:	He didn't say she threatened. And you let her threaten you?
198 MR. P:	And what would you have me do? Say, "All right. This is yours," and walk out?
199 MRS. P:	(sarcastically) What do you think she's gonna do? What do you think she's really gonna hire somebody else that's in there? . . . (voices overlap)
200 MR. P:	Sally . . . they're around. There are people that can be hired. I could be replaced. I can be replaced.
201 MRS. P:	(disbelievingly) Well, you think you can be! And you think . . . (overlap)
202 MR. P:	(high pitch) I know I can be . . . there's nobody who's infallible.
203 MRS. P:	And you're this far from getting the axe.
204 MR. P:	Well I may be. I don't know.
205 MRS. P:	(tearful) And I can't live with your anxiety. (sobs) I'm anxious enough myself!
206 THERAPIST:	(softly) Sally, what you really are saying to him is that when he gets anxious, you fall apart. (silence) So how come you fall apart—you are asking *him* not to go into a slump? 'Cause then you've-*you* behave as if the world were coming to an end . . . and there'd be no more jobs . . . and no more security, which is really a counterpart to what Jack is seeming to express in the way he goes down.
207 MRS. P:	(bitterly) There's more danger of his throwing up his hands (Mr. P.: Sally . . . I . . . I . . .) than there is of his losing his job.
208 THERAPIST:	Has he thrown up his hands in the years you have known him?
209 MR. P:	(excitedly) I have threatened to . . . I have threatened to. . . .
210 MRS. P:	Not in quitting . . . but there is more danger to me in what he does than if he would, you know, tell them—"Go blow" and get another job. And . . . I-I don't . . . (chokes up).
211 THERAPIST:	You say there is more danger for you?

36

212 MRS. P: Yes, I feel more threatened by that. (overlap)

213 THERAPIST: Well, let's see . . . let's see what . . . what the danger is real—and it may be—or the danger feels imminent because of Jack's way of receiving whatever criticism there is—in what "real" or "not real" situations he's facing. You say he's never blown . . . thrown up his hands and gone off?

214 MRS. P: No, he never has.

215 THERAPIST: Well, where do you think this feeling comes from?

216 MRS. P: On my part? (Therapist: Yeah.) Or his part?

217 THERAPIST: No, no. *Your* feeling that things are going to explode.

218 MRS. P: No, I didn't . . . by "throwing up his hands" I didn't mean that he'd quit his job.

219 THERAPIST: What then?

220 MRS. P: But he was just . . . that this was the end of the world!

221 THERAPIST: (interjects) For a moment!

222 MRS. P: (deep bitterness) And I have seen the end of the world for Jack so many times.

223 THERAPIST: But has it turned out to be "the end of the world"?

224 MRS. P: No! And why I can't get used to it I don't know. (Therapist: (reinforces) Hm-hm.) It's like when he wouldn't come home at night. Why . . . you know, it took me like five months to finally get used to the idea that Jack was not going to come in that door tonight (becomes tearful). He's not going to be there. I keep waiting for someday, for him to . . . .

225 THERAPIST: But, Sally, can we stay with this one element here?

226 MRS. P: Yeah.

227 THERAPIST: Of the feeling that when he is down in the dumps and this seems way down, that even though in the past he's been that way and has not thrown up the hands, to you it feels the imminent, next door, around-the-corner threat. So somewhere this must be repeating something for you . . . 'cause in reality it isn't a threat. (overlap)

228 MRS. P: Well, it's . . . it's like the . . . the night he called me (Therapist: Hm.) and had been drinking. It's been like every other night that he's been calling me and been drinking. Or not come home. Or . . . I . . . they all do the same thing to me! (tears) I think that . . . maybe *this* time will be the . . . (chokes up).

229 THERAPIST: They all do what to you? The feeling is that he will not come, he will not be able to manage?

37

230 MRS. P:	(tearful) He always seems to be on the edge of doing something.
231 THERAPIST:	Your father used to go off and drink, I think you mentioned several times.
232 MRS. P:	He was in bars or else he just sat right in front of me and drunk. He was a harmless drinker. But Jack, there's a threat in my mind about Jack. It's never materialized in our life (Therapist: No.) together . . . but because I know of about how he lived before he met me, there's this feeling that . . . holy crow! . . . you know, maybe it could happen.
233 THERAPIST:	Well, how did he live before. (addresses Mr. P.) How *did* you live before, Jack?
234 MR. P:	(to Sally) Are you talking about when I was in the hospital? . . . Or when I went into the hospital? (hardly audible)
235 THERAPIST:	What happened before that episode?
236 MR. P:	(becomes guarded) Before, you mean, when I went . . . ?
237 THERAPIST:	Yes . . . the subway incident, uh . . . had life been piling up?
238 MR. P:	Ya . . . an . . .
239 THERAPIST:	What? What was exactly going on for you?
240 MR. P:	Well, guess I was pretty lonely. I guess the culminating thing was some gal I was going around with who . . . threw me overboard.
241 THERAPIST:	She threw you overboard and you threw yourself in front of the subway.
242 MR. P:	(almost whispered) Ya. I guess so.
243 THERAPIST:	Must have had a tremendous impact on you.
244 MR. P:	And yet, you know, in reality, I didn't throw myself in front of the subway. I did something I was sure I was gonna get caught at, as I'm sure most people do.
245 THERAPIST:	You did something that you were gonna get caught at?
246 MR. P:	Yeh! I'm sure. . . .
247 THERAPIST:	What do you mean?
248 MR. P:	Well, I started down a catwalk, you know . . . subway employee sees someone start down a catwalk, you know, they're going to grab him right away and this is exactly what he did.
249 THERAPIST:	But how did you feel when she threw you overboard? This is somebody you loved very much or you knew?
250 MR. P:	I don't know, you know, whether you can call it love, ya know. I guess at the time I thought I did.

251 THERAPIST: Ya, well, at that time you did.

252 MR. P: Uh . . . and . . . uh . . . I really don't know how I felt . . . I was very . . . uh . . . angry with her. Uh . . . life was really pretty horrible, I guess. Or at least I thought it was.

253 THERAPIST: Why?

254 MR. P: I had gone to a basketball game. I was on my way home from a basketball game when I did it.

255 THERAPIST: You were angry with her and when you were angry with her, you were going to either do yourself in or threatened to do yourself in.

256 MR. P: (in muted tone) Ya. . . . (pause) . . . I don't think I've ever threatened this to you, Sally.

257 THERAPIST: But this is some of the feeling that comes across to her.

258 MR. P: (rushes to defend self) Yeh . . . but-b . . . but . . . but . . . have I ever . . . you know?

259 MRS. P: No, you haven't. And why that doesn't make sense to me . . . that you have never been, you know, that way. . . .

260 MR. P: It's been a long time since I've had that feeling about myself. Now I may do it in other ways . . . but I mean the feeling that I'm aware of that this is what I want to do.

261 THERAPIST: But when you get very angry or upset, you drowned yourself in liquor. (overlap)

262 MR. P: I mean drink, ya . . . ya. . . .

263 THERAPIST: You drowned yourself.

264 MR. P: (self-mockingly) Mrs. Menninger's little ' suicide. . . . Hm. That's right. (fades out)

265 THERAPIST: Well, you know, I think we may want to understand more of this, not only for Sally's sake, certainly also for yours.

266 MR. P: But . . . if I . . . if I may just for a minute . . . yes, what you're saying about, you know, the night that, you know, I had this conference with —— (employer) and I got all boozed up and so forth at home. But . . . how do I . . . well, on a night like last Wednesday night, when I just want to sit down and talk to you. I certainly wasn't angry about anything. I wasn't upset about anything.

267 THERAPIST: You weren't upset?

268 MR. P: Last Wed. . . .

269 THERAPIST: Upset about the job?

270 MR. P: As such, no . . . I mean I had no incident. Let me put it to you this way, it had me upset. (stammers, broken sentences)

39

		No . . . I-I . . . (in high register) You know . . . yes, I'm concerned . . . I'm, you know. . . .
271	THERAPIST:	And upset about the job.
272	MR. P:	(talks rapidly and anxiously) Yeh! But, but I mean I wasn't, ya know, off on any deep end. Let me put it to you, let me put it in this manner. If I can distinguish between the two. (to Sally) And I just wanted to sit down and *talk* to you about it. And this is what I was trying to *do*. And I get the feeling that . . . heh . . . you know, quite obvious from you that, you know, when I start talking about it and, yes, I di—have a habit of getting into details. Maybe it isn't necessary but I think it is. Uh . . . and . . . and you . . . you become impatient. Y-y-you find . . . you know, you don't find this interesting. . . . What the hell am I going to do?
273	MRS. P:	(hardly audible) I don't know.
274	MR. P:	Now I certainly wasn't drunk. Was I?
275	MRS. P:	(murmurs) No.
276	MR. P:	I certainly was lucid. And I knew what I was doing. I'd had two drinks. I think I had a third as we sat down to dinner. In fact I know I had a third as we sat down to dinner. And that was it. Didn't pursue it after dinner or anything like this.
277	THERAPIST:	You didn't pursue the drinking?
278	MR. P:	The drinking, yeh.
279	THERAPIST:	But it isn't the drinking. It's what comes when you're feeling intimate and wish to lean on Sally. And this doesn't make it wrong for you to want somebody to listen to you. But we're . . . what happens is that she gets scared. And so there are two pieces to this.
280	MRS. P:	I-I was thinking yesterday, why . . . when I met Jack he didn't drink at all. He didn't drink at all. If we went out in the evening he had a coke or something like that.
281	THERAPIST:	You were a teetotaler at that time?
282	MR. P:	This was shortly after I came out of the hospital.
283	THERAPIST:	Oh, so you stayed away from drink.
284	MRS. P:	And he was fine . . . and I don't know why it couldn't be like that again!
285	THERAPIST:	Well, wait a moment. What you are really asking of him is not so much the not drinking but for him not to be *upset*. Because his being upset rocks the boat for you.
286	MRS. P:	(barely audible) Maybe it's, I don't know, it seems for me it

seems like the, you know, the drinking (Therapist: Hm-m.) brings the red flag.

287 THERAPIST: What actually happened with your father? He would avoid, escape from the cares of his world through drink, too? So that even though he'd be wonderful about poetry, that he was really not there for you. He was absorbed in himself.

288 MRS. P: Yes, if my aunt was running things and it didn't suit my father, he would never stand up and fight (Therapist: Hm.) . . . never! You know, attempt to assert himself. He just sat there and felt sorry for himself and (laughs with embarrassment) made remarks. And, uh, you know, he was never rowdy or disorderly, very seldom, you know. He just got sleepier and sleepier and went off to bed.

289 THERAPIST: Well, what were you . . . what were your feelings at that time? You have pretty intense feelings about it with Jack. What went on for you? You were so much littler and so much less capable of protecting yourself.

290 MRS. P: No . . . I was, I was, this was like, like in my teens when he did that. (Therapist: Well.) Before that he was just out of the house. . . . Well, like he was an embarrassment to me, when my friends were around. Otherwise, that's the way he was and, uh. . . .

291 THERAPIST: It didn't bother you that he didn't stand up and. . . .

292 MRS. P: Yah, that bothered me.

293 THERAPIST: . . . fight for you and fight for his rights?

294 MRS. P: Yeh . . . yeh.

295 THERAPIST: I would imagine that, uh, fighting for you would be out of the question then since he couldn't fight for himself. (overlap)

296 MRS. P: Just because he didn't have much self-respect, that's all. But I felt well. . . .

297 THERAPIST: That's all you felt? Never *you* . . . never . . . never standing up for you? No sense of loss about that? Or anger or anything?

298 MRS. P: No. When I was younger and he was away from the house a lot. . . . This is when I was, you know, resentful of him. But the older I got, the less I felt that I needed to, you know, look to him. I could . . . by this time I was doing as I wanted to do. You know, I was going around my aunt, you know, if I needed to. I accommodated to that. I didn't look to him to (laughs)

41

		rescue me from anything anymore. I'd think I had better do it by myself. . . . (fades out)
299	THERAPIST:	It's awfully hard to live with that though.
300	MRS. P:	I felt it was just him and his problem. It was very sad to me. He just didn't care about himself. And I understood why probably, you know.
301	THERAPIST:	I wonder whether you could understand why at that age.
302	MRS. P:	(hardly audible) Well, you know . . . I was being philosophical. But whether I really down deep understood, I don't know. I can't understand him now, probably . . . (fades out).
303	THERAPIST:	But you know, you have such a profound reaction of many parts of anger and disappointment in Jack. So if we read the story backwards, it's hard to imagine that it left you just resigned. Because in resignation there can be sadness, and loneliness, and not just acceptance.
304	MRS. P:	(sighs) I don't know what it's got to do with Jack. I don't see an excuse for Jack. . . .
305	THERAPIST:	Well . . . you're asking him to stand up and fight!
306	MRS. P:	Yes! Jack hasn't had any shattering blows in his life that, you know . . . (laughs ironically) would cause him to . . . to despair!
307	THERAPIST:	How do . . . how can one know this, Sally?
308	MRS. P:	Well, not any external. Maybe psychological blows, you know, like we've all had. But. . . .
309	THERAPIST:	Maybe his proving . . . needing to prove himself has something to do with the past inability to prove himself. You know, what . . . do we really know what it meant to Jack to have a father who didn't listen and a mother who wanted to make things right? And a sister and brothers who all seem to be marching on to success? Do we really know? I don't. . . .
310	MRS. P:	No. And I don't. That's Jack's side of it. Now, I have my own background and my own peculiarities. And how do we work out some kind of meeting ground so he can tolerate . . . I can't see myself giving like this—unless I change an awful lot.
311	THERAPIST:	Uh-m. Well, you're right. This means finding a way of coping with the uncertainty which he evokes in you which is your angle.
312	MRS. P:	I feel now as if I'm supposed to say: "All right, I've got a man and he's a certain way, and if I want to live with him, I've got

	to put up with this. And I've got to learn how to live with this." Which is all right, except it means that all of the accommodation is on my part and there's no understanding . . . (tears) of . . . of . . .
313 THERAPIST:	No understanding of . . . ?
314 MRS. P:	Of the fact that, uh . . . that *I* am involved, too!
315 THERAPIST:	When you married Jack you really had a sense you were marrying a-a very dependable (measured tones), cultured man who would bring into your life what you had not had.
316 MRS. P:	(in low register) He'd make it possible for me to get the things I wanted . . . I wouldn't use the word "cultured" with Jack. In the sense that I mean—and that isn't a derogation of Jack—it's just that I don't think he comes from a *cultured* family. He comes from a *privileged* family. But he doesn't come from a cultured family. . . . But I think Jack is (unclear) What about the other things? Dependable? I don't expect Jack to, to want the things I want but (laughs) I do expect him to somehow allow me to get them for myself.
317 THERAPIST:	Like what?
318 MRS. P:	(tearful) Which is pretty selfish.
319 THERAPIST:	Not all selfishness is bad. You say you expect him to let you get . . . allow you to get what you want for yourself. In what way do you mean that?
320 MRS. P:	The things I want to do. I would like, you know, really . . . (tears and long silence) . . . I would just like to do certain things.
321 MR. P:	Like what? Would you like to go back to school? Darling, you can do that.
322 MRS. P:	(tearfully) No, I can't.
323 MR. P:	Why can't you? Get those children out of the house and in two years you can go back to school. In the two years they will all be in the house (corrects self) in school all day.
324 MRS. P:	(tearfully) It costs money to go to school, Jack, and we've got to put them through school, that's something else that costs . . . we've got debts to pay off . . .
325 MR. P:	Sally, we've got sixteen years—well not sixteen—how long before Mary goes to college before we have to worry about paying—not that we shouldn't start worrying now. But what I am saying, it is not something that is that imminent.
326 THERAPIST:	But you do have difficulties in managing (Mr. P.: Yeah.)

financially now . . . (Mr. P.: Yeh.) without even including college.

327 MR. P: (stammers) I . . . I . . . if . . . if Sally (embarrassed laugh) would like to go back to school.

328 THERAPIST: (incredulous) How will you manage going back to school—going to do without her income?

329 MR. P: Not . . . not right now. Two years from now I could. (to Mrs. P.) And you can certainly go to one of the free schools in terms of, you know, I don't know . . . on the . . . on the Island or in the city or what.

330 THERAPIST: What is the basis for you thinking in two years?

331 MR. P: Our youngest child will be in grade school . . . in grade school all day.

332 THERAPIST: But how about needing Sally's income in order to. . . . Even with Sally's income, the both incomes don't manage to cover all of your needs . . . there are difficulties there.

333 MR. P: (subdued) I hope in two years I am able to do this. It's possible on my part.

334 THERAPIST: What I hear, Jack, is a wish to satisfy Sally and to encourage her to pursue this and in the prog . . . at the same time, maybe a realistic hope, maybe you're going to work on this, you know, business of coping with the kinds of problems that managing money has . . . emerged for you.

335 MR. P: (hesitantly) Well my thought, uh, really, uh, what I'm . . . yeh . . . and I understand what you're saying. . . . But what I'm also saying is that "This is not so farfetched if this is what you wanted to do." An . . . and . . . I'm not gonna say it *can* be done. But, on the other hand, I don't think it is so farfetched.

336 THERAPIST: Is it your feeling, Sally, that when Jack acts . . . is so vulnerable . . . and he is so *down*, then the feeling overtakes you that life is always going to be this troubled and this hard? This is what you're feeling . . . (silence).

337 MRS. P: (sniffs tears) My going back to school is just . . . you know . . . in the realm of a fantasy . . . it's. . . .

338 THERAPIST: You know. . . .

339 MR. P: I know this is something you've always wanted to do.

340 MRS. P: Yeah, and it isn't anything I woul-I need to do now—I think I know that. But it's (not very clear) also like anything else.

341 MR. P: Huh? I don't understand.

342 MRS. P: It's just like anything else you know, it's like when you go to the football game. You've always had to . . . well (quoting Mr. P.) "You get yourself a series ticket, for concerts that go on in the afternoon . . . I go to the game, you can go to the concert." I've never done it. 'Cause I know there is just so much money and there's . . . you know . . . And I've never done it. It's a wonderful idea and it sounds great, but when you come down to it, I can't do it. I'm not able to go out and . . . you know, take a certain amount of money and buy . . . you know, series tickets (laughs) to the concert like Jack can take money—I can't do it. (voices overlap)

343 THERAPIST: Well are you saying that he can indulge his pleasures or his fant . . . fancies but. . . . (Mrs. P.: No.) And says (Mrs. P.: I'm not able.) "Go ahead and do it," but there's really no way of doing it.

344 MRS. P: There's no way . . . an . . . and I don't know if I could make a way or if I just wouldn't let myself make a way.

345 MR. P: Now this is what I'm questioning. Because I (stammers) I . . . it's. . . .

346 MRS. P: (interrupts) Now there isn't any money. There's not even enough money for you to go to the football games for that matter. But you are able to do it and I. . . .

347 MR. P: We-l-l, I agree (laughs with embarrassment) but I also say we both, pardon the expression, piss away enough money that these two things should be no problems.

348 THERAPIST: Well, maybe we need to attend to the "pissing away the money," and also this very real problem between you of your abject depression and what's entailed in that and on Sally's part, her alarm. Because you . . . and then what happens between you is . . . communication breaks down. Because you want something from Sally. She gets scared. Whether Sally can provide it or not remains to be seen, but then she vanishes from you and you feel . . . what you feel I don't know. Do you feel angry? Do you feel despair? Do you feel rejected by her? This time, you didn't run . . . run away. You felt yourself withdrawing. But something happens for you, too . . . (deep breath). Okay. (terminating interview, changes tone) Now look Jack, what is your address? . . . (Some discussion about Mr. P.'s address.) See you on Monday next week.

45

349 MR. P: (to Mrs. P.) Monday night is all right with you? Right?
350 MRS. P: Yeah.
351 MR. P: Huh?
352 MRS. P: Yeah.
353 MR. P: (in jocular tone) Got nothing to do?
354 MRS. P: There is something, but I can't think of it . . . Oh no . .
                okay.

(*everyone says goodbye.*)

Treatment issues in session one

1*   Is it unusual for a patient to immediately plunge into a "problem at issue" in the marriage as the opening gambit of a conjoint session?

5–21   What inner representation of self does Mrs. Porter convey as she complains of her husband's being more open when he drinks and the sense of loss of support she experiences? What might be the sources of some of the feelings she expresses?

24   Why did the therapist turn to Mr. Porter at this point?

33–45   How would you interpret the nature of the communication problem revealed by the Porters here?

74   How does Mrs. Porter's anxiety contribute to the communication problem in the marriage?

95   Can you speculate why Mrs. Porter did not want her husband to talk when they were having intercourse? Why did she react with such anger at his attempt to be verbally affectionate?

102   Why do you think the therapist changed the subject at this point? What is your assessment of her action?

162–164   The therapist brings in Mrs. Porter at this point. Why do you think she did this?

179   What does Mrs. Porter's use of the phrase "slit your wrists" signify?

205–206   How do you assess the therapist's approach of contrasting Mrs. Porter's anxiety with that of her husband?

233   After the therapist has repeatedly probed into the effect of Mr. Porter's drinking on Mrs. Porter, she now suggests a

* Numbers correspond to numbered utterances in the clinical session.

connection with the past and Mrs. Porter rejects this. Does this signify that Mrs. Porter was not ready for such an inter-pretation? How would you have proceeded in the face of Mrs. Porter's response?

241　　How do you evaluate the therapist's directness here in referring to Mr. Porter's previous suicide episode?

266　　Do you think Mr. Porter accepted the interpretation that he turns his angry feelings against himself and that drinking is like drowning himself? What is the evidence for this?

287–303　　In what way has Mrs. Porter's childhood experience of being raised by a father with a serious drinking problem left its mark on her?

309　　Did you get the impression that the therapist was talking *to* Mrs. Porter *about* Mr. Porter, or did she address herself to both at the same time?

330　　Do you feel Mr. Porter was expressing warm feelings toward his wife? Do you think the therapist was on the right track in responding to the reality of the financial situation rather than the feelings Mr. Porter expressed?

348　　Do you believe that the therapist's summing up of the important issues of this interview was a good way to end the session?

General questions

1. In the playback session, the therapist was particularly self-critical about something she had done in this session. What do you think this error was?

2. How would you characterize the overall dynamics in the relationship between the Porters that has emerged in this session?

3. What aspects of communication difficulty does this session reveal?

4. Is there any similarity in the impairments shown by the Porters?

5. How do you evaluate the therapist's use of past history in this session?

SESSION TWO

*Outside attachments
and loyalty to the marriage*

THE PORTERS *have been reunited for several months. They
are making a great effort to rebuild their marriage. Yet problems beset them which lead to dissatisfaction and unhappiness
in the marriage. In this session* * *the issue of their basic commitment and potential loyalty to each other pervades their verbal transactions. Mr. Porter begins by announcing he has
tendered his resignation from his job because his emotional
involvement with a female co-worker—which predates the
reunion—has created unmanageable work problems. Mrs.
Porter denies feeling hurt by her husband's admission of
residual feelings for another woman because she hopes he
will understand her having this feeling for another man. She
is candid in revealing her sense that Mr. Porter doesn't
meet all of her desires and expectations of a man and speaks
of her inner wish for platonic, intellectual relationships with
other men. Mr. Porter overflows with anger about his wife's
revelation and ties this in with her rebuff of his sexual advances, on the alleged grounds that his breath smells and he is
unbathed. Mrs. Porter defends herself tearfully and coin-
cidentally reveals strong hostility to women with whom she
could never enjoy such platonic relationships. The session ends
with angry, hurt feelings unresolved.*

* Session of May 16, 1966

(Preliminary discussion about how to work the tape recorder)

1 MR. P: (seems to struggle with welter of emotions) Well . . . I have a number of things I want to talk about . . . (pause). Uh . . . this morning I asked uh . . . (employer) for a . . . uh . . . conference this afternoon. (voice rises) Which I went to (sighs) and which . . . uh, I tendered my resignation at my firm. No hanky-panky. Just did it (voice fades out).

2 THERAPIST: You mean you had gone there with that expectation? . . .

3 MR. P: Yeah.

4 THERAPIST: Or it happened at the spur of the moment?

5 MR. P: (in low register) No. With that expectation. (more firmly) I went to do it!

6 THERAPIST: Oh.

7 MR. P: Uh-m, in terms of the time factor, the . . . um, soonest it can happen is Su . . . is September 1st. Uh (sighs) and I said, if at all possible . . . it'd be January 1st. I was quite honest with her in saying that I did not have a job at this point. I had nothing to go to. Uh . . . but . . . I wanted her to know quite honestly I was going to be looking. I wanted to feel free to say, "You may call my employer and check my references," uh, because I wanted to come up with the best situation that I could come up with. Now, of course, the question comes up, "Why?" . . . (long pause) Over . . . the past two months or so (suppressed volume conveys difficulty in revealing material) I've been living with the situation at work which has gotten rather sticky. It's a personal situation of my own making, but it has gotten sticky.

8 THERAPIST: (very softly) Can you say what it was?

9 MR. P: (subdued) Uh? The young lady that I was involved . . . with. Uh . . . I think this is on both of our parts. I will not sit here an . . . and say it's on one part or the other. I think we both have, uh . . . realistically perhaps some feeling

51

	for one another. Not strong feeling, but feelings. It has interfered extremely with the work. So much so that, you know, every day I'm having arguments about something.

10 THERAPIST: With her or with others?

11 MR. P: With her, with others, with everyone.

12 THERAPIST: She is, in a sense, responsible to you on this job, too?

13 MR. P: Well, she's not responsible for me, we're on a par, an. . . .

14 THERAPIST: Oh.

15 MR. P: (flat, suppressed tone). . . . and uh . . . in terms of responsibility. And, uh . . . we've conflicted . . . just, any number of times and I'm not always sure, you know, whether sometimes it's me, sometimes it's her, you know, and I don't know. I think this is something I need to examine but I don't know if this is apropos to what we're talking about right now. Uh . . . I think Sally has been aware . . . that I've come home and I've started to talk about this . . . uh . . . I have b . . . sometimes been fearful of talking about it, and (to Sally) I'm not trying to cast aspersions at you, Sally, but I didn't want to weigh her down with these problems. But in thinking about it . . . with myself, I really feel, you know, that in order to (self-interruption) . . . I go in and—and sometimes I just can't describe to you, uh, you know, to *either* one of you, uh . . . the arguments that I get into (speeds up stream of speech) and I'm not so sure it's all a result of this relationship. Uh, I think a great deal of it is part of management which I . . . I'm finding, you know, I'm becoming less and less enchanted with. (increases volume and tempo) So, I went down and I talked with her (sighs).

16 THERAPIST: With whom?

17 MR. P: My employer. Told her exactly what . . . I felt. Told her. . . .

18 THERAPIST: (interrupts) Mentioning this, too?

19 MR. P: Mentioning this, too. 'Cause she's been aware of (unclear) She's asked me any number of times, "What has happened with you and Nancy? Why . . ." you know, "The two of you have had the closest of relationships."

20 THERAPIST: The other one is . . . ?

21 MR. P: No. No. (laughs) Uhmm . . . you know, there isn't the closeness of the relationship yo . . . the two of . . . uh, an . . . and she wasn't talking of the personal, working relationship.

52

Though she may have been talking personal, but I wasn't talking personal. . . . (fades)

22 THERAPIST: Was she aware of any personal relationship?

23 MR. P: Oh, I think everybody around the firm has basically been—been aware of it, you know.

I mean they . . . they have all conjectured (voice gets very soft), let me put it to you that way. Uh . . . but there have been disagreements and, you know, *real* disagreements about the way things should be done and so forth. And . . . quite frankly and quite truthfully, the cap was last night . . . which was my birthday.

24 THERAPIST: (surprise) Oh.

25 MR. P: (barely audible) Uhh . . . I had said to Sally that I would be late getting home. Uh . . . because the young man that works with me . . . uh, had had a death in the family and he had to go to a wake. Uh. But I didn't expect to be as late as I was and I got home . . . I caught the . . . uhm . . . and maybe I'm wrong in this and . . . I've been told a dozen times this evening, between four o'clock and a quarter to nine when I got here, that I was wrong about this. Um. But suddenly certain things had to be done last night that *I* felt, in my judgment, from where I sat, could be put off, and. . . .

26 THERAPIST: Who . . . who felt that it could be . . . had to be done? Nancy or your employer?

27 MR. P: Uh, Nancy started it and then my employer agreed with her. And, I frankly exploded at both of them last night. And then, you know, I . . . I'd been thinking this a long time and I just decided that, you know, I really, I was gonna . . . I wanted *out*. Uh, it's not good for *me* because I go in there and, you know, I'm so churned up at the end of the day that I, you know, I'm worth nothing. So, this is what I've done. I hope, to Sally, you know, that this doesn't become threatening.

28 THERAPIST: Which part of it?

29 MR. P: My quitting the job. You know, giving my resignation. . . .

30 THERAPIST: (softly) Well she's here. Ask her.

31 MR. P: Uh . . . I . . . have, you know, a rather (hesitant laugh) definite plan of action that I'm gonna pursue, and I'm, you know, I'm going (voice trembles) to come out of this as best I can. I mean in terms of . . . of another job . . . (pause).

53

32	THERAPIST:	Are you asking her for a response?
33	MR. P:	Yeah, yeah.
34	MRS. P:	(barely audible) I think whatever you want is all right with me.
35	THERAPIST:	(softly) But doesn't it affect you in any way? . . .
36	MRS. P:	(subdued) Of course I'm affected, but I will go along with whatever he decides. He knows the situation better than I do.
37	THERAPIST:	Can you share with us how you experience what, you know, Jack's talking about? After all, he's saying several things. He's saying, one, he has to have another job and even though he has some time (asks Mr. P.) they granted you. . . .
38	MR. P:	Uh, we, we agreed that the earliest anything would happen would be September 1st. . .
38A	THERAPIST:	Uh-hm.
39	MR. P:	Uh, the outside date would be January 1st.
40	THERAPIST:	So they granted you both? (voices overlap)
41	MR. P:	Yeah, yeah.
42	MRS. P:	What?
43	THERAPIST:	He's saying two things. One, the loss of something definite without anything positive there, anything assuring. And he's saying he was still in a way attracted to Nancy.
44	MRS. P:	Well, Jack has *resigned* before. If this . . . if he had quit . . . tomorrow . . . or tonight or ever, at the end I might be upset. But there's enough time for him to find a job if he wants to and if this is just another threat—not to me, to his employer, as it was before—then it will pass. But there's time to think and I'm not particularly upset about it. The other business is . . . Jack's business.
45	THERAPIST:	(surprised tone) Not yours? Doesn't affect you, too?
46	MRS. P:	Uh uh.
47	THERAPIST:	(surprised) How can this be? You mean you're so disinterested in . . . in Jack affectionately that his affection for another woman and the fact that it still continues to play a part in this instance, really negatively, in his career, and his life, his moods. . . .
48	MRS. P:	(in subdued, low register) I'm not surprised . . . and a . . . to hear it. It's only natural that you just don't stop feeling things for someone if you have problems. You don't just stop. And I know that many times when there is someone you care for, you can . . . you can be angry with them or disagree with

	them just because you do care for them. Now . . . but that is Jack's problem in that his feelings are his problems and if he can't work with this situation . . . and . . . or if his feelings for her are so strong that he must leave, then he must leave.
49 THERAPIST:	How do you feel about his feelings being so strong? Is it a relief to you to know this, or is it a disappointment or is it a . . . (voices overlap).
50 MRS. P:	No it just makes me. . . .
51 THERAPIST:	. . . threat to you?
52 MRS. P:	. . . wonder why he is so. . . . (voices overlap)
53 MR. P:	I can . . .
54 MRS. P:	If his feelings aren't strong enough that he wants to live with (hesitates) us . . . I. . . .
55 MR. P:	No, no, wait a minute, wait a minute. Let me make one thing clear. At least I hope I . . . I make this clear. I'm not always sure . . . yes, some of my feelings come involved in this. There's no question about this and I make no, you know, no bones about this. I'm not sure that it is always me. I think, you know, I am made to react at times.
56 MRS. P:	Uhmm. . . . It can be very awkward.
57 MR. P:	Yeah. And-an-and, you know, I find myself, you know, uh. Friday night I came home. I'd had an argument. Uh . . . I didn't want to n-n-not burden . . . eh . . . eh . . . I . . . don't mean to . . . no, I *do* mean it in that way . . . uh, because I felt, you know, you was, you was so emotionally involved in something else, you know. I mean thi-this business of this committee and so forth and you were so wrought with that. I started to talk to you about it, but then I . . . I pulled back and I think you recall when I did this. Uh . . . I was not happy, you know, one *damn* bit in having to (faint laugh) stay there last night and I made no bones about it, you know. And, you know, quite honestly and quite truthfully, said it to, you know, all that were involved.
58 THERAPIST:	You had planned something very special for. . . .
59 MR. P:	(interrupts) No-o! It was (squeezes voice into high pitch) just my birthday. I wanted to be home! And you know. . . .
60 THERAPIST:	Well, fine. . . .
61 MR. P:	And, you know, i-it was just. . . . (voices overlap)
62 THERAPIST:	You were entitled to it.
63 MR. P:	(obviously under strain) You know, it was just really as simple

	as that. (retreats) I'm sorry. I don't mean to raise my voice, but I . . . I've been (voices overlap)
64 THERAPIST:	Well, why shouldn't you raise your voice?
65 MR. P:	(louder) I've . . . I've been through this *all night!* (angrily) Tonight, you know, an . . . and. . . .
66 THERAPIST:	Jack, why shouldn't you raise your voice here?
67 MR. P:	Ahh . . . ahh . . . course I should. But (laughs with embarrassment). . . .
68 THERAPIST:	You know, what's—what's so forbidding here, you know?
69 MR. P:	No. (loudly) Bu-but, you know, I-I-I, uh . . . I-I-I been going through this all night. I mean, this, that, you know. Um, why did I get angry about last night. Yo-You know, it's (laughs lightly) very simple. I wanted to be out.
70 THERAPIST:	Jack, are you having any reaction to my probing and inquiring with Sally, here, as to whether she has any reaction to your attachment, slight or much as it may be, to Nancy? Does it make you uncomfortable?
71 MR. P:	(thoughtfully) I guess maybe in a sense it does.
72 THERAPIST:	Can you say in what way?
73 MR. P:	(draws in breath) Well (slight, nervous laugh), you know, I think Sally and I have . . . begun to really, I think, for the first time in a long time, you know, really, you know, really, in a real long time in our marriage, beginning to *build* something. (Therapist: Uh-huh.) And, uh, you know, here I come along and I throw this at her . . . an . . . an . . . and I . . . in one sense I'm . . . I'm hesitant about it.
74 THERAPIST:	Umm. I can appreciate that.
75 MR. P:	(in quivering voice) Uh, because I don't want to upset any applecart. I don't wanna, I don't wanna hurt her feelings. God knows I don't. Um, you know, in this respect. I don't want to sound threatening or an-anything like this. But yet I want to be honest about it. And, you know, if I came in and said, you know, "I-I quit the job today," and not s-said why or what my feelings were about it. Uh, you know, this wouldn't get us anywhere either.
76 THERAPIST:	But do you feel on one level, on the other hand, that by my inquiring, that this may be stirring up some angry feelings in Sally which would upset the feeling you have that you're building on something?
77 MR. P:	This may be. But, I, you know, I hope, you know, this is all I

	can say is that, that if it does, you know, it's something else we have to work out an . . . and I'm willing to work it out.
78 THERAPIST:	Well, I can see that you'd be apprehensive about it, but my observation has been that, in part, the trouble between you has been that resentments have smoldered underneath and, for the first time in your lives, you are communicating *openly* and attempting to work and understand what goes on for each of you. I don't mean to suggest that you have, you know, opened up all the doors . . . (Mr. P.: Uhm) . . . uh, and to ignore, for instance, there was a period when you were very furious with Sally when she had told you about her attachment (Mr. P.: Uhm.) to this other man.
79 MR. P:	(softly) Um. Um.
80 THERAPIST:	I don't know whether the anger ever really, where it finally went. Uh, it seemed to dis . . . diminish sufficiently for you to be able to get back into the house. Whether you had left-over feelings I don't know. We might. . . .
81 MR. P:	Um.
82 THERAPIST:	. . . at some point understand this. But it *is* rather important, it seems to me, if you can *build* on, you know, what you have now, for feelings to be more open so that you know ho . . . what you're dealing with instead of shadows.
83 MR. P:	Um.
84 THERAPIST:	And that's. . . .
85 MR. P:	Frankly, this is my feeling and this is why I . . . I, you know. . . .
86 THERAPIST:	And this is why I'm asking you, Sally. 'Cause I really don't know whether it may be a relief or it may not, you know.
87 MRS. P:	Th-the only, the only way I'm really affected is that I am glad in a way that Jack still (choked up, voice quivers with emotion) feels this for her because I still feel this for someone.
88 THERAPIST:	Um-hm.
89 MRS. P:	And I would . . . (becomes choked and is unable to continue)
90 THERAPIST:	(softly) What are you choking down, Sally?
91 MRS. P:	(crying softly) Can I have a tissue?
92 THERAPIST:	Sure. (long pause)
93 MRS. P:	It isn't hard for me to understand that. . . . if it's a limited kind of feeling.
94 THERAPIST:	How do you mean that?

95 MRS. P:	(in quivering voice) Because I know that there has to be a residue of some kind of-of feeling for anybody after something . . . has happened between you and I can understand that . . . as long as that is what it is, because I would want this to be appreciated in me, too.
96 THERAPIST:	Um-hm.
97 MRS. P:	Because I have felt, um, since Jack has been back home, that I have just got to turn over (takes a deep breath) *everything* to him and not. . . .
98 THERAPIST:	(in low register) And that's (unclear)
99 MRS. P:	That I've got to be (picks up speed) some fairy-tale woman again (moves into exaggerated intonation) of loving my husband and not feeling affection for other, you know, any . . . anybody else. And it isn't the way I feel!
	But I am afraid that he will think that. . . . (voice fades tearfully and becomes unclear)
100 THERAPIST:	(softly) I'm sorry. . . . You're afraid he would feel what?
101 MRS. P:	(falteringly) That he would think that I didn't want him because I . . . because I'm fond of somebody else doesn't mean that I am not fond of Jack, but, but most people are so narrow in their definitions of things that it doesn't allow, you know, if you're married to someone then this has got to be the only relationship you have. And I felt very guilty because this isn't all that I want.
102 THERAPIST:	(softly) Well, can you say what you want? Since you talk about limits and then you talk about what you want—and, maybe we can try to understand.
103 MRS. P:	There . . . there are certain people that I know, men that I know, since I met—since Jack was away. They're not men that I have a physical relationship with but there are men that interest me in different ways. Uh (picks up speed), now for them it may be something else, I'm not going to kid (laughs lightly) anybody about that, but, for me, there . . . there are people that I have interests with in common, that do different things for me, that stimulate me in certain ways. And I don't want to have to give that up just because I'm married to Jack and I don't mean it to . . . to be . . . to diminish our relationship in any way if we can build one. Now maybe I'm asking for something that just can't be. But rather than . . . than expecting Jack to be everything. . . . I don't see why I

can't have Jack the way he is. . . . and have other relationships too, and I would think he would . . . I would hope he would want that with me because I know I'm not perfect. Maybe this lets me off the hook (laughs) then from not being . . . you know, perfect all the time, but. . . .

104 THERAPIST: Wait a minute. You use the word "perfect" and you also . . . by "perfect" you mean. . . .

105 MRS. P: You know. . . .

106 THERAPIST: . . . just with your eyes glued on one man.

107 MRS. P: Yes, 'cause, you know, one woman being everything to . . . I can't be everything to Jack and I'm so conscious of this all the time. And I wouldn't resent him finding other (voice quivers with emotion) things in other women as long as there was a basic loyalty that we had to each other.

108 THERAPIST: Well, what's in loyalty? 'Cause . . . both of you have had physical (Mrs. P.: Yeah.) relationships as—and with people you both have liked. . . .

109 MRS. P: Yeah. . . .

110 THERAPIST: . . . as—additionally as people. Right?

111 MRS. P: Right.

112 THERAPIST: So. . . .

113 MRS. P: I-I don't . . . I don't . . . necessarily want a physical relationship with anybody . . . (voice fades, unclear) . . . A-again I . . . I may be kidding myself. I don't . . . I don't know. But I don't think that I do.

114 THERAPIST: So the thing that comes through is, in a sense, some sense of relief that you don't have to play a, you know, a fictitious role here. That if Jack can understand this—maybe he can understand your needs, too. . . .

115 MRS. P: Yes.

116 THERAPIST: . . . and you can be more open with him?

117 MRS. P: (very faintly) Yeah.

118 THERAPIST: (to Mr. P.) How does it feel to you, what Sally was saying?

119 MR. P: I *don't* understand it.

120 THERAPIST: All right, so ask.

121 MR. P: I-I-I just don't understand it!

122 THERAPIST: What don't you understand? (short pause)

123 MR. P: I'm sorry. I-I'm . . . uh . . . (becomes blocked). . . . for whatever it is, for whatever I, you know, it is, I-I-I don't *need* anybody else, and I haven't *needed* anybody else,

haven't *looked* for anybody else . . . uh, since I returned home. I-I-I don't understand it.

124 THERAPIST: In other words, it isn't as easy for you to understand. . . .

125 MR. P: No.

126 THERAPIST: . . . what Sally was asking?

127 MR. P: No. I don't know what she's asking.

128 THERAPIST: Well, here we are! Good time to try to understand it.

129 MR. P: I mean, I-I-I-I-I recognize . . . *my* situation, uh, in that, uh, obviously my reacting i-in . . . a . . . a . . . with, uh, Nancy is-is-is a, uh, certainly a carryover from that, uh, what I am saying here, um, at least what I (short laugh) am consciously saying here and what I am certainly have no intentions from, uh (small explosive laugh) deviating from is that, uh, I'm not asking, uh, to rekindle a relationship or anything like this. (speeds up) I'm doing, you know, in fact, I'm-I'm far from it.

130 THERAPIST: You're running from it.

131 MR. P: (moves into high register) Sure, I'm running from it! I recognize there are certain weaknesses in me.

132 THERAPIST: Weaknesses?

133 MR. P: Oh, well I call them weaknesses.

134 THERAPIST: What is the weakness? I'm . . . I want . . . want to understand what you mean by this.

135 MR. P: Well, you know, I like girls. I like girls, you know, make no mistake about it. You know, I. . . .

136 THERAPIST: Well even that I don't understand, when you say you like girls.

137 MR. P: (glottalizes in high register) Ah-h-h-h . . . I . . . I-I-I-I . . . the chase, the capture, the . . . the . . . (voice becomes firmer and louder) whatever you want to call it, I mean, this I know about myself! But also, I-I know that, uh, I only want to be one place. I have made a decision. I made a very—firm decisions in . . . decision in *my* mind that this is where I wanted to be. And whatever I look for . . . in companionship and in . . . a personal relationship, I look for in my wife and . . . and no place else.

138 THERAPIST: So what you're asking is why then does she want. . . .

139 MR. P: Um!

140 THERAPIST: . . . interest in any other man.

141 MR. P: Um!

142 MR. P: (long silence) And yet, you know, I-I, you know, this doesn't surprise me. I'm sure Sally . . . (fades out).

143 THERAPIST: What doesn't surprise you?

144 MR. P: Uhm . . . her reaction here.

145 THERAPIST: I don't understand why not. 'Cause on one hand you feel . . . you sound surprised that with all of the pulls for you, but you're willing . . . (voices overlap).

146 MR. P: No, I am, I-I-I-I-I-I thought.

147 THERAPIST: . . . drop it (unclear)

148 MR. P: I find. . . . At least, you know, recently in a physical sense I find, you know, uh . . . basically, there are no oth . . . no other ways to say it you know, that Sally finds her . . . self . . . a-a-a-unattracted to me, or . . . or something.

    I-I don't quite understand what, uh . . . you know, you know, suddenly my breath stinks, . . . uh, and my timing is always off . . . I-I don't know.

149 THERAPIST: When suddenly? For a while after you returned home, it was better and now it's different again?

150 MR. P: No. I . . . recent . . . I mean, you know, since I've been back home, all the time my breath stinks and this is . . . uh . . . I . . . this is a problem I never had or one I'd never been aware of. And yet, uh, I am sensitive about these things!

151 THERAPIST: Um-hm.

152 MR. P: And, you know, if I . . . maybe I got a, you know, my gums have been bleeding and I think I should go back to the dentist. I was there about three weeks ago, and maybe there's something wrong. I don't know. But I, you know, uh . . . but, you know.

153 THERAPIST: (overlaps) But you're expecting that. . . .

154 MR. P: I would attempt . . . I would attempt to kiss my wife and, and you know, I would be rebuffed. An . . . (goes into low register) and I don't understand this. And, I'm not trying to be funny (Sally laughs in background), Sally, you know.

155 MRS. P: (softly) I'm not laughing, Jack.

156 THERAPIST: (deliberatively) So that with all of your efforts, feeling unacceptable, what has that left you with?

157 MR. P: I (very quietly) didn't, uh . . . I don't understand.

158 THERAPIST: Well, you say it makes you feel funny and I'm trying to understand "funny" in what way. I don't. . . .

159 MR. P: (interrupts) That I'm not wanted! I mean, you know, in . . . (glottalizes) in a personal i-i-in . . . in a close, personal intimate relationship.

160 THERAPIST:	Yeah, but does it make you feel sad, angry, depressed, uhh, 'cause you're going, you know, you've been pitching. You've been going on and you've *both* been pitching! All I'm, you know, trying to ferret out is what the feelings are under these circumstances . . . 'cause for one reason or another being unacceptable must, you know. . . . (voices overlap)
161 MR. P:	My initial reaction is to. . . .
162 THERAPIST:	You're human!
163 MR. P:	. . . My initial reaction is one of anger and, the . . . the . . . uh . . . calculated action is one of . . . of, uh, what is important. And . . . an' in terms of my s-s-feelings and thoughts, you know, keeping the home together is very important. And so, you know, uh, I have to learn.
164 THERAPIST:	What do you have to learn? To live with this part of it in order to keep the home together?
165 MR. P:	(barely audible) That's right.
166 THERAPIST:	Instead of finding out why you're so unacceptable and what this does to you?
167 MR. P:	Well, no . . . no. We're doing that now (voices overlap and Mr. P. gets louder). But I mean . . . I'm-I'm-I'm-I'm . . . in terms of the immediate reaction and . . . and the immediate, uh. . . .
168 THERAPIST:	Oh, I see what you mean. . . .
169 MR. P:	Yeah.
170 THERAPIST:	You don't walk off in a huff. . . .
171 MR. P:	Yeah.
172 THERAPIST:	. . . or in a rage . . . or in a . . . (lapses into silence).
173 MRS. P:	(in low register) Yeah. Well one thing has got nothing to do with the other. I only told you that about your breath because you never have been like that and I thought . . . (voice conveys strain) I really think something is *wrong;* you either have stomach trouble or something because I *never* in all the years we've been married have noticed this about you, and I have in the last few months. (Mr. and Mrs. P.'s voices in strident overlap with each refusing to give way to the other) And I thought you would like to know about it.
174 MR. P:	(voice choked, rises into high pitch) You may be . . . you may be . . . you may . . . Sally, you may be absolutely right. You may be absolutely right and I will not *argue* with you

about it. I wi . . . you know, I will try to (voice high) find out about it because I am concerned about it. I'm . . . I'm as concerned about it, too, but I also, you know, recognize . . . put this together with a couple of other things. . . .

175 MRS. P: (interrupts) Well that had nothing to do with that night.

176 MR. P: Oh . . . all right (sulkily concedes). Not that night, you know, there've been other times, you know.

177 THERAPIST: I think what Jack is . . . Jack, what you're saying is that you want to know what . . . you'd like to understand why, if it isn't the breath it's som . . . it's something else and what this is all about.

178 MR. P: Hm! (prolonged silence)

179 MRS. P: (quietly) I don't really know what it's all about. I know that when I'm upset I don't want to sleep with you, and I have been very tired and upset lately, but that isn't, that isn't all of it. . . . You know (voice becomes somewhat tearful) this business about my father that you were talking about the last time. . . .

180 THERAPIST: Uh-hm.

181 MRS. P: One night—and I'm only telling this because it . . . it's connected. I'm not saying this again to hurt you or anything like that. But there was a night Jack got in bed. I don't think he had been drinking. I don't—by that I mean excessively— maybe he'd had a drink or two. I don't know. You were very tired. Jack got in bed with his underwear on, laid out on the bed, spread-eagled like this . . . (gestures) whiskers, everything, and it (laughs agitatedly) really was my father!

182 THERAPIST: Um.

183 MRS. P: (voice quivering conveying mixture of laughing and crying) I mean it's just the way he used to sit around the house!

184 THERAPIST: Um.

185 MRS. P: And I can't bear it! (voice becomes very choked) And I don't want anything to do with you when you're like that. And it doesn't go away. I remember it! I made this big . . . thing about pajamas and you thought it was some kind of superficial thing. It's a very real thing with me!

186 MR. P: (voice rises to squeal) Yeah. All right. I know this! Now— now I understand this.

187 THERAPIST: What do you understand?

63

188 MR. P:	(voice is firm, in high register) At least . . . (short laugh) that thi . . . yeah, that at least that my laying there in shorts has a real effect.
189 THERAPIST:	And that it has less to do with you than Sally's. . . .
190 MR. P:	Yeah!
191 THERAPIST:	. . . experience. (to Mrs. P.) But what happens to you is that then Jack turns almost completely, totally into. . . .
192 MRS. P:	(interrupts) He's just (voices overlap—unclear) . . . one more slob!
193 THERAPIST:	. . . terrible.
194 MRS. P:	(voice quivers with emotion) . . . You know, I didn't have much respect for my father and I felt sorry for him. And I don't want to have to have a husband that I don't respect and that I feel sorry for. Now, I don't want Jack to be like some toothpaste ad, some kind of plastic person, but there's some kind of minimal mode of conduct.
195 THERAPIST:	(softly, almost not audible) Wait a moment, Sally, let's see if we can understand it a little more precisely. When this happens, when you see Jack this way . . . are you, are you suggesting that then any other aspect of him which in other ways you do regard and do respect, gets wiped out?
196 MRS. P:	Yeah. I'm just overcome by this . . . revulsion.
197 THERAPIST:	Because that's the important part, that, you know, there is such revulsion that you lose all so . . . all sight (Mrs. P.: Yeah.), lose sight of *anything* else. . . .
198 MRS. P:	Yes. . . .
199 THERAPIST:	. . . that Jack convey . . . you know, means to you.
200 MRS. P:	Agreed. Yeah.
201 THERAPIST:	(softly but firmly) Well, that's really not Jack's problem. That's yours.
202 MRS. P:	(with trace of annoyance) I know!
203 THERAPIST:	(whispered) Yeah. It helps us to see it.
204 MRS. P:	But by the same token I (slight laugh) don't know why. . . . You know, before I come to bed, I either take a shower—I at least wash up. I don't come to bed after being up all day, being sweaty and every . . . I just don't do it. (squeezes voice, conveys frustration) And I don't know why Jack can't do this, too! It's . . . if nothing else it's lack of manners.
205 THERAPIST:	You mean it feels to you like a lack of regard for you.

206 MRS. P: Yes.

207 THERAPIST: . . . of . . . that's what you mean by the manners?

208 MRS. P: Yeah. (silence)

209 THERAPIST: Your father would do this pretty constantly?

210 MRS. P: Yeah.

211 THERAPIST: Whether people were in the house, I think you once said, or not.

212 MRS. P: Yeah.

213 THERAPIST: And even when you were a growing young woman.

214 MRS. P: (hardly audible) Especially then because that's when he was sick. Before that he was all right, or he wasn't around very much.

215 THERAPIST: Must have been pretty uncomfortable in many ways; here you were a teenager, your father exposing himself. He would plunk down like this in the living room with people and you around?

216 MRS. P: (whispered) And his bedroom was like off the, the living room. So that in order to go to the bathroom and he were asleep, he'd have to go through (laughingly) the whole house to get to the bathroom which was at the back of the house—he would go straight back.

217 THERAPIST: But. . . .

218 MRS. P: But he was, you know, a sick man and he was *old*. But Jack isn't sick and he isn't old and I don't know why he does the same thing.

219 THERAPIST: Except that you have your feelings not of under, you know, of the unreasonable attitude, "My father was old and he couldn't help it," but he affected you in a very alive way whether he was old or not! Because obviously it was a most uncomfortable, to put it mildly, situation for you since you have such strong feelings about it with Jack who in so many ways is different from your father. And yet he turns into your father when he is spread-eagled and not, you know, freshly bathed.

220 MRS. P: (voice hardens) You know, all that is true. But I try and think of any woman I know, if she without this history of a father like this, would want this either.

221 MR. P: Sally, maybe you—heck, I hate to bore you with (laughs) statistics, but the pajama industry in America for men is in

65

dire straits because men from twenty years ago are still sleeping in their skivvies as they did—a habit they developed in, during the war.

And this was just a (laughs) recent article in the New York *Times.* An-an-and . . . and I don't (becomes louder) know that I'm so different than . . . than they are, in this respect!

222 THERAPIST: And some men sleep in their, you know, no . . . with nothing on, in the nude.

223 MR. P: (voice in high register) That's right! That's right!

224 THERAPIST: So let's see what this is, seeing Jack exposed 'cause, you know, the image that you conveyed to me is of a dirty old man. . . .

225 MRS. P: (overlaps) He's not exposed, he's got on a crumby, very crumby underwear, I mean, he's had on all day. It isn't as if it were clean underwear!

226 THERAPIST: You mean it feels dirty to you. . . .

227 MRS. P: (emphatically) It's *dirty!* Yeah.

228 THERAPIST: And you're—because the sense you conveyed was this dirty old man.

229 MRS. P: Yeah.

230 MR. P: You will admit the fact that I bathe every morning.

231 MRS. P: (in low register) Yeah—like twelve hours later then come to sleep with me. 'Cause you work hard, you know.

232 THERAPIST: You mean there is so much stench around?

233 MRS. P: No. But it's just human smell in excess (to Mr. P.) plus the fact that you seldom wash your hands and you work hard.

234 MR. P: Oh, I wash my hands, Sally.

235 MRS. P: Very seldom.

236 MR. P: Come on.

237 THERAPIST: You wash your hands particularly much before you come here?

238 MR. P: I didn't tonight because I rushed out of Forty-third.

239 THERAPIST: They're . . . they're dirtier than they are now, Sally?

240 MRS. P: Sometimes.

241 MR. P: I rushed out . . . I washed up and rushed out of . . . ah . . . my place down to——Street tonight.

242 THERAPIST: (softly modulated) You know, it's understandable that the revulsion is there since the image and the association with your father is so clear. This I can appreciate. But I think we need to understand what more goes into this 'cause everything else goes out the window. 'Cause you had in the past

	talked when the three of us were together about two months ago or so back that, uh. . . . I don't remember whether it had anything to do with toileting and with washing up (becomes hardly audible) the whole feeling was, you know, the real, you know, a feeling for you this was real filth.
243 MRS. P:	(almost hushed tone) I don't remember that. I'm not particularly a fastidious person.
244 THERAPIST:	About your body?
245 MRS. P:	Yeah. And I'm-I'm sloppier in my surroundings (laughs) than Jack is some of the time. Uh, my house is not a-a-an overly clean house. I'm not that. . . .
246 MR. P:	(interrupts) Yeah. But you're talking about your person.
247 MRS. P:	Yeah.
248 THERAPIST:	We're talking now about your, you know, your body.
249 MRS. P:	Yeah.
250 THERAPIST:	Are you saying that you're no . . . you're not as fastidious as you'd like him to be bodily?
251 MRS. P:	No. And some people are I'm saying, so I don't think I have exceptionally high standards in this area (fades out). (sustained silence)
252 MR. P:	Well, can we get back to this other business 'cause I-I . . . that, you know, really disturbs me. You know, it's of concern to me and I don't understand what you meant about this. . . .
253 MRS. P:	Well, let's just forget that because then, you know . . . (fades out and becomes unclear).
254 MR. P:	(high pitch) No! I mean I can't forget that. Who can forget that?
255 THERAPIST:	Why can we . . . why should we forget this?
256 MRS. P:	Well, you know, uh. . . .
257 THERAPIST:	Sally! This is the easiest road to disruption . . . to forget. .´. .
258 MRS. P:	(interrupts) Okay. (sighing) All right? So I feel (voices overlap). . . .
259 THERAPIST:	It may be hard (unclear).
260 MRS. P:	. . . that way and it's very lovely; it's a nice dream. But it isn't practical and (slight laugh) I really didn't think, you know, you were going to swallow it anyway.
261 THERAPIST:	(emphatically) Well, wait a moment. You say it isn't practical —Jack is saying because (overlaps with Mr. P.) . . . it's unacceptable. . . .

67

262 MR. P: (overlaps with therapist) Uh . . . I-I-(squeezes voice and goes into high register) I-I . . . find it unacceptable, but I'd also like to understand it.

263 MRS. P: Well, I can't explain it anymore than I have. I've been exceptionally honest for me (voice shows tension). . . .

264 THERAPIST: Yes, that's true.

265 MRS P: And I have laid myself wide open (sounds teary).

266 THERAPIST: For what?

267 MR. P: (with firmness and anger) You haven't laid yourself wide open for anything. Now stop that foolishness (voices overlap).

268 MRS. P: I *feel* that way. (sighing and close to tears) By telling you that . . . and that is all I want to say, there's nothing more that you can say about it.

269 THERAPIST: What's the danger? How have you laid yourself open?

270 MRS. P: I don't know.

271 THERAPIST: You've laid . . . you've mentioned the fact that there are some men who interest you. You've mentioned the fact that there's still a feeling for this other man, and what's the danger, Sally, 'cause there is apparently?

272 MRS. P: (voice sounds hollow) That Jack will just find this totally unacceptable. I don't fit into the mold.

273 MR. P: (in high register) All right! I don't understand it. I'm sittin' here trying to understand it.

274 MRS. P: (faintly) Okay.

275 THERAPIST: Are you trying to understand why you're not interesting enough to Sally to fill the bill completely. . . .

276 MR. P: (interrupts) Well, yeah. This is part of it. Certainly. (voice vibrates in high register) I'd just like to understand.

277 MRS. P: You see, the way you say that makes it . . . seem as if I'm dissatisfied with you.

278 MR. P: Well, obviously, you are!

279 MRS. P: No, I'm *not!*

280 MR. P: Now, Sally, don't sit here and say that 'cause you are. . . . I . . . uh . . . you know, not dissatisfied. . . .

281 MRS. P: (interrupts) You are not the whole *world* to me. Maybe that's a terrible thing to say (voices overlap).

282 MR. P: (becomes shrill) Well, all right! (normal voice) I'd like to find out why I'm not.

283 THERAPIST: Would you like to be the whole world to Sally?

284 MR. P: Certainly I would!

285	THERAPIST:	All right. So it's not only. . . .
286	MR. P:	(interrupts) 'Cause I want her to be the whole world to me.
287	MRS. P:	(tearfully) I'm not able to be the whole world to you. . . . You . . . I dissatisfy you in so many ways, Jack!
288	MR. P:	(irritated) Oh Sally stop it! (voices overlap) You know that I . . . you know, dammit, you know this kind of thing hasn't . . . wh . . . in what ways do you dissatisfy me?
289	THERAPIST:	Well, she's certainly not receiving your affections.
290	MR. P:	Agreed. Agreed.
291	THERAPIST:	Boy, I would think that would dissatisfy you enormously.
292	MR. P:	Fine. (tensely) It does.
293	THERAPIST:	Why are you making so light of that?
294	MR. P:	(snaps angrily) I'm *not* making light of it! She's referring to something else, she's not referring to . . . in that area.
295	THERAPIST:	Oh.
296	MR. P:	And I'm sure she's not. And I'm sorry, I . . . uh . . . you know. . . .
297	THERAPIST:	What are you sorry about?
298	MR. P:	Well, didn't mean to contradict you, but she. . . .
299	THERAPIST:	(interrupts) What's the matter, why can't you contradict me?
300	MR. P:	(hardly audible) I don't know. I can't contradict you (laughs), you know.
301	THERAPIST:	(not clear) Absurd.
302	MR. P:	My Southern manners.
303	THERAPIST:	We need to spend some time on that pretty soon.
304	MR. P:	My Southern manners.
305	THERAPIST:	Uh-hum. Maybe. I don't know. Maybe something is involved in your . . . in your Southern manners here.
306	MRS. P:	(choked voice) Jack, it's not your fault that I'm the way I am.
307	MR. P:	(high pitched) Well, Jesus, it's not your fault tha-that the way . . . I'm the way I am. I'm trying to (very rapid) understand you. You trying to understand me.
308	MRS. P:	Well, then, why can't you understand that I am . . . *strange!*
309	THERAPIST:	That you're strange?
310	MRS. P:	I'm different than you are.
311	MR. P:	Certain . . . every . . . every human being is different. You got-you-you-yo-you-yo. . . .
312	MRS. P:	(voice quivering) Look, I'll tell you something. What I told you tonight . . . I don't know any woman—there's no woman

	in my acquaintance that has ever said to me they feel this way. (tearfully) And there is no woman I have ever told that I feel this way.
313 MR. P:	(high register and low volume) Well, fine, fine.
314 THERAPIST:	That you feel which way, Sally, that you'd like to be interested in other men?
315 MRS. P:	I told you. Yes!
316 THERAPIST:	Oh, there are thousands (voices overlap). . . .
317 MRS. P:	Now maybe they exist. . . .
318 THERAPIST:	. . . of other women.
319 MRS. P:	. . . but I don't know if in your world they exist.
320 MR. P:	(high pitched) Sally, I-I-I haven't said a thing yet.
321 MRS. P:	No, I *know* you haven't said a thing.
322 THERAPIST:	Oh, you've said a lot.
323 MRS. P:	I don't know what I'm trying to explain. I told you how I feel. . . .
324 THERAPIST:	Sally, you know, to say . . . to live in a world, for both of you to live in a world where you both think that to not have an interest in having a friendship with another man or woman, the question is what kind of friendship, how intense, what you're feeling you're missing, what you're feeling that Jack isn't supplying. This is what we're trying to work out.
325 MRS. P:	All right. There's . . . there's a man I know that I could call tomorrow—I never have—but I know I could call tomorrow and he would go to the museum with me. *Take* me to the (light laugh) museum and we could spend the afternoon at the museum and that would be it! And it would be (squeezes voice) very nice . . . and there is nothing wrong in that except if you think there's something wrong in it.
326 MR. P:	(very low register) Fine.
327 THERAPIST:	Is it really "fine"? (voices overlap) You didn't think it was "fine" before.
328 MR. P:	No. I . . . I say "fine."
329 MRS. P:	(in ringing tones) If you don't approve as my husband then there is something wrong in it. I would wish that you would (voices overlap). . . .
330 MR. P:	(interrupts) It's nobody that I know, unfortunately.
331 MRS. P:	(angrily) You don't *know* that it's anybody you know, and it doesn't make any difference.

332 MR. P:	(high pitched) Well, it *does* make a difference. (in high register) Makes a *big* difference!
333 THERAPIST:	What's the difference, Jack?
334 MRS. P:	Well, I'm not interested in anybody that you know.
335 THERAPIST:	Jack, what's the difference?
	(Mr. and Mrs. P. overlap loudly)
336 MR. P:	Just, ju . . . .
337 MRS. P:	(unclear) . . . a friend or something like that.
338 THERAPIST:	But can you say what the difference is?
339 MR. P:	(high pitched) I'm sorry, I-I-I'm a man and I know man's ways and man's thinking and, uh, you know, I'm sorry. I just can't buy this clear out of the blue!
340 THERAPIST:	What can't you buy?
341 MR. P:	That some man is going to take my wife to a . . . a museum and that's it.
342 THERAPIST:	Oh, you mean that he would have other interests . . .
343 MR. P:	(exclaims) That's right!
344 THERAPIST:	Oh. Well, how about it being a friend? Apparently that makes even more of a difference than if it's a stranger.
345 MR. P:	(talks in low register, almost mumbling) No, it does make a difference. A friend I wouldn't min. . . .
346 THERAPIST:	You asked then?
347 MR. P:	No! I . . . well, when I saying, I was saying it's someone I didn't know.
348 THERAPIST:	Jack, you may be very clear but can you help me understand? You did say, "Is it a friend or not a friend," and apparently it made some difference to you. . . . (voices overlap)
349 MR. P:	(interrupts) If it was someone I knew then, an . . . and . . . you know, fine!
350 THERAPIST:	Oh, you mean if it were a friend. . . .
351 MR. P:	Yeah, if it were a friend.
352 THERAPIST:	. . . then you would feel safer about it?
353 MR. P:	Yeah. Sure.
354 THERAPIST:	Oh.
355 MR. P:	I have no question about it.
356 THERAPIST:	(quietly) Oh. (silence)
357 MRS. P:	We don't have any friends that aren't married, you know, and I can't see their wives buying anything like that.
358 MR. P:	Umm, then you know how I feel.

359 MRS. P: (voices overlap) . . . I know. . . .

360 MR. P: You expect me to buy this?

361 MRS. P: (raises voice) I *don't* expect you. I said it knowing that you probably wouldn't accept it.

362 MR. P: (attempts to speak but is cut off) No more. . . .

363 THERAPIST: Sally, let me ask you something. . . . There's some feeling about going with a man to a museum, and this may sound like I'm saying to you, "Mustn't want another man," and it's not what I'm saying. I'm trying to understand. How is it that if the wish is the museum and to have company, why it . . . can't it be a man or a woman? For you the feeling is a man.

364 MRS. P: (speaks quietly, barely audible) I get along better with men. I don't know of any woman that I'd ever ask to do anything . . . (fades out) I don't like to meet women for lunch.

365 THERAPIST: I think there's . . . there's something here we ought to eventually. . . .

366 MRS. P: And I know many women who feel like that.

367 THERAPIST: . . . try to understand.

368 MRS. P: I mean (unclear) at base I don't know. It may be *sexual*. I don't know. Maybe I'm kidding myself that it's the intellectual stimulation that I want. I don't know. I work with women all day long, you know, and uh (hissing sigh). . . .

369 THERAPIST: Women leave you pretty cold.

370 MRS. P: Yeah. (barely audible) . . . I've had my fill of them, let's put it that way.

371 THERAPIST: (voices overlap and unclear) Are you talking about your adult "fill" or your childhood "fill"?

372 MRS. P: (in measured hollow tones) There are not many women that I know who are straight and aboveboard. Who don't waste time on nonsense. . . . All of them.

373 THERAPIST: (turns to Mr. P.) What's happening, Jack, do you know? Something else is happening (voices overlap) . . . your irritation.

374 MR. P: I-I . . . yeah. You know. Sa-Sally says things like that and my God I can name six gals off the top of my head that she knows that aren't this way. At least not in my experience with them.

375 MRS. P: I had said before here there are women that I like for certain things, they are fine. But I'm not going to spend an afternoon going to a museum with Beverly Hall even though I know Beverly likes to go to museums.

376 MR. P:	What about Sandy Kroll?
377 MRS. P:	(slightly pouting) No! I don't . . . I have. . . .
378 THERAPIST:	What's missing?
379 MRS. P:	I don't know. She's a certain type of person and I can take her under certain circumstances, but I won't seek her out because we have a very limited, uh. . . .
380 THERAPIST:	Look, I think one thing that is getting clearer and clearer is that there is something about women that leaves you uncertain, uncomfortable, resentful, I don't know what combinations, what ways—uh, what I mean to say is in what combinations. Uh . . . whether this is the time to try to understand what there is—there'll be time for it. We can do it now, we can do it later.
381 MRS. P:	We can do it later. Much later. Because it's no news to me at all.
382 THERAPIST:	Oh, I know. I've gotten this from you! I'm not telling you anything new (voices overlap).
383 MRS. P:	And it isn't something I particularly want to change and I don't think this is the place to change it anyway.
384 THERAPIST:	Oh?
385 MRS. P:	(with determination) No. Because nobody's going to undo what's been done in that area, too.
386 THERAPIST:	You mean you want to hold on to that?
387 MRS. P:	I see no reason and I-I haven't met anyone to, you know, make me change my mind. I take individuals one by one. I either like them or I don't and I go to museums with them or I don't. This is all pointless. . . .
388 MR. P:	(interrupts) It's not pointless, *dammit!* You know, you-yo-you're sitting here and saying it's pointless. It's not pointless. . . . Very frankly I sit here and I say to you, either you *do* or you *don't*, and by that I mean, you know.
389 MRS. P:	What?
390 MR. P:	Get us help, get us straight or don't get us help, get us straight.
391 MRS. P:	Jack, I haven't gone anywhere with anybody else. I haven't done anything (voices overlap).
392 MR. P:	(high pitch) I'm not *saying* that! What I'm saying, you know, whatever it is you feel, or whatever it is I feel, Jesus, if we can't sit here and *talk* about it. . . .
393 MRS. P:	Well, I've been talking about it. I *told* you about it.

73

394 THERAPIST: Well, you know, I also have another question here which should have occurred to me maybe earlier. Here I am a woman and through the help of this woman many things which have been trying for you have been emerging. How do you feel about having to work with a woman?

395 MRS. P: (low voice) I'm not particularly crazy about it. . . . (unclear) You start with a terrific handicap with me as far as (voices overlap). . . .

396 THERAPIST: Yeah, and I think we ought to appreciate that.

397 MRS. P: As far as, you know, I . . . you know . . . I'm sorry but that's true.

398 THERAPIST: I'm not taking any of this personally.

399 MRS. P: All right. (light laugh) But, you know, I know you now and I like you. But you, in my mind, I . . . you know, not you, as a woman you had a couple of strikes (laughingly) against you when I walked in the door and that's the way I am.

And now that I know you it's different. Uh, I think perhaps there are times in conversations when this creeps in again. . . .

400 THERAPIST: Um-hm.

401 MRS. P: . . . and where I would give a man (laughs lightly) the benefit of the doubt, I won't for you, you know. And I'm not particularly happy that I don't always get along with you all the time because I want everybody to love me and it's easier to make a man love me than a woman (laughingly).

402 THERAPIST: And if we're not getting along the immediate feeling is that you're being unloved.

403 MRS. P: Yeah. Yeah. It's very hard for me to . . . to . . . I'm very uneasy about our relationship because we don't get along often and I'm much more comfortable in a. . . .

404 THERAPIST: When you say we don't get along, how do you mean?

405 MRS. P: We don't agree, or I don't feel . . . um (unclear—I think about agreeing and disagreeing). You have remained very neutral in all of this and very fair I think and I would like you to be (laughing) on my side. You know, I really still feel that way.

406 THERAPIST: Yeah. Well, I can understand that. (to Mr. P.) Can you understand that?

407 MR. P: Yeah, I understand that.

408 MRS. P: Why don't we forget about this other idea of mine. All right?

409 MR. P: (shouts) No, I'm not going to forget. I can't forget about it. You ask me to forget about something, it's very important.

410 THERAPIST: Sally, you're making trouble for yourself. Umm, the hope would be that by dismissing it, you're, you know, it's not going to emerge, but it will emerge in many ways. It will emerge as a sadness, of the depression, as a loss, of your having to give in . . . of having to be perfect and, you know, we don't really begin to understand what's involved in this. And you're really—it's not only a question of being unfair to Jack, it's being so unfair to you.

411 MRS. P: All right, so what do I have to do . . . (voices overlap).

412 THERAPIST: It may be painf. . . .

413 MRS P: . . . do I have to justify . . . I feel that way and I've told you and I don't know what the next step in this process is. If Jack is to understand why I feel like this, what do I do next? Do I justify why I feel like this? I have no reasons.

414 MR. P: I'm not asking you to justify . . . I'm just (voices overlap).

415 MRS. P: (coldly) Then what do you want from me?

416 MR. P: I'm just asking you to talk about it so *I* can understand it.

417 MRS. P: I've been doing all the talking. You've been doing the questioning, so what . . . you know (unclear). . . .

418 MR. P: (mutters inaudibly) . . . really. . . .

419 THERAPIST: You know, Sally, I think you feel on the spot. Hold it a minute, Jack. Sally, I think you feel s-you know, on the spot as you said before; all this self-revelation and you've taken courage in your hand and increasingly been, you know, taking more risks (phone rings) in an area where you actually feel very vulnerable. (Therapist: on phone: Hello! Yes Ma'am . . . two minutes). And I really think (sighingly) we ought to allow ourselves more you know, time for this because it's only going to make trouble. Uh, Jack will go on with a doubt as to whether you're there really for him, you'll go on, you know, with a doubt as to, you know, ah, what he is depriving you of because you want to be loyal and good and it . . . it's not likely to work too well.

420 MRS. P: (poutingly) He's gonna be mad all week now . . . (fades out).

421 THERAPIST: Are you? . . . Suppose he is mad? . . . (to Mr. P.) Are you

that disturbed about it, Jack? You apparently are. That was a kind of foolish question.

422 MR. P:　　Yeah, yeah, somewhat. We'll get (unclear) Nothing drastic will happen . . . I assure you.

(*couple departs*)

Treatment issues in session two

54　　What feeling does Mrs. Porter express in responding to the reasons her husband gives for quitting his job? Would you say there is a congruence between her words and tone of voice? Did she answer her husband's question?

63–70　　What is your assessment of how the therapist deals with Mr. Porter's apology for having raised his voice?

76–78　　Is Mr. Porter experiencing the therapist as a benign or threatening person as she inquires into his feelings about her interventions? Do you have any question about her approach?

97–117　　What are the dynamics involved in Mrs. Porter's explanation of why she feels a sense of relief in learning that her husband has vestigial feelings for a female employee in his firm?

129–141　　What signs would indicate that Mr. Porter is upset here? What is disturbing him?

160　　Can you say why the therapist used the term "pitching" here when referring to the spouses' efforts to live together again?

148–174　　What is your estimate of the dynamics of Mrs. Porter's reported rebuff of her husband's sexual advances? How would you assess his statement that he does not want to become angry with his wife when she treats him this way?

179–196　　How would you assess the dynamics of Mrs. Porter's association of her husband's drinking and appearing "spread-eagled" in bed with her image of her father? Does the association explain her strong reaction to her husband's drinking?

219　　Why would the therapist continue to pursue Mrs. Porter's reactions toward her father and toward her husband?

240　　Do you think the therapist is "checking out" reality when asking Mr. Porter whether he washed his hands before coming to this session? How did Mr. Porter respond to this question?

251　　How do you interpret this silence: a) As Mrs. Porter's plea for assurance that she is not unreasonable? b) As an expression of anger? c) As resignation? d) Other?

224–233   What do you make of Mrs. Porter's emphasis upon cleanliness? What are the likely roots of such feelings?

252   Why is Mr. Porter changing the subject at this point?

265   Why does Mrs. Porter feel she has "laid myself wide open?"

271–287   What is Mrs. Porter conveying when she tells her husband, "You are not the whole world to me"? Is the couple struggling about an issue that lies below the surface?

291–305   What therapeutic principle is the therapist acting upon in this exchange? Do you agree with her handling of Mr. Porter's loss of control?

325   What might be the nature of the fantasy that underlies Mrs. Porter's expressed desire for a platonic relationship with a man outside of the marriage?

339–341   Is there a reality basis to Mr. Porter's skepticism about the intentions of other men to his wife?

363–401   In dynamic terms, what might be the source of Mrs. Porter's expressed antagonism toward women? What implications does the fact that the therapist is a female have for the course of treatment?

405   Do you think the therapist's probing was productive?

410   Do you agree with the therapist's interpretation of not encouraging Mrs. Porter to "forget it" with reference to her earlier expressed desire to have relationships with other men?

General questions

1. What would you regard as the central issue in this session?

2. How valid is the emphasis upon earlier experience as a source of explanation of Mrs. Porter's attitudes about drinking and cleanliness?

3. Would you characterize the interventions of the therapist as equally supportive of both spouses or more of one than the other?

4. Is there anything in the material you have heard which makes you suspect that Mrs. Porter's expressed revulsion against her husband may be connected with his blackness?

If you do, is it because of something made explicit by the communications, or because of something implied?

5. In what way, if any, does the session display the value of conjoint treatment for this couple?

SESSION THREE

Just pop a casserole

into the oven

Session THREE * *begins with Jack Porter presenting a check to pay for accumulated fees. The therapist detects some feelings of misgiving about money going out for therapy and encourages open discussion of this. It turns out that there is a sense of discouragement about where the marriage is headed which was exacerbated by a quarrelsome weekend. The Porters had undertaken to entertain friends on the weekend and had run into communication difficulties about their desires and inclinations with respect to being hosts on such occasions. Mrs. Porter found herself feeling overburdened and resentful at having to entertain on one of the two days she had off. Mr. Porter, in turn, resented her lack of graciousness in being a hostess and consoled himself with a few drinks with resulting diminishment of his performance as a host. The weekend was thus one of strain and hurt feelings. Mrs. Porter expressed her resentment in a dramatic way during the night. The therapist attempts to use the experience of the weekend to get the Porters to examine how each contributed to the debacle. The session is characterized by a high degree of emotionality and ends with Mr. Porter continuing to express doubts about the potential effectiveness of treatment. He sees his wife's behavior as part of an over-all stance of total disregard for his feelings.*

* Session of October 13, 1966

(*Therapist tests tape recorder.*)

1 THERAPIST:	October the 13th. . . . one, two, three, four.
2 MR. P:	(expels air with gusto, waves receipt for payment of back fees) I thought you'd get a letter from me before I'd return. . . .
3 MRS. P:	(laughs with slight embarrassment)
4 MR. P:	. . . I'm sorry . . . (slightly unclear) . . . I didn't get to it . . . (fades out).
5 THERAPIST:	(referring to bill sent to the P.'s) Well, maybe you felt like throwing it at me.
6 MR. P:	(laughingly with Mrs. P. joining in) Well . . . yeh . . . maybe I did, I don't know.
7 THERAPIST:	(laughs in staccato fashion) What do you think? Don't you think you might have felt . . . like throwing it at me!
8 MR. P:	Ah . . . as good as ever as of. . . .
9 THERAPIST:	You've gotten the whole thing cleared up?
10 MR. P:	Yeah. As of the 24th of October.
11 THERAPIST:	That's dated for next week.
12 MR. P:	Right.
13 THERAPIST:	Well, do you feel good about this? Or are—'cause last week you sounded as if (voices overlap) it were like the, uh. . . .
14 MR. P:	(talks in low key, somewhat unclear) I'm struggling, I'm struggling to get (unclear, laughs) debt paid the way I can. (talks under breath) You know. I can do without having to worry about the hundred, whatever it is, hundred twenty-five, you know, I have to pay here this month (fades out). (deep breath) Certainly it's worth it (sigh).
15 THERAPIST:	Well, wait a minute. . . . There was almost a question mark in your statement.
16 MR. P:	No question mark (extends check).
17 THERAPIST:	Will you give it to the person downstairs so you can get a . . . receipt for it (voices overlap) 'cause I don't have receipts here.

18 MR. P:	Well, no, we-e-we'll—got the canceled check but that's all right. I'll give it to her. Uh. . . .
19 THERAPIST:	Well . . . you know. . . . 'cause when you said, you know, you're sure it's worth it, there was an element of, "I'm not so sure it's worth it," as I heard it.
20 MR. P:	Well, it's just, i . . . you know, I-I . . . (sighs) it woulda been a little easier with this and uh, maybe I could have gotten a little more done this month than I had planned to get done, but, you know.
21 THERAPIST:	Well, what about it though, Jack? You know, let's stay with this for a while.
	(silence, 18 seconds)
22 MR. P:	(barely audible) Well, I don't know what about it, you know (unclear). I mean, I. . . .
23 THERAPIST:	What does it do to you not to have the plan work out the way, you know, you visualized it as getting it settled? And, uh, coming, you know, continuing here because you had a plan of halting for a month.
24 MR. P:	Well, it's just that it makes it much harder to do the things I would like to see us do; reach some of the goals I have in my mind for us . . . (fades out).
25 THERAPIST:	You mean being caught up? Or other goals?
26 MR. P:	Getting caught up and other goals also.
27 THERAPIST:	Can you share those—what you mean by. . . .
28 MR. P:	Oh, I think they're some things we need to get done around the house, I'd like to see us get done. I'd like to, you know, see us have our first (laughs) Christmas back together, one which is free of at least this kind of, you know, problem. And this is what I've been sort of shooting for.
29 THERAPIST:	You wanted this coming Christmas to be free of all the past debts, is that it?
30 MR. P:	Yeah.
31 THERAPIST:	Be kind of. . . .
32 MR. P:	Yeah. You know, so that Sally could feel free to have the kind of Christmas that she wants in terms of the children and the things she'd want to get; and wouldn't have to think about scrimping and scraping, this kind of thing. Maybe this is more myself than for Sally.
33 THERAPIST:	(softly) Well, Sally is here. You can ask her. We can ask her, you know.

34 MRS. P:	(in cheerful tone) Yeah. It would be nice to have, you know, the one Christmas not . . . well, what it . . . we didn't do it for two years, but we used to charge everything (slight laugh) at Christmas time and then January would just be dreadful. It would just be nice to not have to do that.
35 THERAPIST:	And you're anticipating that this is what again you'll have to do?
36 MRS. P:	Well, I don't know. We, uh . . . may have more sense. We didn't do it for two years. (suppresses laugh) We used to feel we had to really make a big splurge with, not only the children but other people, too, at Christmas time. And we've kind of gotten over that (voices overlap).
37 THERAPIST:	Over. . . .
38 MRS. P:	More realistic about, you know, the things we give people.
39 THERAPIST:	But . . . I hear a hankering for it, though, on (interrupted). . . .
40 MR. P:	Well, we (unclear) well, I mean, I don't know that it's a hankering. It-I-I just, within reason, you know, I'm not saying that it's going to be, you know, anything unlimited. I'm not trying to project it into that. But at least to feel that, you know, here it is . . . whatever it is that we have and you can go out and spend this with a, with a free mind or do with it, you know, without any fear of, you know, the mortgage not being paid or (sighs) this not being paid and this kind of thing. This is . . . (fades out).
41 THERAPIST:	What (unclear), so let's get back. You know, we can talk about realities (voices overlap). . . .
42 MR. P:	Well (unclear).
43 THERAPIST:	. . . too, but, uh, I get the sense almost as if you were snared or lured into, uh, junking your plan and going on here and, uh, undertaking another hundred and a quarter a month against your will. Against, you know, part of you. Not all of you, but a part of you.
44 MR. P:	Yeah.
45 THERAPIST:	'Cause this, in a sense, is what you're saying. Well, what about that?
46 MR. P:	I just think I could have come a little closer to making this realization that I just . . . or this dream that I had, or whatever you want to call it.
47 THERAPIST:	Well, why didn't you go ahead with this plan, you know.

	True (with light spoofing) Sally and I are very strong women here, huh?
48 MR. P:	(haltingly and not too clear) No, I-I . . . not that. I-I think really the thing that made me go along, it-it-I had felt that Sally, uh . . . concurred, or maybe it's, you know, my lack of communication with her in talking to her about these things more, uh, uh . . . uh, but when I did talk to her about it (speaks in low register, hardly audible) which was the day, I guess, we were coming here, uh . . . you know, she didn't seem to think it was such a good idea and didn't express any, uh, thing particularly in favor of it other than, "If that's what you think, okay." And, you know, uh, maybe my idea wasn't such a good idea.
49 THERAPIST:	Now wait. What . . . what you're saying is that if Sally didn't concur—we're not saying now whether she's right or she was wrong—but for you in feeling it set some doubts going about whether your plan was a good one.
50 MR. P:	Yeah. . . .
51 THERAPIST:	Well, does this always happen to you, that if you have a . . . a conviction about something, if Sally or somebody else. . . .
52 MR. P:	If it's someone I respect, sure.
53 THERAPIST:	Then you begin to doubt—have misgivings about your own. . . .
54 MR. P:	Second thoughts, at least.
55 THERAPIST:	Well, the second thoughts seem to be one of self-doubt rather than of its being valid.
	You know, it's being, uh, in truth, something you hadn't thought about and therefore a new set of facts which make you concur. What I get is that it upsets your own, uh, sense of, uh, comfort in your judgment.
56 MR. P:	(too low to hear)
57 THERAPIST:	Hm?
58 MR. P:	(repeats) I said it may, I don't know.
59 THERAPIST:	Oh.
60 MR. P:	(speaks with uncertainty) Uh-uh, you know, I guess it does . . . I, uh . . . 'cause you know I-I have a . . . ability or whatever, I don't know what you call it (goes into low register) uh, of, uh . . . perhaps losing sight of the seriousness of certain things, uh. In my mind the most important thing was to get these things cleared up so that, uh, we could both stop

feeling this, you know, the tightness under which we're . . . we're living, Sally and myself. Uh . . . and, uh, you know, I came up with the plan to sort of, you know, get us out of this. On the other hand, uh, there certainly is value in us continuing here and not breaking the string. Uh, you know, what more can I say? And I think perhaps in reality this is the more valuable of the two.

61 MRS. P: (softly modulated) You think we should still keep coming here?

62 MR. P: I think so.

63 MRS. P: Um.

64 THERAPIST: You have some other thoughts about it, Sally?

65 MRS. P: No. I just wasn't sure that Jack really felt we should still be coming, you know (voice fades). It just occurred to me.

66 THERAPIST: I don't quite—you mean whether there is still the same feeling about wishing to stop for a month, or wishing to stop altogether, or . . . ?

67 MRS. P: No. I just didn't know whether he felt we really needed to come anymore. I just had, you know, a hunch that maybe this was behind this.

68 THERAPIST: Uh-huh.

69 MRS. P: And that it wasn't really that important . . .

70 THERAPIST: This isn't your feeling you said, but you think it was, might have been his.

71 MRS. P: Might have been his, yes. It's not mine. I'm just curious to know whether it was his.

72 MR. P: We talked. . . .

73 THERAPIST: (to Mr. P.) Would you feel free to say so if you thought so?

74 MR. P: (hesitant and lacks fluency) Uh-huh. I think that, uh . . . (moves into high register) there's a lot we can learn here, each of us. Uh, and, you know, we are learning. . . . Uh . . . on the other hand, I-I really wonder sometimes how much each of us has really learned how to, uh . . . I . . . and so, you know, it . . . it leads to another conclusion, well, you know, uh . . . maybe we haven't learned as much as perhaps we should.

75 THERAPIST: Maybe it isn't worth it, all the effort.

76 MR. P: (overlaps therapist) Yeah, yeah. On the other hand, you know, we've reached a point, at least, where basically we can live with one another and, uh, life isn't so bad, you know,

85

we're not at one another's throats and we're not at the children's throats, uh, you know.

77 THERAPIST: But somewhere there's some dissatisfaction here. Jack, can you talk about that?

78 MR. P: Yeah . . . Uh, there's dissatisfaction in terms of a-a reality, uh, reality being that, uh, sure I think we've come a long way in the nine months or whatever it is financially and probably emotionally . . . (corrects self) and emotionally; not probably, and emotionally.

79 THERAPIST: But you said, "probably." (voices overlap)

80 MR. P: I mean. . . .

81 THERAPIST: And you also meant maybe "We haven't learned as much. . . ."

82 MR. P: Yeah.

83 THERAPIST: So, let's see what, you know, your . . . your doubts or your misgivings or your dissatisfactions. Aren't these . . . you know . . . you're sure entitled to them! To talk about them. To share them if you wish. 'Cause you're feeling them. And it'll only make trouble for you if they stay inside. You know, that you're being masterminded while you're having misgivings. You had enough of that in your life, heavens knows, when you were young. Why repeat it? (pause)

84 MR. P: Oh, the-the giv . . . the misgiving is that in-in that I don't know that either one of us—although we do on the surface, I think, do very well—uh, honestly and truthfully appreciates how the other feels about many things which are very important.

85 THERAPIST: Are you talking about you in relation to Sally or Sally in relation to you? Which?

86 MR. P: Both ways. Uh, on the other hand, I think each of us has learned to, uh . . . (clears throat) soft-soap our objections and our feelings about it. Maybe this isn't the best way, you know. Certainly a lot of people go through life like this. And maybe, you know . . . (voice fades away).

87 THERAPIST: (voice is soft and sympathetic) But it makes for some dissatisfaction for you. So let's see. You apparently wish you could be understood in greater depth or more extensively. Can you talk about that?

88 MR. P: (voice very low) I have nothing very specific in mind at this point. Just the feeling.

89 THERAPIST: Just a general uneasiness rather than anything.

90 MR. P: Uh-hm.

91 THERAPIST:	Any one different way that you'd like. . . .
92 MR. P:	Hm-m?
93 THERAPIST:	. . . to be appreciated? . . . (15 seconds of silence) No "For instances," no? . . .
94 MR. P:	Nothing very specific at this point.
95 THERAPIST:	What point did you have then?
96 MR. P:	(high voice) I don't know. Uh (clears throat, speaks somewhat incoherently) currently I was, uh . . . uh, you know, uh . . . specifics . . . are . . . not very important or maybe it is important, I don't know. Uh, apparently I was a great embarrassment to Sally on (to Mrs. P.) when? Sunday? Uh, we had some friends out, uh, we watched the football game together; we all had a (light, embarrassed laugh) few drinks and I perhaps had too much . . . uh . . . I . . . have no blank spot or such in terms of the evening.
97 THERAPIST:	You mean you weren't . . . drunk?
98 MR. P:	Yeahh. Uh, until I went to bed. You know, and once I woke up with the startle of the telephone, I didn't know who was calling but I just, you know . . . uh, when I went back to bed. . . . Uh. . . . (tone is somewhat depressed) Because the next thing I knew I woke up, as I will do when I have a lot to drink, in the middle of the night and uh, only to find my wife sleeping on the floor.
99 THERAPIST:	(hollow note of disbelief) On the floor? . . .
100 MR. P:	Uh, the first thought occurred to me: "My God," you know, "What did I do?" "Did I get abusive to her and do something?" You know. And when I asked her about it, uh . . . uh, she didn't indicate that I had been particularly abusive to her or *had* been abusive to her, uh, but rather, she just didn't like the whole evening and the way I acted and so forth. Uh, on the other hand, uh . . . I, too, was all very uneasy about the whole day.
101 THERAPIST:	Whole day of the evening or the next day?
102 MR. P:	No, when th-these people came out to us. I think as I was walking out of here, I don't even know if it was on the tape, but I said something to Sally about, "Did you call up so-and-so to make sure they were coming out?" She said, "I'll call them tomorrow morning." Tomorrow morning passed, Saturday passed, and Sunday passed until they arrived. Well, you know, I thought that—yes, I had talked to the husband, and *I*

had been the one that had done the inviting two weeks prior. But I just felt that it was only right that Sally call and, you know, make sure that they understood that they were to come to dinner, or come out for the afternoon and stay for dinner. And, uh, she didn't. And wouldn't. . . .

103 THERAPIST: These people that you did-weren't very pleased to have, Sally?

104 MRS. P: No, they're friends of ours.

105 THERAPIST: You had some question about it?

106 MRS. P: (low voiced) I just did not feel like having company.

107 THERAPIST: Uh-huh. (to Mr. P.) And you knew that?

108 MR. P: (with trace of anger) Well, yeah. I-I find this out on, you know, like Saturday when I invited them two weeks before.

109 THERAPIST: Well, how come there was no dis . . . the message didn't reach you? Or are you saying that Sally didn't let on?

110 MR. P: Sally didn't indicate a thing to me, you know, when I mentioned it to her. (to Sally) Did you?

111 MRS. P: (very low, barely audible) No.

112 THERAPIST: Sally, you're taking on a kind of frozen voice and face and I can't tell whether this was . . . you were feeling trapped or you're feeling that, uh. . . .

113 MRS. P: (in clipped, biting manner) No, I just did not want company! (fades out) That's all.

114 THERAPIST: You didn't feel you could tell this to Jack? Or you felt he should have known that?

115 MRS. P: At the time I didn't know what he told them either, um . . . (fades out).

116 MR. P: It was two weeks before.

117 MRS. P: Something about "I talked to Walter and asked him to come out," but that was two weeks, you know, from the time that it was supposed to happen and then as the time drew closer I just didn't want company. Two or three weeks ago we had company on Sunday and I wound up . . . "shlepping" around the kitchen all day Sunday waiting on people; trying to feed the children. And I really did not want to do it again this week. I don't want company on Sundays anymore. I didn't say this to Jack, but we began to argue about it on Sunday and I told him then. I didn't . . . and I guess the reason . . . the reason I didn't call is because I don't, I di-I don't like to call people.

118	MR. P:	(with bitter edge to voice) Oh come on. You know you say that but you know it's not true.

118 MR. P: (with bitter edge to voice) Oh come on. You know you say that but you know it's not true.

119 THERAPIST: (overlaps Mr. P.) Well, you know, Sally, you may not like to call people. . . .

120 MR. P: I'm sick of that . . . I get sick of that!

121 THERAPIST: Get sick of what?

122 MR. P: This "I don't like to call." Boy, you let her get something on her bonnet and she'll be on the phone for an hour!

123 MRS. P: (with choked emotion) I call people if I have a reason. But I don't call people just to say "hello" and to schmooze with them. And I don't think you can remember since we've been married when I called anybody just to say "hello" (voice rises to angry pitch), and I'm sorry I'm just not that way!

124 THERAPIST: Well, you know, I don't think (voice overlaps with Mr. P.) the issue is your calling.

125 MR. P: (moves to very high, squeezed sound) This isn't a question of calling and saying "hello." This is a question of confirming of . . . of someone coming out to your home.

126 THERAPIST: But wait a moment! You know, it seems to me that we're putting the cart before the horse here. It seems—there seems to be two issues here, two problems. One, that Sally didn't feel up to or wish to have company on a Sunday, but neither did she communicate this to you. What isn't clear is why she couldn't tell you this; whether you would . . . I don't know whether you . . . she felt that . . . you'd come down on her like a ton of bricks or be very disapproving of her.

127 MR. P: I certainly wouldn't if she told. . . .

128 MRS. P: (interrupts) He had already made the arrangements! (voices in strident overlap)

129 MR. P: I said I. . . .

130 MRS. P: You had talked to Walter and made the arrangements.

131 MR. P: Yeah, but . . . yeah, but I told Sally to call back on Walter and say . . .

132 MRS. P: And say what? "Sally doesn't want you out."

133 MR. P: No! "Could we make it on a Saturday?" or "Could we make it on a Friday night?" I was out of base!

134 THERAPIST: So what you really saw was yourself really being the patsy and the bad one. Sally, in this instance, that somehow it

would get over to these friends that you didn't want them.

135 MRS. P: Yeah. Which is true. I mean, that I just didn't want them to know, I guess.

136 THERAPIST: Yeah, I can understand you're not wanting them to know. So what's so terrible about people knowing that a Sunday is not convenient for you and that another day would be better? Unless you didn't want them at all, and that brings up another. . . .

137 MRS. P: No, I didn't . . . it wasn't that I didn't want them at all.

138 THERAPIST: Oh. So what's so terrible? You know, it's so terrible for people to know that Sunday is not a good day for you? Uh, doesn't make a, uh, sinful person out of you or a bad person out of you. But apparently the lack of communication had something then to do with your question as to how it would reflect on you. What do you think?

139 MRS. P: I don't know. Sometimes I don't see other ways out of things except my own solutions.

140 THERAPIST: Which is what? Not to do anything?

141 MRS. P: I don't know. I didn't have any solution. So I didn't think there was one, you know.

142 THERAPIST: It was really fated for problem, this . . . this arrangement, you know. Nei . . . you couldn't talk to each other about it and then, you know, this might very easily then leave you feeling put upon and trapped. (to Mr. P.) But I have to ask you something else.

Knowing Sally, you've had no sense about Sunday being a bad time for Sally?

143 MR. P: No. She never said anything.

144 THERAPIST: Or not a day she enjoys having people?

145 MR. P: She has never indicated this. (to Mrs. P.) Have you?

146 MRS. P: You know I enjoyed having Terry and Mike that day, don't you?

147 THERAPIST: Meaning that he should know that you didn't?

148 MRS. P: Yeah.

149 THERAPIST: Now, I wouldn't have known, except from what we've been saying, that you really meant the opposite.

150 MRS. P: (sighs in exasperation) Well, I did mean the opposite (louder and petulantly), and he should know by the kind of, you know, time it was and by what I . . . (voices overlap) said. . . .

151 MR. P: (interrupts) That was that particular group of people, what the heck has that got to do with somebody else?

152 MRS. P: (tearfully) It was the same kind of situation. I spend all Sunday afternoon . . . working.

153 MR. P: (moves into low register) Sally, you never said that . . . (fades out). (pause)

154 MRS. P: Well you know it now.

155 MR. P: I know it. . . .

156 MRS. P: And doesn't really make a-a bit of difference, does it?

157 MR. P: Yes it does. You know, I told you the other day. . . .

158 MRS. P: (interrupts in clipped style) No more company.

159 MR. P: No more company; forget it.

160 THERAPIST: Oh well then it's—wait a minute. You must, you were really very furious with Sally. 'Cause Sally is talking about com-no company on Sunday . . . and you're talking. . . .

161 MR. P: (interrupts) Look, Mrs. ——, eh, you know . . . you know (in loud strained voice) these are all excuses and I, and-an . . . you know, and I frankly get sick of them! Sally had all Saturday. If she wanted . . . i-i-if her spending all day in the kitchen is a big problem, she could have planned the menu for Sunday that all she had to do was pop in the oven an-and it's done every day in the week, so that she could be out with everybody else, if this is her problem. And you know, d-d-you know, the rest of it is excuses as far as I'm concerned.

162 THERAPIST: (in moderate, thoughtful tone) Let's see, what is it that both of you are saying? You're saying that entertaining is . . . requires very little extra effort.

163 MR. P: It re . . . no. I'm not saying that. It requires effort. Sally's argument is that, "I spend all day in the kitchen." Now if that's the argument, Sally is clever enough, in terms of food, to have done something on Saturday that on 4 o'clock Sa-Sunday afternoon she could have popped back into the oven, heat it up, and there's a meal. . . . Now, I've seen her do it. She knows how to do it. So I don't accept that as any excuse.

164 THERAPIST: Well what do you think of that?

165 MR. P: (continues in agitated fashion) Saturday, Saturday, as far as I am concerned, an-and I'm sure Friday is the same as far as she is concerned, is certainly no night to be entertaining any-

91

one because that's, you know, usually, as-as things go our first night home. Sally with her meetings, me with my work. Saturday we're doing things around the house and so forth. Sure, late supper is fine. But not the kind of people like you're talking about who've got kids and little kids and so forth as was the case with this couple.

166 THERAPIST: You mean they couldn't get away?

167 MR. P: Ye . . . oh, yeah, I mean, they bring their child along. So Saturday night is certainly, you know, no different. Or Saturday is no different, and if you're having people in on Sunday, damn it, you planned it, plan it in this way and you cook a roast or you make a casserole, or whatever it is, so that you can pop it in the oven on Saturday afternoon at 4 o'clock and you can serve dinner at 5. Now what's the big deal?

168 THERAPIST: He's saying it's no big deal and that there must be some other reasons. He's implying you don't want company, Sally. (coughs) I didn't hear this from you. So what . . . can you explain to him what the difference is to you? . . . (57 seconds of silence) You're swallowing all your tears. I think feeling very angry. (Mrs. P. makes crying sound) I really don't know what you're feeling.

(10 seconds of silence)

169 MRS. P: (tearful and angry) I'm supposed to sit here and defend myself now and explain myself!

170 THERAPIST: Well, wait a moment, Sally. Are you at a tribunal or are we trying to arrive at some mutual understanding of what goes on? Why does it always happen, or so often happen that this is a defense of yourself at the court of law?

171 MRS. P: (angrily) Because I am so imperfect, as Jack has so aptly pointed out.

172 THERAPIST: (softly modulated) Sure you're imperfect. So what? He's so perfect? I'm so perfect? (Mrs. P. sniffling). . . . But you know these silences and the feeling of a court of law kind of puts, you know, I can only tell you how I respond to this. It's as if I've got to be very careful with the way you feel so that you shouldn't feel more hurt. And it kind of, you know, leaves a person feeling paralyzed.

173 MRS. P: (in crying, plaintive manner) I don't know! What am I supposed to say? Huh? No, I am really not a foo . . . a poor manager? Is it really, yes, I really want company? What . . . (voices overlap) It's not true.

174 THERAPIST: I don't think it's a question of what you should say; I think it's a question of what you do wish and what you do feel.

175 MRS. P: (in angry, tearful voice) I don't want people in my house on Sunday. I want Sunday for myself to relax. I haven't read the Sunday paper in four weeks . . . at least! And Sunday night, I don't want to spend Sunday night in the kitchen clearing away ta . . . the table and putting dishes away and pots and pans and don't tell me I should leave it for Edith because I won't do that. You might, but I won't! That's not the way I want to spend one of my two days off. And I don't care if we never see Walter and Barbara. If they're too goddamn cheap to pay a babysitter and come out without their child, then they can stay away! But my life is to be run for the convenience of you and everybody else. . . . You "pop a casserole in the oven," huh? And nothing else? You don't see anything else?

176 THERAPIST: Well tell him what else there is. Maybe he's shortsighted.

177 MRS. P: The preparation that goes into a casserole. I had a roast! You don't just eat meat. You eat other things, too. You set the table, you get things ready. You feed three children who want to eat, plus a fourth. . . . And you serve hors d'œuvres and you take care of people and tell them where things are when your husband starts drinking too much and can't navigate for himself and suddenly gets lost.

And then you eat a meal apologizing for him because he's saying ridiculous, irritating things! And that's my Sunday!

178 MR. P: (in low-voiced, menacing anger) Don't ever apologize for me, all right?

179 MRS. P: All right. No, that I'll skip, you know.

180 THERAPIST: Well, you're both furious with each other. . . . (to Mr. P.) Was part of the drinking to do with your anger and embarrassment, 'cause you talked about being embarrassed that Sally had not called them. Was this what was happening for you? That you were (Mr. P.: Yes. Yes.) furious with Sally?

181 MR. P: (very low and depressed sounding) Yeah, I guess so. What difference does it make?

182 THERAPIST: Now, you know, right now you're saying life is bleak, we haven't gotten anything. . . .

183 MR. P: (interrupts with slight laugh) I'm not saying that life is bleak. . . .

184 THERAPIST: Oh, you're saying that life between us is bleak, "we've-I've

93

plunked down all this goddamn money and for what?" This is really what you're saying. So that in a sense Sally was catching something before, that you seemed to be feeling.

Now, so let's see what's going on. You go to bed, ah, you know, kind of blank to what was going on, and Sally puts herself on the floor. She feels ignored (picks up tempo) and she puts herself down on the floor. (to Mrs. P.) You put yourself on the floor even, you know, what, to symbolize your position of being left out?

185 MRS. P: (sullenly) No, it was the only place I could sleep without anybody else in the house knowing it. That's all.

186 THERAPIST: You mean you couldn't stand the sight of him in bed? He was so . . . (unclear).

187 MRS. P: He smelled! . . . of booze. . . .

188 THERAPIST: It doesn't take much to smell of booze. You mean he was pretty repulsive to you is the message.

189 MRS. P: Well, he had done some repulsive things that I just, you know. . . .

190 THERAPIST: What did he do?

191 MRS. P: He started to . . . (voice fades out).

192 THERAPIST: Hm?

193 MRS. P: He was making all kinds of remarks.

194 THERAPIST: You mean to people during the, uh, evening?

195 MRS. P: (barely audible) Yes.

196 THERAPIST: What kind of remarks were so terri . . . so embarrassing to you? (changes direction) I think that's even again putting the cart before the horse. I think more important we should pay some attention to what preceded this.

Sally, were you saying before that somehow it is easier to put yourself out regardless of the same amount of care and work that it takes whether you entertain on Friday or Saturday? I couldn't tell whether it was the presence of another child or whether they. . . .

197 MRS. P: (interrupts) We had, we had people in to dinner two weeks ago, on Saturday night.

198 THERAPIST: Hm.

199 MRS. P: And it was beautiful. It was very nice. The food was good, the table was set (voices overlap).

200 THERAPIST: Well, I remember you both. . . .

201 MRS. P: My children were in bed. It was fine!

202	THERAPIST:	They were in bed already.
203	MRS. P:	It was fine. (with vehemence) They have four children and they didn't bring *any* of 'em! And I told them I didn't want thei . . . I didn't want a family dinner! I, you know, I wanted a nice dinner! These people who came Sunday have come before. They need a lot of catering. (slight laugh) They're very good friends, but they're—for some reason I feel on, more on edge with them than I do with strangers.
204	THERAPIST:	Why? You have any idea what there is about them?
205	MRS. P:	Well, when we go to their home everything is very lovely; very, you know, lovely. We leave the children at home when we go. We always have a nice, quiet dinner. They have one child and they put her to bed and we eat a nice quiet dinner.
206	THERAPIST:	Well, do you feel kind of having to match them in what they make available . . . (Mrs. P. overlaps).
207	MRS. P:	(unclear) I would like to see how it, you know. . . .
208	THERAPIST:	But wait a minute, Sally. In connection with these people, do you feel kind of on edge because, you know . . . you're-you feel less polished and less the hostess and less competent than they and then you have to kind of, you feel you have to match them?
209	MRS. P:	I don't think it's that. It's just that . . . (fades out).
210	THERAPIST:	Then why do you say they need more catering to than other people?
211	MRS. P:	Well, you know, Walter makes remarks and he jokes all the time, but you know, like they'll come at 1:30 or 2 o'clock and he'll say, "What do you have to eat?"
212	THERAPIST:	Um.
213	MRS. P:	Well, you know, I'm ready for them (Mr. P. attempts to comment). . . . He's done this to me! Repeatedly.
214	MR. P:	Why can't you say to him, just like you said before, "Walter, go on out in the kitchen and find what's in the (Mrs. P.'s voice overlaps) refrigerator. Help yourself!"
215	MRS. P:	. . . In the, in the past I have made efforts to have things there so if he, if he does this I've got food for him to eat, when he comes in, plus having dinner for him.
216	THERAPIST:	Well, does it feel like an extra burden, an extra demand with a guy who's this informal?
217	MRS. P:	You know . . . I know he's kidding in the things he says but . . . (interrupted).

95

218 THERAPIST:	What other things does he say than other . . . than, "What do you have?" 'Cause it does something to you, Sally. Doesn't give you any pleasure that he is informal, wh . . . it gives you only a sense of irritation and burden and anger. Or anxiety first before anything else happens.
219 MRS. P:	I don't know. It's just that even though I know he's joking, it's serious to me and I want to be able to produce and I can't.
220 THERAPIST:	Why do you have to produce?
221 MRS. P:	I always have to produce.
222 MR. P:	(high voice) You don't have to go to. . . .
223 THERAPIST:	(interrupts) Wait. I'm sorry. Wait a minute, Jack, I'm sorry to cut you off. We're trying to understand what this "produce" means for Sally.
	You can be more, you know, casual about it, maybe because in your family people would drop in (Mr. P. expels air in disgust) and, you know, there'd be kind of an easy give and take. . . .
224 MR. P:	(interrupts in ringing tones) You know, the situations aren't even comparable and this is what I can't seem to get over to Sally. We invite them out for the day or for, like from 1 o'clock till they have to go home—8 or 9 o'clock at night. . . .
225 THERAPIST:	It's a long day.
226 MR. P:	(echoes) It's a long day. We go there—to their house—primarily on a specific invitation to dinner. I . . . you know, to come for dinner at 8, so you arrive, you know, 7:30, quarter to 8.
227 THERAPIST:	But I think you're missing something of what Sally is saying, Jack. Sally is saying if she has them over, or anybody over, just for dinner, she can collect herself, she can get the kids out of the way. She can then concentrate on being the hostess and feeling good about it, as she did two weeks ago. What she is telling us now is that when they descend on her as a family . . . she's kind of torn in many directions. They want food now. It doesn't feel easy for her to just say, "Go and take something." It means that she'd have to prepare something to have. She feels demanded of more. So the comp . . . the fact that it isn't comparable . . . the point is that she's feeling some extra burden in this—when people come a whole day. And I think maybe it's hard for you to sense, you know,

what these extra demands feel like to her. 'Cause they're not much of a chore for you. I don't mean because you don't want to pitch in, although this instance Sally felt by your drinking you kind of faded out. . . .

Uh. . . . (43 seconds of silence, clock ticks in background) What was happening during the day while you were busy, Sally? Were you . . . where was Jack in all this?

228	MR. P:	In watching the football game on TV, and so was Sally.
229	MRS. P:	(very softly) You mean when they first came?
230	MR. P:	Hm?
231	MRS. P:	When they first came?
232	MR. P:	H-m-m.
233	THERAPIST:	They don't even come after lunch. They come really around lunch time.
234	MRS. P:	(barely audible) They came around 2:30, a quarter to 3 or . . . (becomes inaudible) They've come earlier before.
235	THERAPIST:	Hm-m?
236	MRS. P:	They've come earlier before.
237	THERAPIST:	Oh.
238	MRS. P:	They didn't come until later.
239	MR. P:	It's usually at my invitation, "Come early."
240	THERAPIST:	(to Mr. P.) So maybe one of the difficulties is that you don't, you know, have a sense of the kind of job it is for Sally when you, you know, when you, out of the bigness of your generosity and hospitality and sociability, say, "Come early." Maybe knowing Sally, it's important to know what this does. You may not like it, even after knowing it, but you seem not to understand it. . . . Sally, you don't feel comfortable in just being informal and just saying, you know, "Okay, go help yourselves."
241	MRS. P:	No. They . . . (fades out).
242	THERAPIST:	Can you say what this is? Is it the extra expense of the food that they'd be eating? Or is it that you're feeling you're letting them down as a hostess? That you should have everything in kind of, uh, partyish order for them? (pause)
243	MRS. P:	(in low register) I don't know. I really don't. Part of it, I suppose, is that I just want things to be nice if I have people in. Uh . . . Um.
244	THERAPIST:	But "nice" means a certain kind of orderliness and quiet.

97

245	MRS. P:	Yeh . . . (pause).
246	THERAPIST:	And somehow I also get the sense that, uh, the presence of the children acts as another irritant for you.
247	MRS. P:	Yeah. Our children were out of the house though, it's just that they're very careful with their child and they don't let her go outside and they don't let her go here and they don't. . . . It was a much better visit this time than it ever was before. Before it's always, "She can't go here" and "She can't go there."
248	MR. P:	(voice in high register, squeezed) Oh my God, the child's two and a half years old, three years old, what do you expect?
249	THERAPIST:	Oh!
250	MRS. P:	And she's walking around!
251	MR. P:	(high register) So what?
252	MRS. P:	So she can go out in the back yard and play. My kids played in the back yard.
253	MR. P:	Yeh, but your kids are used to the back yard, you know . . . (mutters comment under breath with tone of disgust). (Mrs. P. and Therapist overlap)
254	THERAPIST:	What are you so furious with her for?
255	MRS. P:	They don't want her to get her hands dirty. They don't want her to touch this. . . .
256	MR. P:	(mutters angry words unintelligibly)
257	THERAPIST:	Well, wait a moment. You're making nothing out of Sally right now. What are you so . . . what's so . . .
258	MR. P:	(interrupts) You know, I-I-I don't understand it. I honest to God, I don't. You know, eh, eh . . . you know . . . (fades out, becomes unintelligible).
259	THERAPIST:	What don't you understand, Jack?
260	MR. P:	I-I just don't understand that kinda attitude. You know, Jesus! She doesn't remember when she was that way.
261	THERAPIST:	When she was being what? This anxious about. . . .
262	MR. P:	Hm. About Mary.*
263	MRS. P:	I was never like that with any of my children, Jack.
264	MR. P:	You were anxious about Mary when she went someplace strange when she was that age.
265	MRS. P:	I let her play! And I didn't care if she got her hands dirty.
266	MR. P:	(interrupts in shrill outburst) They let her play! They let her play! (voice becomes normally modulated) No, not outside.

* The Porters' oldest daughter.

98

Barbara doesn't feel comfortable about it. Well, this is Barbara, you know. Jesus Christ! Ya-you learn to, uh, know what you expect from certain people!

267 MRS. P: Yeah, I do (sighs deeply in resignation).

268 THERAPIST: Sounds as. . . .

269 MRS. P: (continues) While you watch television.

270 MR. P: (echoes) While I watch television.

271 MRS. P: (with irony) And I know what to expect from you, too.

272 MR. P: (flatly) That's right. Nothing.

273 MRS. P: That's right.

274 THERAPIST: Were you hoping that Jack, instead of watching television, would have . . . taken care of some of the guest's needs?

275 MRS. P: I don't know. I a . . . (voice becomes lighter) my anxiety, as always, was greater than the reality because it turned out to be a comfortable visit. Uh . . . but, I still, I had a lot to do! (voices overlap)

276 THERAPIST: So it was. . . .

277 MRS. P: If I had my choice, I wouldn't spend my Sunday that way.

278 THERAPIST: All right, so maybe we can pay attention to the anxiety because the anxiety can be more wearing—the anticipation and all the energy that goes into it—than the actual fact. Can you . . . t . . . help me understand why their particular view and attitude toward their child is such a nuisance to you? After all, they're the ones who are doing it. Doe-does it put you on your *guard* more? Does it make you feel like a careless mother in ca-ca . . . terms of your own kids? Why is it such an issue for you—what their kid is like?

279 MRS. P: (deep sigh) I don't know. I really don't.

280 THERAPIST: Care to try to find out?

281 MRS. P: (whisper-like) No. It's just that . . . (fades out with sigh). (pause)

282 THERAPIST: Does it set up a stream of feeling that if they're this fussy about their kid, they're going to be critical of you if you're not absolutely on your toes about everything?

283 MRS. P: I . . . they're just fussy about everything. That's just the way they are.

284 THERAPIST: I know. But what it does to you is our question. 'Cause they, you know, it affects you in a certain way.

285 MRS. P: I don't know. You know, I had butter in the house. I had butter in it because I knew Walter would say (with mock-

99

ing exaggeration) "Is that butter or oleo?" So I had my butter ready! I don't know why.

286 THERAPIST: Well, then there must be something to do with—I think you can guess why yourself without even my telling you. Sometimes we will have things that we like our guests to have to enjoy, but I don't get the sense that that's why you had the butter. Somewhere they stand for the great big . . . what? Standard bearers for you?

287 MRS. P: I don't know, it's . . . (fades out expelling air in frustration). (pause)

288 THERAPIST: You know, Jack, in your background you had different, uh, obstacles to overcome. Would you behave in a way which would displease your sh . . . or sh . . . embarrass your parents? And boy, you know, we know a little bit about that.

289 MR. P: I'm sure I did.

290 THERAPIST: Hmmm?

291 MR. P: I said I'm sure I did.

292 THERAPIST: You're sure you did what?

293 MR. P: (light sigh) That I *did* embarrass them on occasions.

294 THERAPIST: Yeah, but the point is that it affected you in certain ways when, you know, certain behavior went underground, certain feelings went underground and you had to kind of . . . in a rebellious kind of way get yourself into trouble. Sally, in her growing up, had her embarrassments with her father and the kinds of discomfort she had when coming home, there wasn't any ease with which people came and were entertained. Uh, you know, so there she has. It isn't as if she behaves as if she's learned that she can be really a competent person. She has her anxieties from way back! You have yours. Exactly how they operate in a similar situation, I don't know, but, you know, when you get mad—what do you do? You drink yourself into kind of a lethargy or if you get anxious. And Sally has the doldrums in advance in her way. The sad part of it is that, you know, you both want something together. You can't communicate it and you both feel misunderstood and, of course, you know, I can see why you would feel "What in the hell is this all about?" And I think maybe, you know, Sally might also feel "What the hell is this about? What are we paying money for?" Uh. . . . But I think, Sally, that somehow these people represent by their being so, you know, proper

100

and careful, at the same time that they're so casual when coming into your house, they must feel like, uh, invaders.

295 MRS. P: (tearfully) You know, I don't understand—especially with Walter because he was a friend of ours. You know when we were first married, he wasn't married and he was at the house all the time. And he ate with us and he watched television with us; he was, he was always living there.

296 THERAPIST: This is an old friend of yours, Jack?

297 MR. P: Yeah.

298 MRS. P: And I don't know why I'm . . . (fades out).

299 THERAPIST: Why you're what? So on hook . . . on tenterhooks about. . . .

300 MRS. P: . . . so worried about.

301 THERAPIST: Well, let's see if we can find out! Is it the wife whom you're worried about or were you always on tenterhooks with Walter before?

302 MRS. P: No!

303 THERAPIST: (echoes) No. And yet it's Walter who wants butter.

304 MRS. P: Yeah. But he came out and he made the gravy for me.

305 MR. P: Walter's . . . Walter's a gourmet. You know, Walter . . . Walter knows the best restaurants, eats at 'em on occasions . . . Walter knows food.

306 THERAPIST: The question is whether Sally feels she has to provide it just 'cause Walter is.

307 MR. P: Well I think this is what she feels. . . . (pause)

308 MRS. P: (tearfully) You know, I . . . I know how to do things right . . . but I don't always do them right because I don't really care that much, but some people just make me—(to husband) *you* do it, *they* do it—I just got to show them that I can do it right (dissolves into crying). . . .

309 THERAPIST: You have to do it right all the time?

310 MRS. P: That I'm not a slob. I don't care about my children the way they do about that child. (poutingly) And I hope I never do!

311 THERAPIST: But, yeah, on the one hand, you hope you never do, but, on the other hand, there seems to be a niggling doubt, self-doubt, that you . . . that you don't.

312 MRS. P: Well, it's just that every occasion, you know, kind of . . . I come off badly by contrast (overlap of voices) at least. . . .

313 THERAPIST: In whose eyes?

314 MRS. P: . . . in my own eyes.

315 THERAPIST: Uh-h-h. So let's see. How come? . . . (to Mr. P.) Do you

wish that Sally were more like these people with their child?

316 MR. P: Barbara . . . Barbara is a real bitch. I wouldn't have two cents to do with her. You know, I've expressed this to Sally.

317 THERAPIST: So, so it's on her own.

318 MRS. P: She keeps a nice, neat house, a clean house. You never see her house dirty, and you never see that child dirty.

319 THERAPIST: (with mild sarcasm) Well, isn't that wonderful. When does the child. . . . (three voices overlap)

320 MRS. P: That's what Jack wants!

321 MR. P: (in high register) I'm not around Barbara twenty-four hours a day; so I don't know what Barbara does! So how in the hell can you make a judgment like that?

322 THERAPIST: Well, wait a moment. She says that's what you want.

323 MR. P: Sh. . . .

324 MRS. P: You-you were, that day, you were out there and you went out to the garage. You decided you were going to "check the garage" while I was getting stuff ready and *fussing* and *fuming* about why "somebody" hadn't cleaned that garage. I don't know who you wanted.

325 MR. P: No. No . . . I. . . .

326 MRS. P: Edith? * Or me?

327 MR. P: No, no, wait a minute. That . . . that is not what I said.

328 MRS. P: And fussing about "goddamn junk all over the garage!" And why? . . . I don't know who you thought was supposed to do it?

329 THERAPIST: Jack, you say that this was not what you were fussing about. (pause)

330 MR. P: Not what I said.

331 THERAPIST: Oh? What did you say? . . .

332 MR. P: (speaks in carefully metered fashion conveying suppressed anger) We've got a car . . . with a big hole in the roof! And that doesn't necess-necessarily have to have a hole in the roof.

333 THERAPIST: What? Where's the hole? In the car or in the garage?

334 MR. P: In the roof, in the roof.

335 MRS. P: It's a sun top, you know, canvas.

336 THERAPIST: Oh.

337 MR. P: (declaims dramatically) Because, goddamn it, it's been left

* The Porters' housekeeper who cares for the home while Mrs. Porter is at work.

outside of the house. The windows have been left open. It is *rainin'*. And we are riding around in something that is damn unsafe because you wouldn't put a car in the garage! Or you wouldn't tell the children to move their bikes back. Or you wouldn't tell them, "Don't mess up the garage so you can get a car in it." (in stinging tones) Now you want to know what I'm fussing about? That's what I'm fussing about because goddamn it, I gotta go out and buy another car for us to drive around in. . . .

338	THERAPIST:	So what you're saying, it's all Sally's carelessness. . . .
339	MR. P:	Well, you're damn right. . . .
340	THERAPIST:	. . . that the car's deteriorated.
341	MR. P:	. . . 'cause Sally's very, very careless. (moves into high pitched declamation) There is nothing, not a thing, not a single, solitary thing that we've got that has been taken care of. Our furniture looks like hell. Dishes that we had that were nice, are all gone! Everything. Just everything. You name it, it's happened. Sally doesn't care. I care . . . (becomes pseudo-philosophical) But, you know, that's life and it will be that way and what the hell's the point in worrying about it.
342	MRS. P:	You know, Jack, I had that car in the garage two weeks ago (phone rings).
343	THERAPIST:	Excuse me. (over phone) Yes.
344	MR. P:	For what? Once?
345	THERAPIST:	(over phone) Yes, but, uh, would you tell her that I'll call her back. I'll be another five minutes.
346	MRS. P:	I put . . . I cleared all the bikes to the side, I put the gr- grass-cutter in the back. . . .
347	MR. P:	(interrupts, shouting) That-that-that's now. That's now!
348	MRS. P:	(angrily) That was two weeks ago, that I did that. (overlap)
349	MR. P:	That's now. What-what about all the nights that it was left out in snowstorms and rainstorms and the whole bit?
350	MRS. P:	I don't feel it's my job to clean the garage.
351	MR. P:	I didn't say clean the garage, I said put the door . . . car . . . in the garage.
352	MRS. P:	In order to do that you have to move bikes, you have to move this, you have to move that.
353	MR. P:	Okay (fades out in disgust).

103

354	THERAPIST:	Well, why is, wait a minute. Why is now the past becoming. . . .
355	MR. P:	(interrupts) Because it's all part of a pattern, you know, an-an-and I'm frankly very sick of it! You know, *I don't care* and, you know, let it go, all go to hell! Because, uh, it really doesn't matter, and, and I-I, I'm just sick of it! You know.
356	THERAPIST:	You know what you're saying, Jack, to me at least. You're saying—and this ties in with what you said earlier about understanding each other—what you're saying is that "Sally doesn't care about a thing that's important to me."
357	MR. P:	That's right.
358	THERAPIST:	Whether it's nice dishes or whether it's keeping . . . keeping. . . .
359	MR. P:	(interrupts and gropes for words) Whether it . . . whether-whether it's, uh, whether it's, uh. . . .
360	THERAPIST:	(interrupts) Or having company. . . .
361	MR. P:	Or a coat that she buys for her daughter that she loses four buttons off of and gettin' them replaced. . . . None of these things does Sally care about.
362		(someone sighs)
363	MR. P:	And I've just sort of had it.
364	THERAPIST:	You mean you're ready to give up the ship?
365	MR. P:	Um-hm.
366	THERAPIST:	Boy! That's an easy giving up. Are you saying that. . . .
367	MR. P:	(interrupts) Very easy to give up. (pause)
368	THERAPIST:	I wonder whether, in part, you're feeling . . . you, uh . . . so hopeless about it has to do with the welter of expenses and your question about getting them. . . .
369	MR. P:	(interjects) Sure it does.
370	THERAPIST:	. . . uh, you know, cleared up and all of a sudden Sally becomes the great big cause of all of your difficulties.
371	MR. P:	Sure it does.
372	THERAPIST:	Well, you're sure it does? Uh, after all, some of these hang-ups on the money were not only hers, her doings. But why you would choose at this particular time to be so futile about it and so furious about it, you know, is worth understanding.
373	MR. P:	It's just something I've been feeling, that's all.
374	THERAPIST:	You mean something you've been feeling, but keeping to yourself? . . . Why have you been keeping it to yourself and why does it all come out now?

375	MR. P:	(becomes jocular) I don't know. Maybe because I stopped and had two drinks.
376	THERAPIST:	Because you what?
377	MR. P:	Stopped and had two drinks before I came here.
378	THERAPIST:	Well, maybe it's also because you feel that, uh, you're doing something you don't want to do. You know, in part. You feel, Sally feels that she was ignored and it's true she did nothing in an open way to let you know about Sunday, and then she let you know in a very open way that she found you very . . . unacceptable. She left your bed and I, you know, I don't know whether you . . . what this did to you. But I suggest that we go into this next week some more. (to Mr. P.) Feel like doing that?
379	MR. P:	Yeh.
380	THERAPIST:	Or are you ready to blow?
381	MR. P:	(rapid condensed speech, barely intelligible) Oh, I guess I'll be in next week, who knows?
382	THERAPIST:	"Who knows," means that you don't know.
383	MR. P:	(sotto voce) Yah, I guess I'll be here. Don't know anything right now.
384	THERAPIST:	You mean you don't know whether it's worth going on?
385	MR. P:	Very much so.
386	THERAPIST:	Yeah . . . the question would be, Jack, *why* at this particular juncture? Last week you were. . . .
387	MR. P:	(interrupts) (unclear) Look, Mrs.——, I don't think we're making much headway.
388	THERAPIST:	Well, it may feel this way at this point and it may periodically feel this way at this point . . . (becomes hesitant).
389	MR. P:	(interrupts) Yeah, you know, I-I-I've unfortunately, I've been through situations in my personal life like this and, you know, maybe I just don't feel like going through it again.
390	THERAPIST:	I don't know what you mean you've been this way in your personal life.
391	MR. P:	I mean, you know, psychotherapy and things of this nature and maybe . . . (trails off).
392	THERAPIST:	I think you're saying something to me. I think you're saying, "Look, I'm pretty mad at you, too."
393	MR. P:	No, I'm not saying that to you.
394	THERAPIST:	I thin . . . that's the message I get.

105

395 MR. P:	(unclear) . . . the whole situation at this point—it's jus . . . just not worth it to me.
396 THERAPIST:	Well, you know, let's find out about that.
397 MR. P:	Okay.
398 MRS. P:	(barely audible) So long.
399 THERAPIST:	So long.

(*sound of couple departing*)

Treatment issues in session three

15–23	Why did the therapist focus upon the doubt she heard in Mr. Porter's voice?
33	The therapist suggests Mrs. Porter be brought into the discussion. Her words are: "Well, Sally is here. You can ask her. We can ask her, you know." What do these words tell you about the therapist's approach?
50	The therapist makes a distinction between doubt about a decision and self-doubt with reference to Mr. Porter's plan to stop therapy for a month. What might be the therapist's reasoning? Do you think she should have intervened differently?
61–65	What is Mrs. Porter's purpose in suggesting that she is not sure her husband desires to continue in therapy?
95	Why, do you feel, the therapist persisted in probing Mr. Porter's feelings about therapy: a) Because she thought Mr. Porter had not disclosed all his feelings? b) Because Mrs. Porter had not been satisfied with the answer he gave her? c) Because the therapist wanted them to continue in therapy?
98–100	How would you interpret the dynamics of Mrs. Porter's decision to sleep on the floor over the weekend?
102	What did Mr. Porter experience when his wife failed to call their friends to remind them of their weekend appointment?
112	What do you think the therapist was trying to achieve with this comment?
124	What *is* the issue here?
142	The therapist probes the area of the spouses' miscommunication. Do you feel this was helpful? Would you have approached this problem differently?
169–175	What does Mrs. Porter's outburst indicate about where she

is dynamically at this point? What is the effect of Mrs. Porter's tears and silence upon her husband?

180   Do you agree with the therapist's interpretation of why Mr. Porter overdrank after the guests arrived?

184   The therapist links the upsetness of the Porters around the weekend conflict and Mr. Porter's discouragement at the beginning of the session. What is your view of the validity of her interpretation?

196   The therapist makes the decision to explore Mrs. Porter's feelings about entertaining, rather than stay with the marital relationship. As the therapist, would you have done the same? Why?

205–208   What are the dynamics underlying the self-doubts Mrs. Porter experiences as a hostess?

227   How would you characterize what the therapist is doing at this point?

247–253   Why is Mrs. Porter upset by the visitors' hovering attention to their child?

308   What do Mrs. Porter's tears convey to you: a) A feeling of worthlessness? b) Anger? c) A need to control?

332–361   Mr. Porter complains about his wife's indifference about their possessions, how their daughter is dressed, and so forth. What deeper issue in the marriage is reflected in his denunciation?

372–378   What mechanisms are involved in Mr. Porter's having kept his discontents to himself?

380   How would you appraise the way in which the therapist uses vernacular speech here? As opposed to formal speech, what purpose does the vernacular form serve in therapy?

392   Do you agree with the therapist's interpretation that Mr. Porter is expressing anger at her also?

399   Would you predict that Mr. Porter will stop therapy? What is your judgment based on?

General questions

1. Was Mr. Porter's drinking while the couple entertained triggered off by any specific event?

2. How did Mrs. Porter communicate to her husband that she did not want company on Sunday?

3. Did the message reach him and did he ignore it deliberately, or was there a breakdown in communication?

4. What deeper significance does good hosting have for each of the spouses? How do the social embarrassments of the Porters dovetail?

5. To what extent are the problems revealed by the Porters around entertaining guests reflective of normal problems faced by all married couples? To what extent do they reflect unique pathological elements in their backgrounds?

6. Was Mrs. Porter's gesture of sleeping on the floor directed *against* her husband, or an attempt to protect herself?

7. How would you link Mr. Porter's questions about the worthwhileness of continuing in therapy at the opening of the session and the events of the previous week?

SESSION FOUR

The country club
episode

IN THIS SESSION,* *Mr. Porter is late and his wife and the therapist are able to review how things are going at home. Mrs. Porter expresses good feeling about how they are getting along and speaks of her husband as being very considerate to her, particularly in connection with her disability from a recent injury. The discussion moves to the matter of Mrs. Porter's need to be alone, a phenomenon that has come up in earlier sessions. She expresses resentment about the therapist's tendency to see her need for withdrawal and isolation as a problem to be scrutinized. When Mr. Porter comes, he is welcomed and filled in on some of the earlier discussion. He becomes embarrassed at the mention of his being in a good mood at home and attentive to his wife and plays this down. Around the issue of her negative reaction to the intrusion of others, the therapist encourages Mr. Porter to reflect upon his own patterns of reacting, particularly to others in authority. He reveals the nature of his defenses and apparently is conscious of his need to weigh carefully his own thoughts before expressing himself on a subject. When the therapist asks for an example of how this pattern works, he hesitatingly cites a recent encounter with his wife in which the full depth of his feelings were not revealed. Their daughter had asked why they could not join a local country club. Mr. Porter had started to tell her about Negroes not being accepted at the club, but his wife indicated her unhappiness with this line of explanation and he dropped it. Much emotion is discharged in the session about the meaning of the issue. Mrs. Porter feels a big deal is being made of an incident she can hardly remember. Mr. Porter expresses the view that this is the way she has handled the race issue throughout their marriage. The therapist persists in exploring the issue despite Mrs. Porter's strong desire to get away from it.*

* Session of February 16, 1967

109

1 THERAPIST:	(announcing of session) . . . "All right, we seem to be having trouble with this (referring to the tape recorder) February the 16th . . . Mr. and Mrs. P. . . . Mr. P. is not here yet! . . . But he'll be here soon . . . one, two, three, four." Okay . . . we're set.
2 MRS. P:	I talked to Jack earlier and he's very busy and he's, you know, I said, "Well, I'll see you later then." And (he said), "Ahhhhh I don't even know if I can make it." And I said, you know, "Come on," so he said he'd be here. But I have a feeling he'll be late, you know.
3 THERAPIST:	Do you think he is reaching a kind of impasse, kind of feeling disgruntled about something . . . in coming here?
4 MRS. P:	No. I think it's probably . . . oh he may be, but I think this is just because, uh, you know, more that they moved over the weekend . . . (Therapist: Oh . . .) . . . and, uh, Mon . . . Tuesday and Wednesday were . . . were very good days but today evidently didn't go very well (laughs). So . . . he's not in a very good mood and he wants to stay there. You know. . . .
5 THERAPIST:	(earnest and softly modulated) How has this period been for you though, Sally? You know, we were talking so much about Jack and how, uh, the job is affecting him and what's going on; how is it for you to be living through this with Jack at this time? When he's been in such a mood and . . . and so unhappy?
6 MRS. P:	(soft and warm, reflecting Therapist's voice) I don't know. Jack generally really has been very good. He hasn't been miserable to live with or anything like that. He's, uh . . . this has been a very anxious time, but he's been very good at home.
7 THERAPIST:	How do you mean "good"?
8 MRS. P:	I mean good-humored.

111

9 THERAPIST:	(surprised) Oh!
10 MRS. P:	You know, he's been good-humored.
11 THERAPIST:	You mean the kind of feeling he expressed here isn't what he takes home?
12 MRS. P:	No. No.
13 THERAPIST:	Hmm.
14 MRS. P:	Uhm. You know, he may tell me about a few things but he doesn't, um, he doesn't seem to carry over when he's with the children. He's gone ice skating a couple of times. Well, since this happened, I think he's been ice skating three times. We've had . . . you know, friends out . . . (voice fades).
15 THERAPIST:	Since what happened? Your injury?
16 MRS. P:	Since I . . . since I've been ice skating with him. Since that he's been by himself (Therapist: Hm-hm.) two or three times. Once he took the children. Other times we went with friends. And so the weekends have been very good. During the week there isn't much of anything, you know. Generally, though, he's been of a . . . in a very good mood.
17 THERAPIST:	Well is that what's helped it for you, that he takes the children out of the house for a while and you kind of feel that you can call your world your own for a while?
18 MRS. P:	No, it isn't that. It's just that he's in a good humor (Therapist: Uh-huh.) and when he is, you know, I am usually. And I haven't been feeling that well so it helps when he's been, you know, in a good frame of mind. (hardly clear) But, uh, (becomes pensive) . . . I don't know. We had . . . an argument a while back. (unclear) Oh, uh, not last Thursday, but the Thursday when we weren't here. . . .
19 THERAPIST:	Uh-hm.
20 MRS. P:	But that's, you know, kind of forgotten.
21 THERAPIST:	What sort of an argument? Care to talk about it?
22 MRS. P:	Jack just went out and, and, uh-uh . . . you know, stayed out and came home I don't know . . . about 11 o'clock (voice fades). No it must have been later than that. Must have been 12 o'clock (overlaps Therapist).
23 THERAPIST:	That was that Thursday that he said he. . . .
24 MRS. P:	Yeah, he just went out and . . . and this man brought him home. This man in town that we know was on the train with him; they were in the bar car.
25 THERAPIST:	(not sure of what she is hearing) He brought him home?

26 MRS. P:	And he brought him home in the car, you know (voice fading) and, uh, his wife had been at the station to meet him. . . .
27 THERAPIST:	For the moment it sounds like he brought him home because he was too drunk to come under his own steam.
28 MRS. P:	Well, he was pretty shot, you know.
	And . . . he did bring him home because he didn't stay. He had to leave. And, uh . . . (long pause) I don't know, I had my usual reaction to that, you know. I jus' got all upset and. . . .
29 THERAPIST:	Well, what hap-. . . .
30 MRS. P:	(hurried tone) Not really upset. I just got very quiet, you know, which (laughs lightly) is what I do when I'm upset. I'm just. . . .
31 THERAPIST:	So you were upset.
32 MRS. P:	I was steaming. Yeah.
33 THERAPIST:	Well, what were you steaming about?
34 MRS. P:	I don't know. When they came in I thought, oh, you know (mocking sing-song intonation), I've got to take this in stride and, you know, this is just one day in all the other days and the man was there so I smiled and, you know, tried (laughs) to show I was a good sport. And I couldn't keep it up very long, you know, and Jack was, you know, he runs on when he . . . when he's like this. He just talks and gabbles and. . . .
35 THERAPIST:	But what were you . . . were you steamed up by the time they came home?
36 MRS. P:	No. No.
37 THERAPIST:	You mean during the period you. . . .
38 MRS. P:	(overlaps Therapist) I expected him home, but when he didn't come home I wasn't upset.
39 THERAPIST:	You weren't? Why not? (Mrs. P.: No.) How come?
40 MRS. P:	I don't . . . I don't know.
41 THERAPIST:	Because you, you know, when you and I talked on the phone, the day before, and you were telling me about your injury, uh . . . you were saying that you thought Jack would be coming home; that he would prefer to come home. (Mrs. P.: Yeah.) So here . . . now we're back two weeks ago Thursday (Mrs. P.: Yeah.) and he didn't come home.
42 MRS. P:	No.

113

43 THERAPIST:	So—and you say it didn't bother you. (voices overlap)
44 MRS. P:	And I had the feeling he hadn't come here. I just had . . . when I called him back after I spoke with you and said (Therapist: Hm-m.), you know, that he should call you, and he said, "Ahhhh-uhhhhh" (imitates husband's incoherence), and it was just the way we left it. I just had a feeling he wouldn't come anyway. And, uh, so that when he didn't come home I wasn't too surprised really. I just had a feeling. . . . (Therapist: Well, what did you have the feeling?) (voices overlap) . . . (laughs) It was going to be one of those nights. I don't know, you know.
45 THERAPIST:	Well, what sort of a feeling? That he was going to stay out all night? He didn't stay out all night.
46 MRS. P:	No. I just knew he hadn't had a good day and, and, that, that he (falters) didn't want to come here if I wasn't going to be coming. . . .
47 THERAPIST:	Well, how did that feel to you? Did that affect you in any way?
48 MRS. P:	I don't know. I ju . . . I just understand these things. I don't know (laughs). They, you know, I don't think it bothered me in any way. I just knew it, you know, it was so.
49 THERAPIST:	(voice is firm and interrogatory) Are you saying that the only thing that bothered you was that he was, you know, running from the mouth because he'd had a few drinks and this is how he is? Is that (Mrs. P.: No.) the only thing that bothered you when he came in with the man and his wife?
50 MRS. P:	No, what bothered me I think was probably the fact that I knew he had been on the train like this, you know, and uh, this man particularly we don't know very well, but, um . . . you know, he leads his own life here in the city and I know, you know, a little bit of what this is about. He hangs out in bars and things like that.
51 THERAPIST:	This other man?
52 MRS. P:	Yes. So he isn't anybody I would feel, you know, worried about seeing Jack like this 'cause I'm sure he's been like this many times himself.
53 THERAPIST:	So who were you worried about?
54 MRS. P:	(voices overlap)But my thought was, "Well I wonder who else was on the train." And then I think back to all the other times Jack's been on the train.

114

55 THERAPIST: So your feeling of embarrassment (Mrs. P.: Yeah.) is that he'd be exposing himself and you. 'Cause somewhere you get involved in this.

56 MRS. P: Yah . . . yah . . . yeah.

57 THERAPIST: (thoughtfully) Can we talk about that a little bit? 'Cause you're not—you say you weren't angry (rise-fall intonation) that he didn't come home. You were not feeling well. He wasn't there to minister to you . . . to talk to you. . . . Yet . . .

58 MRS. P: No, I didn't . . . that I. . . .

59 THERAPIST: This you didn't bother?

60 MRS. P: (voices overlap) No, that doesn't bother me.

61 THERAPIST: That doesn't bother you at all?

62 MRS. P: When I'm not feeling well, I prefer to be alone.

63 THERAPIST: When you're not feeling well, you prefer. . . .

64 MRS. P: No, it meant that I didn't have to, you know, cook anything for him.

65 THERAPIST: Well, if you weren't feeling well. . . .

66 MRS. P: You know, so it had its advantages.

67 THERAPIST: Well, couldn't he cook for himself when you're not feeling well?

68 MRS. P: Yeah, I guess . . . and he has been, you know, he had been cooking his meat, I guess.

69 THERAPIST: (somewhat challengingly) So why do you need to be alone when you're not feeling well?

70 MRS. P: (light gasping laugh indicating exasperation with therapist)

71 THERAPIST: (stated firmly) You know, Sally, this is par for the course . . . (voice drowned out by Mrs. P.). (strident overlap)

72 MRS. P: (high tone) I don't know! . . . Yeah, so I like being alone (laughingly). Some people can't stand to be alone and I don't mind to be alone. So I don't know which is worse, you know . . . (unclear).

73 THERAPIST: The only reason I'm pursuing this, Sally, and I'm . . . you know, I can only say I'm sorry that it . . . it feels like such a pain in the neck and I'm so nosy, and so intrusive, but part of my job is, with you, if I'm going to help you, because you seem to be fighting a battle between being *alone*. You know how, at times, (talks with emphasis) you have felt you wanted to get . . . the family out of the way. . . .

74 MRS. P: Yeah, yeah.

75 THERAPIST: . . . Jack out of the way so you can get to *you* (warm, rea-

115

	sonable tone). That's why I'm pursuing it so that we can understand it better. We don't have to pursue that phase of it now, we can go back to it. We can pursue the business of your being . . . feeling so dreadful about his exposing himself 'cause he's Jack Porter and his image somehow involves your image of yourself. You get that upset. That, you know, that has happened time and again; you're saying this tonight, too.
76 MRS. P:	Hm-m. I wasn't a-as upset this time as I have been in the past. And . . . and, you know, af-finally Jack went to sleep an . . . and I lay there thinking and I thought well, you know, "This really is one day, and think of all of the good days we've had." And we've had some, you know, really good days and Jack has been, you know, very good. And, um . . . with the children, with me, you know, he was attentive when I was sick in bed and so I think, you know, I just have to balance it out and um. . . .
77 THERAPIST:	This is one time where he didn't—it was very different from the times you used to say, when you used to complain you're not well, "Let's get the doctor." He was actually there for you.
78 MRS. P:	Yes. Yes.
79 THERAPIST:	That's quite a difference, isn't it?
80 MRS. P:	Yeah.
81 THERAPIST:	Well, did it please you? Did you feel closer to him because of this? Or not?
82 MRS. P:	Yeah, it pleased me. It . . . it . . . um . . . I knew, of course, that there was something genuinely wrong. At one point, you know (laughs), I was laying—laying there not knowing whether I was just not really able to take it, you know, whether I just had a sore spot and here I was being a big baby, so it kind of made me (laughs) feel better when I . . . when I . . . you know, found I really had something cracked. And then I said to Jack, "You know, now you know I haven't just been putting on," or something like that. And he said, "Well I never thought that!" You know. . . .
83 THERAPIST:	I wonder if you. . . .
84 MRS. P:	But I. . . .
85 THERAPIST:	Why can't you . . . (Mrs. P.: I don't know) what's that about your needing proof of a crack before you can. . . .

116

86 MRS. P:	Yeah, as (laughs) if I, you know (embarrassed laugh), couldn't ask him. I don't know.
87 THERAPIST:	Has this always been your way of meeting illness on your part, or discomfort physical? . . . Kind of had to wait for a fracture-proof before you could feel entitled?
88 MRS. P:	(in low register) I don't know. I've never been sick that much. It's just that it's . . . it's . . . just that when you are sick, you're kind of a nuisance, you know.
89 THERAPIST:	What do you mean?
90 MRS. P:	Well, you know, that people have to wait on you. It's very hard for me to be a patient. You know, to let somebody. . . .
91 THERAPIST:	But whose feeling is it that you're a nuisance?
92 MRS. P:	(very low) It's my own, I guess.
93 THERAPIST:	Well, I don't know whether it's your own or whether this is a feeling from way back. You so often felt a nuisance (telephone rings). You felt a nuisance. . . . That may be Jack. Excuse me. (picks up telephone) Hello. Yes. Would you ask him to please come up. Thank you. Very good. (to Mrs. P.) It's . . . you know, you used to feel a nuisance, a . . . a burden because of the money and I'm wondering whether there was also a question of your feeling so guilty about not feeling well. (footsteps of Mr. P. entering) Hi, Jack.
94 MR. P:	Hi. Sorry I'm late. (notices parcel near Mrs. P.) Been shopping again I see.
95 MRS. P:	Um-hm.
96 THERAPIST:	There goes your money.
97 MRS. P:	(laughs warmly) You've been making it, I've been spending it. Fifty-fifty (laughs).
98 MR. P:	(sighs breathily) Yeah! . . . (pause) Good evening.
99 THERAPIST:	Good evening, Jack.
100 MR. P:	(sighs)
101 THERAPIST:	Boy, you ran, huh?
102 MR. P:	Yeah. (breathes heavily and jokingly expels air) Whew! All right, where are we?
103 THERAPIST:	We were speculating whether you'd be able to get here or not.
104 MR. P:	Yes. (sigh) Well, I said I'd get here. Sorry I was late.
105 THERAPIST:	We missed you.
106 MRS. P:	Yeah. (softly) Do you have to go back?
107 MR. P:	Yeah. (loudly) Why do you think they gave me the job? They

117

	know we got a sucker who'll break their back, break their backs for them . . . all right?
108 THERAPIST:	You really think you're a sucker?
109 MR. P:	No. No (mumbles unclearly).
110 THERAPIST:	Well, are you?
111 MR. P:	I don't know.
112 THERAPIST:	Are you doing more than you . . . your judgment tells you you should be on this? You have to kind of break your back? (Mr. P.'s voice drowned out by bus) We were. . . . (to Mrs. P.) Do you mind if I just say something to Jack about what we were talking about?
113 MRS. P:	No.
114 THERAPIST:	We were talking about Sally's feeling—her own feeling about herself; that she can't, you know, if she's not well, uh, she thought she was a nuisance to you.

You had to reassure her that you didn't see it that way. So we were getting back a little bit into her history to see where this came from because it doesn't, you know, happen overnight. Sally was also saying, Jack, that . . . re . . . despite all of the heartache . . . and strain that you've been going through, that you've been wonderful at home. (measured almost exaggerated slow tempo) Thoughtful . . . patient . . . good-humored for the most part. How do you manage that? It's quite some . . . (fades out).

115 MR. P:	(sotto voce) I dunno . . . I don't know that I've been all these things.
116 THERAPIST:	(surprise) Oh.
117 MR. P:	I haven't been home very much, that's for sure, so (laughs good naturedly) maybe that's when the decent feelings come out. (unclear due to hearty laughing) (Mrs. P. laughs also).
118 THERAPIST:	You really think that's it?
119 MR. P:	I don't know. Wasn't home all last weekend.
120 THERAPIST:	Hm-m-m?
121 MR. P:	(more slowly and articulated carefully) I said I wasn't home all last weekend.
122 THERAPIST:	You were moving. (Mrs. P.: Sunday.) Oh, you were home Sunday?
123 MR. P:	I was home Sunday . . . (pause) so I don't know.
124 THERAPIST:	Didn't feel to you as if you had been home because you'd worked on Saturday.

118

125 MR. P:	(barely audible) Worked all Friday night right through Saturday (unclear).
126 THERAPIST:	Oh.
127 MR. P:	I left work at 10:30 Saturday morning. (laughs) I slept away Saturday night.
128 THERAPIST:	You slept the way, did you say? I didn't hear.
129 MR. P:	Slept away Saturday night.
130 THERAPIST:	By that you mean you slept in town?
131 MR. P:	No, I slept at home, but I mean. . . .
132 MRS. P:	He was here all-all Friday night and Saturday morning and then he came home and went to sleep . . . about noontime.
132A THERAPIST:	Oh, I see.
133 MRS. P:	And he slept till nighttime.
134 THERAPIST:	(sympathetically) Must have been bone, bone weary.
135 MR. P:	Yeah. I'm gettin' wearier. Take a couple of days off next week. (pause) I've been thinking about that. Ya got some time open on Monday? Or Tuesday?
136 THERAPIST:	In the daytime?
137 MR. P:	Anytime. If I take time off I want to take Thursday and Friday.
138 THERAPIST:	(leafing calendar) Do I have any time on Monday? (to Mrs. P.) Can you take time off?
139 MRS. P:	It's not so good in the day. It's better at night.
140 THERAPIST:	At night I don't have any time, except at 9 o'clock.
141 MRS. P:	Well, I can manage during the day.
142 THERAPIST:	You can? All right, so let me take a look at my Monday calendar. (pause) Can you make it at 12:45? Both of you?
143 MR. P:	It's all right.
144 MRS. P:	Um.
145 MR. P:	If I'm fortunate enough to be able to arrange those two days, I'll take Thursday and Friday. (pause) All right?
146 MRS. P:	(agrees) Um-hm.
147 THERAPIST:	Okay, that's clearly out of the way. (long pause—clock ticking in background)
148 MR. P:	Where were we last week? (mumbles) I'm trying to remember.
149 MRS. P:	We were talking about work, your work.
150 MR. P:	(mumbles and laughs) I don't want to talk about my work. Get enough of that.
151 THERAPIST:	(deliberatively) You were quite, um, disgruntled with me last

119

		week for (measured emphasis upon each word) *probing* and *pushing* and trying to get to some of the things that were not very clear about the state that you were in in connection with with job and with Nancy K.* You remember that?
152	MR. P:	Yeah.
153	THERAPIST:	Do you remember being quite miffed with me?
154	MR. P:	Um-hum.
155	THERAPIST:	Do you know what that's about at all? I mean it would be kind of helpful, I think, to understand this.
156	MR. P:	(wearily) Not really.
157	THERAPIST:	(with warmth and animated sincerity) Jack, how do you feel when I, you know . . . Sally has said many a time in a variety of ways the ways in which she minds (moves into rise-fall intonation) my pushing and focusing on her and getting back into her early life and how it might be connected with her present, your present lives, and her present attitudes. How does it feel to you? You know, you showed this time that you didn't like it.
158	MR. P:	(low voiced, barely audible) Well, it was something I, for one reason or another. . . . Last week I was just sort of . . . sick of talking about it, I just. . . .
159	THERAPIST:	Oh.
160	MR. P:	I . . . I . . . you know . . . (Therapist: Well . . .) I guess, I guess I just don't talk about it. You know, shut it off one way or the other.
161	THERAPIST:	Well, what is it about talking? I know your . . . one of your ways is to shut it off.
162	MR. P:	I don't believe I like to talk things out, you know. (pause) I guess, you know, in reality what I do is that, uh, if I find a subject either unpleasant or I'm not sure how I really think or feel about it, I, you know, won't say anything.
163	THERAPIST:	Well, what is it about not being sure? Is it . . . what is it that you risk if you're not sure? 'Cause somewhere . . . (pause) what you're saying is that you have to feel that you've sorted out yourself.
164	MR. P:	(low tone, hardly audible) Yeah, I guess so.
165	THERAPIST:	Well, can we try to understand why it must be, you know, your sorting out and if you're unsure that there's something

---

* Female employee with whom Mr. Porter had previously been emotionally involved.

		about it that's uncomfortable? Is it like finding out something?
166	MR. P:	No. I don't know what it is. I do this about anything.
167	THERAPIST:	I gather!
168	MR. P:	Well, you know, it doesn't have to be something I'm particularly emotionally involved in. It could be anything that. . . .
169	THERAPIST:	(animatedly) Oh, I think that the emotions get involved. I remember how you used to describe, a year and a half ago and a year ago, how you would get things sorted out in your own mind and then you could then go and present it. It's as if, you know, you don't quite—I don't know whether it's you (intones in rise-fall manner) don't *trust* the thoughts that come, uh, to your mind at the moment, whether you feel they're out of control, that you will say more than you will . . . say something you'll be sorry for. You know, I don't understand it, and I think it would be good, particularly since it's in so many places.
170	MR. P:	Oh, I think of a number of aspects of this. One in terms of . . . (pause, struggles with thoughts) I've accustomed myself, let me put it to you this way: In so much of my dealings with people that whatever it is I want to say, I want to say it in the best possible way so that it is shown in the best possible light. This is the only way I could describe it. . . .
171	THERAPIST:	You mean that it will be received?
172	MR. P:	Not that it will necessarily be receive—(interrupts self) well, yeah, that it will be received, but I don't mean necessarily received favorably. But at least I have . . . I want to have the feeling that I have—whatever the case is that I am presenting—I am presenting as best as possible, or whatever the thought is as best as possible.
173	THERAPIST:	You mean, so it will be listened to at least?
174	MR. P:	Yeah.
175	THERAPIST:	You know what this reminds me of, Jack?
176	MR. P:	What?
177	THERAPIST:	I don't know whether you would agree with me, but uh, since this you say has always been, or for a long time been your method, I wonder whether it didn't start a long time ago when you'd be slapped down.
178	MR. P:	(quietly with flatness of effect) Probably so. Probably so. Wouldn't surprise me a bit.
179	THERAPIST:	'Cause why would you be so—yeah, you know, I can under-

stand that we all want to be underst . . . you know, listened to, but for you it is such a (measured tones reflecting his cautiousness) concerted effort to make absolutely sure that your facts are in and every last dot—you have . . . you know, every last "i" is dotted. Uh. . . . (pause) So that I can understand it. But when your thoughts are going in seven different directions, you're not . . . you don't feel as if you can trust yourself to say it or trust the person, or me to really listen to you. Is this it?

180 MR. P: (starts with high register, then lowers voice) I don't think . . . well, I don't think it's quite the same situation. I don't think it's the same situation. I may react that way at times and this is probably because. . . .

181 THERAPIST: Well, what do you think it is?

182 MR. P: . . . You know, years of doing things this way. (Therapist: Uhm.) I don't react that way with my wife. I say pretty much what's on my mind.

183 THERAPIST: And I don't know what that. . . .

184 MRS. P: (laughingly) Sometimes I wish you wouldn't.

185 THERAPIST: (laughs) Oh, you sometimes wish he wouldn't? (Mrs. P.: Hm.)

186 MR. P: No! But (glottalizes) uh-uh-uh-uh-uh-you know, part of my talking about things incessantly at times is . . . is not being guarded, not being, uh, afraid of the reception, but wanting her thoughts or her ideas on whatever it is we're talking about.

187 THERAPIST: But even in the way you've talked with her in the past, it's almost as if you wanted to make absolutely certain that with her help you came out with the right answer. You know (Mr. P.: Ya. Sure.), and this is one of the things that Sally has felt like an *extra* demand on her. I think we also know that in the past, though this doesn't seem to be so much your meth . . . your way of protecting yourself now, you used to . . . if things got too hot and heavy, you used to *fly*. So what do you think it is . . . well . . . let's-let's give you, you know-you know, here I am again making these pronouncements. What's your own think . . . what is your thinking as to why this is?

188 MR. P: Well, I think. . . .

189 THERAPIST: If you're not clear that you know it's. . . .

190 MR. P: Well, I think your initial analysis is probably very accurate.

You know, probably goes back to childhood or whatever it is, and, uh, and (almost inaudible) you know, what you do about it, what I do about it is something else.

191 THERAPIST: Well, one thing we can possibly understand is your own feelings of saying something before you feel it's absolutely pigeonholed and very complete. Because here, for instance, there's really—(intonation suggests effort to be reassuring and reasonable) I'm going to try to understand. I don't know whether . . . how you see me. Whether you think that I will *pounce* on you or be *critical* of you.

192 MR. P: I don't see you that way at all . . . (unclear).

193 THERAPIST: I don't know. Jack, you know, there have been times when, uh, you came out with an idea (bus noise in background; unclear) it felt as though you were subjected to pressure to do something you didn't want, and I'm wondering whether, if you say. . . .

194 MR. P: (laughing) Well, you do some (words unclear).

195 THERAPIST: Yeah, yeah, but, you know, that's (Mr. P.: [coughing] You know that's . . .) . . . we're talking about. . . .

196 MR. P: Well, really! I-uh, I-uh, realize this point, for the moment, or whatever it is for the moment, but I . . . you know, it's certainly nothing lasting, certainly nothing of any earth-shattering. . . .

197 THERAPIST: (contradicts) Oh, this wasn't a moment. This was . . . this went *on* for you in feeling. It lasted a long time. . . . And it came up *again*, uh . . . when we talked about it about a month or two later. (to Mrs. P.) Do you have any thoughts on it, Sally?

198 MRS. P: (almost inaudible) Not really.

199 THERAPIST: I thought you might have some notion because you, too, have your feelings—you know, for instance, the moment before Jack joined us, uh, remember there was a moment when you were feeling that I was really *pressing* you awfully hard.

200 MRS. P: Well, that's only because I-I know I have . . . I'm strange in certain ways, so is Jack, so are you, so is everyone and I don't know why. . . .

201 THERAPIST: Strange?

202 MRS. P: . . . anything has to be—we . . . we all have our peculiarities; things we do. And I don't know that everything that we do necessarily is . . . has to be scrutinized.

123

203 THERAPIST:	But some things you mind and some things you don't mind, or mind less. *Right?*
204 MRS. P:	(animatedly and with intense feeling) Yes, because I enjoy —for instance, we were talking about my liking to be alone. I like to be alone and I don't really want to see *you* (laughs vibrantly) put it in the light of, of some kind of . . . of sickness, or some kind of symptom of . . . (laughs) of . . . because, you know . . . it's . . . it's like anything else, I-I like to be *alone* and I guess I don't want to be thought of as *queer* because I like to be alone. And so I've gotta explain (mocking intonation) why I want to be alone. There are a lot of reasons why. . . .
205 THERAPIST:	(interrupts) Why did you pick that out for queerness rather than something else, huh?
206 MRS. P:	Only because you were, you know, considering it . . . before . . . (words incomprehensible due to overlap).
207 THERAPIST:	I wasn't saying it was queer.
208 MRS. P:	No, but I mean why would you want to examine it unless it . . . you didn't feel there was something unusual about the extent to which I want to be alone?
209 THERAPIST:	(to Mr. P.) You know what my comment . . . my response to Sally was in connection with that? Would you like to tell Jack that?
210 MRS. P:	No (Therapist: Go ahead.), I don't-I don't. . . . What do you mean?
211 THERAPIST:	Why I was asking about why you wanted to be alone.
212 MRS. P:	I'm not . . . I'm not sure I . . . you know, exactly remember.
213 THERAPIST:	I was saying that for Sally so much of her life in the past used to be, and it still is at times, in feeling that she needs to brush all of the intrusions and pressures away from her to feel . . . before she can feel that her soul is her own; (rise-fall intonation) whether it's sometimes you, sometimes it's the kids, sometimes it's all four of you. . . .
214 MRS. P:	Uhh. . . .
215 THERAPIST:	But the important thing is that . . . you know, the . . . also the important thing is the way you feel about it.
216 MRS. P:	(with earnestness and intensity) *Yes.* It's because I've been alone most of my life anyway and I'm more. . . . I'm more used to being alone than I am with people. I'm more comfortable that way. Jack is more comfortable if there are a

lot of people around all the time. And I find it very exhausting. That's just conditioning I think. And I don't . . . you know (laughs) maybe I am being sensitive. I just wish you didn't look on it as something that had to be *explained* or *examined* as if it were something *strange*.

217 THERAPIST: You know, it's funny. You say I'm looking at it. . . . it's-it's one of the areas, one of the problem-making areas in your life together, you know, when (pause) on the one hand you need to be alone and wish to be alone and Jack is intruding.

We need to understand what this intrusion is all about. You say you're always alone. That's interesting. I think you're describing a feeling because you had people around you— sometimes maybe they felt like too many people for too much of the time. It isn't that you grew up alone (Mrs. P.: No.), except maybe in feeling. (to Mr. P.) I don't know about you. Did you feel alone in your family at times; kind of lonely and alone, Jack?

218 MR. P: (hardly audible) Well, I'm sure at times all kids do.

219 THERAPIST: But do you remember?

220 MR. P: Not specific things. (long pause)

221 THERAPIST: It's harder for you to remember your earlier feelings.

222 MR. P: Yeah. I have very little (voice fades). (sustained pause) Like I-I begin to know more about myself in terms of my child-hood, really, in a way by my dealing with the children.

223 THERAPIST: Umm. You mean you recall certain feelings in you?

224 MR. P: (very uncertain and hesitating) Oh, no! I . . . I . . . I . . . I only say this because of . . . I-I'm sure, you know, it's ax-axiomatic; ya act, you act towards your children—or most people do—the way they were brought up. How else did you learn to do or to react or be the way you are? And, uh, so I'm sure that, uh, you know, part of it is this . . . I mean, ya know, this is, this is all . . . this is the real basis of my (voice fades).

225 THERAPIST: Does it work that way for you, too, Sally?

226 MRS. P: No, I don't think it's necessarily true. A lot of people go just in the other direction. I probably do. I don't know about Jack. (pause)

227 THERAPIST: (softly) Can you describe some of the . . . illustrate some of the things you mean, Jack? Because I think there is truth to what both of you are saying.

228 MR. P:	(subdued tone) Yeah. Well, the thing that comes most immediate to mind was, uh, happened a couple of weeks ago. Mary * asked me—Sally was there with the kids. . . .
229 THERAPIST:	Sally was what?
230 MR. P:	Sally was there (unclear) . . . the other two children were there. . . .
231 THERAPIST:	Oh.
232 MR. P:	. . . why we couldn't join a certain country club. And I answered, one, that we didn't have the money to do this, and I wanted to go further in it and say that, you know, there was also another problem (voice drops) . . . that this particular club did not admit Negroes. Sally stopped me . . . (inaudible).
233 THERAPIST:	Why did you stop him? . . . Oh . . . you don't remember stopping him?
234 MRS. P:	No. I'm trying to remember. I. . . .
235 MR. P:	We were in the bedroom. The kids were talking about joining the Southport, I mean, uh, the. . . .
236 MRS. P:	Oh, yeah (appears to remember incident).
237 MR. P:	(hardly audible) There's one next door.
238 THERAPIST:	You did stop him?
239 MRS. P:	(softly) I may have. (voice hardens and rises) I never stop Jack! If he's going to say something, he's going to say it (Mr. P.: Oh, yeah . . .). I may have indicated I didn't want him to continue.
240 THERAPIST:	Well, this is what you mean then (Mr. P.: Yeah.); she nodded, gave you a cue?
241 MR. P:	Hmm.
242 THERAPIST:	(to Mr. P.) Why did you . . . why did you, uh, accept her cue?
243 MR. P:	I just accepted it. I knew probably I would upset her if I went on with it. And yet I think it's . . . (laughs) something somewhere along the line that the children have got to know and understand this, and Mary is certainly old enough to know this.
244 THERAPIST:	(to Mrs. P.) Why . . . what was your feeling? What were your thoughts on it, Sally?
245 MRS. P:	I don't know. I just . . . I-I probably just . . . it was just a spur of the moment thing. I probably thought it was *enough*

* Oldest daughter of the Porters.

first of all they know we don't have the money. It takes money
. . . so why go into a lot of details?

246 THERAPIST: (firmly and deliberately) Sally, I would suggest possibly you
do have some feelings about it, you know, about bringing up
the Negro issue.

247 MRS. P: (remains calm and speaks softly) I do it myself, at times,
when I feel it, you know, it's appropriate.

248 THERAPIST: But when is it not appropriate?

249 MRS. P: I don't know. Sometimes Jack will get very deadly and very
serious about everything and makes it . . . uhm, all out of
proportion . . . instead of handling it lightly.

250 MR. P: It's not out of proportion. See this is where you see it. . . .

251 THERAPIST: But it isn't so light for him.

252 MRS. P: (softly controlled) Well, the . . . you know, there are a lot
of things that we feel strongly about or deeply about and we
don't always have to transfer these things to children. You
don't always . . . you know . . . (trails off).

253 THERAPIST: (also softly) But isn't it a fact of life for them? That this is
(Mrs. P.: Yeah.) also something they contend with? So let's
see what's . . . what's . . . what troubles you about their
knowing it. You feel that Jack makes it a (exaggerated stress)
preachy, miserable, dark future for them?

254 MRS. P: No. It's just . . . I barely remember this incident. (to Mr. P.)
I . . . I accept it because you say it happened. I barely remember it. And it was probably just something that happened and my immediate reaction was, "Don't make such a
big thing out of it." Because they're asking to go to the club
every . . . you know, every time you turn around they want
to go to the club, you know. And there are, you know, a lot
of reasons. Being, you know, Negro is just one of them. (three
voices overlap) (Therapist: But it's. . . .) And you don't
have to sit down and say (exaggerated mocking intonation)
"Now, we're going to talk about the subject now." In some
ways, Jack, you get very preachy, you know. When you decide
to talk about religion to the children, for instance, you know,
you're not . . . (laughs) you're about the least religious person I know, and yet when you decide to talk about religion,
we get out the Bible and we're going to read the Bible and
we're going to do this. And it's a *big.* . . . I don't know.
(lowers voice) It's like a big dishonesty of some kind. (voice

127

	fades) And this is that kind of thing. It's . . . taking it. . . .
255 THERAPIST:	Well, why is this dishonesty? He *is* a Negro—it's not the same as he's not religious, and I don't know what religion . . . maybe religion is. . . .
256 MRS. P:	Well, we don't ever make a great big thing out of it. And to . . . to blow something out of proportion is, it's. . . .
257 THERAPIST:	Well, but you assumed he would.
258 MRS. P:	. . . is foolish.
259 THERAPIST:	(deliberately but softly) Sally, I think maybe you have more of a problem about this than you know.
260 MRS. P:	(angrily) Oh, I think you're making something out of nothing because this is a slight incident and I don't even remember it.
261 MR. P:	(softly with earnestness) But you know this "slight" incident —and we've talked about this kind of thing before—you know, it's . . . it's when do you, when do you—and let's just go back and I'm not trying to bring up anything. But when do you start telling children, "You eat with forks at the dinner table, not with you hands;" when do you say, you know, "This is the way to sit at a table and eat?" (speaks with great deliberateness) These are *all* little things. None of these things (speaks with steady beat) in and of themselves, are necessarily important. But when do you say something?
262 MRS. P:	Hm . . . (vehemently) Yeah, but you make everything a federal case. You do!
263 MR. P:	(defensively) Well, maybe I do.
264 MRS. P:	You know, it just makes, you know, every little thing is like. . . .
265 MR. P:	(voices hardens) Maybe I feel I have to, and this is, you know, this is what we're coming down to.
266 THERAPIST:	Sally, is it possible that . . . (pause) While. . . .
267 MRS. P:	(interrupts) If . . . if one of these children doesn't tell the truth about something, or evades, it's-it's not that they're at this age and they're evading. They're *lying!* It's . . . it's . . .
268 MR. P:	(in high register) Well, what's wrong with that?
269 THERAPIST:	What about. . . .
270 MRS. P:	(voice is shrill and dramatic) You don't see anything wrong with that?! To tell a child he's *lying.* "*Don't you lie to me.*" At that age children don't *lie!*
271 THERAPIST:	Well even. . . .

272 MR. P.:	(stammers . . . defends self) Well, you . . . what do, what-what. . . . How do they learn what's wrong?
273 MRS. P.:	(both voices in strident overlap) . . . all of your grown-up moral implications on the fact that the child may be afraid because you're yelling.
274 THERAPIST:	Well, suppose even he . . . it's a lie, is it what you're saying is that Jack gets so terribly intensely offended by it?
275 MRS. P.:	That's right. It's a *great* . . . *big thing.*
276 THERAPIST:	We're moving away a little bit from the Negro question (Mr. P.: [tries to defend self] It's the same kind of thing. It's the same kind of thing . . .) (voices overlap). But, wait a minute. But, wait. I don't know. Is it the same kind of thing? Because this lying had come up before. Is this something also that was out of your past, about lying?
277 MR. P.:	Sure, it's . . . I, you know, I place great importance on this.
278 THERAPIST:	Were you very often called down for lying and not telling the truth, when you wanted to? . . .
279 MR. P.:	When I was caught at it. Whenever I was caught in something wrong, sure.
280 THERAPIST:	You mean everything became a federal case?
281 MR. P.:	I don't know that everything became a federal case.
282 THERAPIST:	But I mean particularly about not telling the truth. You know, kids will, as Sally says, in order to avoid. . . .
283 MR. P.:	(speaks rapidly, with anger) I don't know that I make a federal case out of it, but when I speak to one of them about something very specific and, Sally, you can't say that I-I do this all the time. (phone rings) When I speak to them about something very specific and there's a. . . . you-you know, I . . . I . . . want an answer whatever, you know, the answer is. I want them to give me the answer.
284 MRS. P.:	(sarcastically) Yeah. You got little Jack there quaking in his boots and *"I want an answer from you now, don't you lie to me!"* That's what it is, you know, and you scare the hell out of him and you wonder why he, you know, he cries at a word from you. And I stay out of it, you know?
285 THERAPIST:	It's interesting you stay out of that, but you don't stay out of the Negro question. But, there . . . you know, this is a problem on several levels. . . .
286 MRS. P.:	(talks under breath) I'm not even aware I was doing anything. What did I do? (fades out) You know?

287 THERAPIST: You know, Sally, it feels like you're being picked on now. This is your response. Instead of our trying to find out what—apparently as, as I see it, there may be some feeling you have about it.

288 MRS. P: Hm . . . well, I don't . . . I don't think I like the idea of picking this out because it happens to involve Negro-ness and, an. . . . (Mr. and Mrs. P.'s voices overlap)

289 MR. P: (hesitantly increasingly firm) Yeah, but Sally . . . Sally, you have never been willing to face *anything* along this line. And when I say to you it is because, uh, my reaction is because . . . and you, you are always minimizing. You are always minimizing.

290 MRS. P: Like what?

291 MR. P: I—I can't. . . .

292 MRS. P: You mean, rake up anything about race?

293 MR. P: Uhm. I can't think of anything specifically, but on the other hand. . . .

294 MRS. P: It just doesn't come up that often (Mr. P.: Eh . . .). We're very frank with the children and whenever this has come up I've been the one that has talked to them about this.

295 THERAPIST: Well, why do you mind. . . .

296 MRS. P: When they ask about the housing and what-what-why is it that we do this and that. We tell them.

297 THERAPIST: But, you know, this can be very safe because you can do it for other people. Here's an instance where Mary says, "Why can't *we?*"

298 MRS. P: I know, but we've related this to our own lives. And I've never hedged with them.

299 MR. P: (high voice) No, I'm not saying you hedged with them. . . .

300 THERAPIST: (interrupts) Well, what do you think that Jack would do with this? What did you think Jack would do?

301 MRS. P: He'd make another one of his. . . .

302 THERAPIST: (interrupts) Well, like what?

303 MRS. P: (explodes) I don't know! Because I don't remember it. You know. . . . you know. . . . (is lost for words)

304 MR. P: All right. All right. You don't remember. What would you imagine I would do in a situation like that?

305 MRS. P: I don't know (very low voice). Go on, you know (pause).

306 THERAPIST: You mean he'd go on and give them, Mary, the whole history of the Negro struggle?

307 MRS. P: No. It's just that, not remembering it, I'll . . . I'll say it's just one in a. . . . (subdued, quiet voice) They want a lot of things that they're not going to have and to take this one thing and-and make it into a racial thing . . . is kind of . . . of, it's really not accurate because there are a whole lot of reasons why we . . . there are a lot of white people who can't belong there either. Granted, you know, this isn't our situation. But it . . . it pertains to us and maybe that is hedging. I don't know. But, I just, you know (voice fades). . . .

308 MR. P: (suppressed anger; expresses self firmly) There is never anything very clear cut in this day and age, my dear, that you can point out and say, it is because of race that this doesn't happen, because, you know, things are changing. But also it is a fact of life that this plays a part in it. And this is all I was trying to say. Or all I wanted to say.

309 THERAPIST: (pause) You apparently have some strong feelings about this. (to Mrs. P.) Do *you* have any feelings about it at all, Sally?

310 MRS. P: What? About the country club?

311 THERAPIST: Umm.

312 MRS. P: (voice quavers with emotion) Look, you know, a long time ago, I, you know, I know I don't have money and I'll never belong to the Southport Country Club. Not for racial reasons. I just won't. And that's enough for me. I don't have to go any step beyond. (to Mr. P.) Now maybe for you it's sumpin' else. Maybe you think, "Well, someday I can . . . I could belong over there if only I weren't Negro," but with me it's enough.

313 THERAPIST: Well, let's see what it is for Jack.

314 MR. P: (high-pitched voice) I'd love to join the South—Southport Country Club if I had the money. (voices overlap)

315 MRS. P: Yes, in your mind it's a possibility—in mine, it's not.

316 THERAPIST: But, you know, Sally. Are you very angry with Jack right now? For bringing this up? Because in a way. . . .

317 MRS. P: (voice is squeezed, absolute exasperation) It's all out of *proportion* again, you know, it. . . .

318 MR. P: (high pitched) What is out of proportion?

319 THERAPIST: (overlaps) What's out of proportion?

320 MRS. P: (sounds almost tearful with rage) This whole big discussion about something that I did offhandedly. Everytime I blink my eyes now I've got to examine my motivation.

131

321 MR. P: (mutters in the background) . . . Come on!

322 THERAPIST: You know, Sally, you feel attacked somehow in this . . . and there are some things about which you feel attacked and others which you don't. Why, in this, do you feel so attacked? I ask myself and of you.

323 MRS. P: (pseudo-humorously) Because of me and my old soft line of being . . . being criticized here. You know, old softy.

324 THERAPIST: "Softy?" Ah-h, I don't see you as "softy" in this.

325 MRS. P: That's what he said, I'm soft on everything. I won't face anything.

326 MR. P: What?

327 MRS. P: You. You said I'm soft and I can never face up to anything. (bitterly) I face up to plenty!

328 MR. P: I'm sure you do.

329 THERAPIST: (softly) Is it possible that this is something that is harder to face up to, Sally?

330 MRS. P: (imitates Therapist's intonation in exaggerated sing-song fashion) No, it's not.

331 THERAPIST: Boy, you're furious with me. You were just making fun of the way I said it to you.

332 MRS. P: I'm just exhausted.

333 THERAPIST: This is your turn today. Last week it was Jack's and his feeling pushed and pounded on.

334 MRS. P: (voice squeezed) It's so *pointless* to waste time on something like *this*.

335 THERAPIST: (voice rings affirmatively) Is it really? Isn't it possible a . . . you know . . . one of the features in your marriage? You know, a couple of weeks ago—it's more than a couple of weeks ago, it's at least a month and a half ago—when we were talking about, uh, the situation between ta-the two of you in bed, uh, and your feeling of revulsion with Jack and his unwashed body sweat and his unchanged underpants, and Jack came through with a feeling of, you know, dirtiness and we got to the question of Negro, uh. There may be more to this than you really know. You . . . I wonder whether it's really a feeling of total attack or whether it's also the question of Negro. I mean, whether you feel, you know, that you're being picked on or whether it's also a sore subject. That is it may be. It's easy for you to go—not easy—but you go and do the battle for the community, but maybe some of it goes right

132

on at home. I think that you . . . you have, you know, un-
doubtedly there is much to what you're saying about the way
Jack may, in other instances, overreact in connection with lies
and table manners and I think we need to get to this. But you
lump it all together.

336 MRS. P: (bitterly conveys sarcasm by throwing out utterance mechan-
ically with flatness of effect) Yeah. I lump it all together. So
that's very significant. This is fine and I'm trying to do something. I don't know what. Ya know.

337 THERAPIST: To me, it's not a sign you're trying to do anything. To me,
it's a sign that there may be some more problem about it
than meets the eye.

338 MRS. P: (icily) Well, you're entitled to your opinion. (hardly audible)
I don't happen to agree with it . . . okay? If anybody does
anything about race in our house, it's me. Talks to our children, it's me.

339 THERAPIST: Oh, Jack is the one who hedges usually?

340 MRS. P: It's just nonexistent.

341 THERAPIST: Oh! Oh, that does turn it around.

342 MRS. P: The only time Jack is Negro is when we have friends come
in who are Negro, or when it's convenient. There's never any
racial talk or anything. Maybe between us—remarks and
things like that.

343 THERAPIST: Between the two of you?

344 MRS. P: Yeah. You know, about television—we see (Therapist: Oh.)
something on television or a joke or something like that. But
there's no other, you know . . . it's nothing in our lives.

345 MR. P: (cautiously stated) I . . . I . . . I think I treat this in exact
same manner in which you do. By that I mean I don't go out
to make a deal about it. I don't go out to bring it up as a subject that has to be necessarily discussed and . . . and so
forth, but in a . . . in a-in a natural situation. You don't sit
down and say, "All right, now we're going to discuss race."
And I wasn't about to do that either. But . . . a . . . a . . .
subject was a . . . a . . . a . . . a . . . opportunity came up!

346 MRS. P: (very quietly conceding) Okay.

347 MR. P: You know, they *don't* come up that often. And I don't want to
make a big deal out of it. But I also think there are certain
(light nervous laugh) facts of life. You know, another five
years, you gonna have to. . . .

133

348 MRS. P:	(suppressed sarcasm) What are the facts of life? Do you know?
349 MR. P:	Huh?
350 MRS. P:	(ironically) What are the facts of life (barely audible) anyway, you know. You got me thinking now.
351 MR. P:	Like what?
352 MRS. P:	What d'ya tell those children, you know, what do you tell them? Is that the kind of thing you're going to tell them everytime they turn around?
353 MR. P:	Have I ever said it to them before?
354 MRS. P:	(in pseudo-agreement) I don't know. Do you—as I said, you've got me thinking now. You know. How many sit-situations are there going to be?
355 THERAPIST:	What do you mean by that?
356 MRS. P:	Country clubs . . . there are a lot of things we can't do.
357 THERAPIST:	Yeah.
358 MRS. P:	You know, for a lot of reasons. There's a . . . a damned good reason (laughs lightly) why you shouldn't go play tennis this summer maybe because we don't have the money.
359 MR. P:	Yeah.
360 MRS. P:	Going to turn that into a racial thing, too? You know, what are you going to do?
361 THERAPIST:	Wait a minute, Sally.
362 MRS. P:	You can't send her to a summer camp, you know.
363 MR. P:	I don't follow what you're saying.
364 THERAPIST:	Uh . . . are you . . . you're going . . . are you feeling very angry right now?
365 MRS. P:	Uhh . . . I'm fed up!
366 THERAPIST:	Why are you so fed up right now? (long pause) Because right now you're hurling some things . . . calling some things. . . .
367 MRS. P:	(exasperated) Ummm. I just wish, you know, if I'm going to be accountable for things I would remember them, that's all. (overlap between Mr. and Mrs. P.)
368 MR. P:	(high-pitched voice) All right. Forget that. I . . . uh . . . you know . . . this is. . . .
369 THERAPIST:	(interrupts) Wait a minute.
370 MR. P:	(shouting) I . . . I don't say forget it. (squeezes voice) I . . . I . . . you know, let's say I'm totally erroneous and this

is a feeling I've got that this is what happened. Ah, can't you discuss it like that?

371 THERAPIST: Well maybe it stirs up certain feelings, not maybe, it apparently *does* stir up all kinds of feelings in Sally and why she feels *attacked* under this. Because what you're doing now is counterattacking and . . . (Mrs. P. makes inaudible comment and therapist laughs) I'm smiling in connection with your smile.

372 MRS. P: (laughingly) Well, I just would like the heat off a while, that's all.

373 THERAPIST: Yeah.

374 MRS. P: You know, I feel like I've done something and I don't remember doing it; like I've stolen you know, a million dollars and I don't remember doing it and now I've got to answer for it.

And now I wonder if I do really have to answer at all for it. Maybe I-I just feel, you know, if I did it, I had my reasons, you know.

375 THERAPIST: But it's interesting, in your counterattack, you bring in other things which you may have a lot of feeling about. You may have a lot of feeling about Jack's going out and spending money on himself.

376 MRS. P: (low voice, hardly audible) Oh boy . . . well I'm just hitting below the belt that's all. I don't mind about his playing tennis.

377 THERAPIST: You don't?

378 MRS. P: No, I really don't. As long as we do certain other things, too.

379 THERAPIST: (to Mr. P.) How do you feel about what's just happened?

380 MR. P: Oh, I. . . .

381 THERAPIST: Hummm?

382 MR. P: (determinedly) I said I don't like it.

383 THERAPIST: What don't you like?

384 MR. P: (angry and discouraged) Because this has been Sally's reaction to this particular subject many, many times.

385 MRS. P: To what?

386 MR. P: And it baffles me. It really *baffles* me!

387 THERAPIST: What subject are you talking about now? Talking about Negroes?

388 MR. P: Race. Yeah.

389 MRS. P: What's been my reaction many times?

390 MR. P: It is quite obvious I don't like my kids walking around the streets in holey pants for one very simple reason: I'm a Negro. And I am under a strict scrutiny and I don't want my kids under . . . in and under this kind of scrutiny, so I want my kids with pants on with holes in them—without holes in them. (bitterly) But you could never understand this.

391 MRS. P: (softly) It wasn't that I couldn't understand it, Jack.

392 MR. P: Well then it didn't mean anything to you then. You know, so you went on and did it as you saw fit, you know. This kind of thing. And you've done it, you've done it in this area the whole time we've been married—unfortunately. (lowered voice) Sorry this came up.

393 THERAPIST: What you're saying is you're sorry to disturb what has been a good feeling between the two of you. I am into this too with you.

394 MR. P: I'm sure the two of us will return. I'm not worried about that. But it's just that . . . that, you know, every time it comes up we end up in the same place, you know. No place.

395 THERAPIST: What are you saying now? Are you saying that every time some issue that is of vital importance to you comes up, we reach an impasse?

396 MR. P: I'm saying on this particular issue.

397 THERAPIST: Well, maybe we can give it some more thought. Maybe Sally can help us understand whether it's out of disregard for you or out of her really not knowing deeply enough how this can feel to you. And it may be very hard. As you yourself were saying about two months ago, Jack, that nobody really can *truly* savor the feeling, really can *understand* the feeling that you have on this. So I don't know whether it's that, whether it's disregard or whether this is truly something which is hard for Sally with all her sympathy to understand. Well maybe we can get a chance if both of you are—can tolerate it—to talk about it some more. See you the next week. Monday.

Treatment issues in session four

20   How does Mrs. Porter's voice sound to you? Is the tone of the voice congruent with the words?

34   Considering Mrs. Porter's strong reaction to her husband's

drinking in the past (see Session One), does her current reaction indicate progress on her part?

69–73   How do you assess the therapist's concern with Mrs. Porter's liking to be alone? Why does the patient show such a strong reaction to this line of inquiry?

87   What insight is the therapist attempting to elicit by this inquiry into Mrs. Porter's need for a "fracture-proof" in order to be entitled to be ill? Why is it hard for Mrs. Porter to be a patient?

107–114   What can you say about Mr. Porter's entry and the reception he receives? Why is the therapist letting Mr. Porter know what had been discussed in the session before his entrance? Do you think it was correct for her to do this?

149   How would you interpret the long silence and Mr. Porter's expressed inability to remember what had been talked about in the last session? Do you think the therapist should have: a) Asked Mr. Porter what he wanted to talk about? b) Asked Mrs. Porter whether she remembered? c) Remained silent?

157   The therapist is focusing upon Mrs. Porter's reactions to her probing. This effort is in the service of what purpose?

162   What does Mr. Porter reveal by the admission that if he finds a subject unpleasant he won't say anything? How would you have responded to him?

174   Does Mr. Porter's explanation ring true?

197–199   Why did the therapist shift the focus to Mrs. Porter at this point?

208   What is your impression of Mrs. Porter's reluctance to let the therapist examine her feelings about being alone? A neurotic defense, or an expression of strength and autonomy?

217   Why did the therapist turn to Mr. Porter at this point?

221   The therapist observes that it is harder for Mr. Porter to remember his earlier feelings. What implications does this have for conjoint therapy?

227   Is the therapist's request for an illustration of Mr. Porter's mode of reacting a useful technique? What does it lead to in this instance? Does Mr. Porter's response indicate he had "business" to bring to the session which was not yet revealed?

252   How would you describe Mrs. Porter's tone of voice when she is talking about the race issue? Is there an incongruity between the words and the manner in which she speaks?

276   The therapist remarks that the discussion is getting away from the Negro question. Mr. Porter says it is the same kind of thing. How do you see it?

289   What are the implications of Mr. Porter's accusation that his wife has minimized the issue of race in the marriage?

300   Mrs. Porter has accused her husband of making a "federal case" out of everything, while he reproaches her for "minimizing situations." In the first instance, the therapist makes a link to Mr. Porter's past; in the second, she stresses the interactional variable. Why did she do this? Do you think it was appropriate?

308–321   What are some of the dynamics underlying this interchange between the Porters? From a therapeutic standpoint, was it useful for them to have this confrontation over the issue of race?

329–331   How would you evaluate this exchange between Mrs. Porter and the therapist?

335   How do you feel about the therapist's directness in dealing with the evidence that Mrs. Porter has harbored ambivalent feelings about her husband's race?

General questions

1. How deep are Mrs. Porter's feelings about her husband's racial difference? What implications do they have for treatment of the marital difficulty?

2. How do you assess the therapist's handling of the racial issue?

3. What defense mechanisms are revealed by the Porters in this session?

4. Do you think feelings about racial difference revealed in conjoint treatment would have come out in more traditional individual encounters?

SESSION FIVE

The world

of work

IN THIS SESSION,* *Mr. Porter's adjustment to his work situation and his wife's reaction to his anxiety constitutes the exclusive theme of the therapeutic hour. Mr. Porter has made significant gains at work having been promoted to a position of increased responsibility and status. With the advancement, however, has come a niggling doubt that he will somehow upset the gains he has achieved. His anxiety has led him to check out many of his decisions with his employers, particularly in areas where he fears he will be held responsible for judgments that backfire. His indecisiveness and insecurity has stimulated his wife to make derogatory remarks about his needing to run to his employers, in the unseemly manner of the tattletale. Out of a need to justify himself and to secure the understanding and acceptance of his wife and the therapist, Mr. Porter tends to dominate the exchanges that take place within Session Five with excess verbalization. He thus provides the basis for a better understanding of the nature of his anxiety as well as some rational explanations for the behavior in which he engages. Simultaneously, Mrs. Porter reveals how undermined she feels when her husband fails to provide her with the sense of strength which she requires in order to cope with her own insecurities.*

* Session of April 14, 1967. The playback session took place the following day.

(Mrs. P. enters out of breath)

1 MRS. P:	Oh! The curse of being punctual! (laughs).
2 THERAPIST:	(laughs sympathetically) Uh-h . . . such a curse?
3 MRS. P:	(breathless) Hi!
4 THERAPIST:	You mean you were running yourself too ragged?
5 MRS. P:	(out of breath, not clear) . . . And I wouldn't have to wait then . . . (fades out).
6 THERAPIST:	You mean I'm not ready and Jack isn't here. . . .
7 MRS. P:	(barely audible) Well, you are but Jack's not.
8 THERAPIST:	Yah. . . . (telephone rings) There he is (Mrs. P. laughs) . . . yes . . . ask him to come up, please. (After a short pause, Mr. P. enters)
9 MR. P:	(buoyantly) What are you yawning about girl? . . . (Mrs. P. laughs) Huh? . . .
10 MRS. P:	I don't know . . . (Mr. P.: Huh?). I don't know. Just sleepy. (Mr. P. getting settled—small talk)
11 MR. P:	(notices no curtains in room) You lost your curtains. (barely audible) I was wondering. . . .
12 MRS. P:	(light laugh) Spring cleaning. (laughs at inaudible comment of husband) . . . grinning, I guess, grinning!
13 THERAPIST:	(part of cheerful exchange) You came in fairly grinning to yourself.
14 MR. P:	(inaudible) . . . bad day.
15 THERAPIST:	Hu-h?
16 MR. P:	(sighs) I had a rough day.
17 THERAPIST:	(sympathetically) Been a rough day. "Rough" in terms of work or? . . .
18 MR. P:	Just work.
19 THERAPIST:	Has that good feeling continued for you?
20 MR. P:	Oh yeh. . . . (sighs) So far I haven't lost the battle, neither have I lost the war (laughing) so . . . (fades out).
21 THERAPIST:	You're ahead.

22 MR. P:	I'm ahead . . . (silence) So . . . where shall we start? (to wife in mock seriousness) You have nothing you wish to discuss tonight? Then we can go home! I've got a lot of work to do.
23 THERAPIST:	Well, she doesn't have anything and I gather you don't have anything.
24 MR. P:	Oh yeh, I've got something for her. . . . (even tone, regulated tempo almost conveys sinister threat) One of these days I'm gonna bust my wife in the nose! When I try to tell her something *good*. Tell her what I have *done*. And perhaps what I do is not give all the details so she can get a complete pi'ture. But she has a very nasty habit of cutting me *dead*.
25 THERAPIST:	That sounds pretty awful. . . . What happened?
26 MR. P:	Nothing very serious . . . Well I-I told her about something the other night. And I told her what I did. You know . . . I was feeling good about it because it (Therapist: Hm-hm.) had been pretty sticky. And . . . uh . . . she didn't like the way I had handled it.
27 THERAPIST:	(surprised) Oh!
28 MR. P:	That was the implication I got. (turns to wife) Yes? . . . No?
29 THERAPIST:	You were disappointed?
30 MR. P:	(in high register) Oh, sure! I was feeling good about it! (silence)
31 THERAPIST:	(to Mrs. P.) He's very serious. . . . You're grinning!
32 MRS. P:	(suppressed laughter) I know . . . I know he's serious. (to husband) You're the person who always talks to me, and wants my opinion . . . and when I give it to you and I tell you something that I see very clearly, whether I'm right or wrong, you don't like it. You . . . you don't want me to say it.
33 MR. P:	I don't think this necessarily was a case where I was looking for something . . . (voices overlap) you know, that this is what's wrong. . . .
34 MRS. P:	(breaks in) . . . you can't pick and choose the time when I'm supposed to, you know, give . . . I should wait I suppose. You know I realized that it made you angry as though I shouldn't have said anything about it at all.
35 MR. P:	No . . . I'm not saying you shouldn't, I . . . I . . . I . . . yo . . . know I-I . . . well . . . I don't know what I . . . you know . . . I was feeling good about it. . . .

(somewhat inaudible) I had a real knock-down drag-out fight with K. (one of his bosses) about something. And I know I had her dead to rights. And I just let her work herself into a trap on the thing. . . . And . . . when I later saw T., one of the other partners, I just went over it with him briefly so that he was aware of the facts.

36 THERAPIST: So he should know that if she comes complaining what it was about.

37 MR. P: Right. And Sally sees this as wrong. Sees this as me being . . . a tattletale . . . or I don't know what.

38 MRS. P: No, only in the sense that you have done it often . . . uh, and then I think there has to come a time when you stop being so anxious about the things you have done, that you had to get to him so that in case she said anything he had all the facts. And, I-I don't think it indicates . . . you know . . . I don't know what! That you're not so secure? Or you're anxious? And that you're worried that she may—you know—get in there first and, and tell her lies, which you know she's going to do anyway. . . .

39 MR. P: (attempts to answer) Ya, but you know. . . .

40 MRS. P: (does not permit interruption) And that you have to run— and you do it repeatedly. And I think it's the same . . . you don't like it in *other* people. And R. becomes a nuisance when he's always bitching about things or he's always . . . people are . . . are so dependent. And yet I've noticed you doing it often. And you do it, always when you . . . when something . . . you've been in the right.

41 MR. P: I'll do it when I'm in the wrong. See, this is what you don't see.

42 MRS. P: Well, I'd . . . either way! If you, if . . . you know. So you had a fight with M. and you settled it. Now, you should be secure enough with these men and the assurances they've given you. . . .

43 THERAPIST: But maybe he isn't.

44 MRS. P: Yeh. Well maybe not. But this is how I see it.

45 THERAPIST: But did this come out . . . kind of with an irritating, uh, problem that Jack has. . . .

46 MRS. P: It's happened repeatedly.

47 THERAPIST: . . . for you . . . I know, but is this something that irritates you?

143

48 MRS. P: Yes, yes it does.

49 THERAPIST: Because I gather there may be a great deal to what you're saying but the way it comes through to Jack, it comes through as a, you know, something that you don't respect him for, or you found fault with.

50 MRS. P: Well, it's not the way I think people should operate. But if he does this, I can't do anything about that.

51 THERAPIST: No wait, you know, it's more than if he does and it's right or wrong. 'Cause it isn't a question of a right or wrong. Maybe you put your finger on something that is quite important here. The question is, you know, what that quality in Jack does to you so that it comes back to him, when you point it out, like a . . . an undercut.

52 MRS. P: Yes! I want him to be *strong!* And to me it's a sign of weakness.

53 THERAPIST: He was pretty strong when he put K. in a trap!

54 MRS. P: Sure he was!

55 THERAPIST: Did you let him know this?

56 MRS. P: And I don't see why he can't just see it through. . . .

57 THERAPIST: (interrupts) Now wait a minute, Sally (to Mr. P.) Did . . . did you get a sense from Sally that she liked the way you handled it with K.?

58 MR. P: (uncertainly) Oh . . . no! I didn't. You know I was telling the story and, you know, and it suddenly . . . (fades out).

59 MRS. P: (voice hardens) My point was that you were completely right with her, and, hell, if she wants to make trouble, fine . . . (inaudible) chances are she . . . you've got her so buffaloed now she'd never open her mouth.

60 MR. P: Now, this isn't true. And you see, this is why I think you are. . . .

61 MRS. P: Well . . . I, uh, don't know the situation.

62 MR. P: (loses fluency) Well, ya, ya know, I think you forget and . . . and, eh, eh, you know, eh, you set me to eh, thinking . . . an . . . an . . . and (voice goes into high register) frankly now, I'm . . . befuddled! I . . . eh . . . I am . . . quite frankly feeling my way and being very honest in saying I'm feeling my way in terms of really developing a knack and a technique and so forth in terms of running this plant. All right? Along comes a peculiar situation where she jumps me, you know, details fortunately not necessarily important,

144

which I had well documented in terms of her. Now, I had one of two choices it seems to me. Either, I make . . . I make my position clear with her, all right? And I drop it. That's one thing . . . and two days later, three days later, four days later, a week later, a month later . . . as has happened, and I'm conditioned by the situation I'm in—I'll hear something about this.

63 THERAPIST: (injects) From whom? From the bosses? Is that. . . .

64 MR. P: Ye-ye-yeh, from, ya know, from one of the three of them. At this point I've got to stop and . . . again re . . . you know, refresh my memory. Now this came up. I think it is going to develop into a sticky situation, because there's money involved and a production technique involved. Now, in my judgment, the job had to be done this way. She didn't see this and didn't expect this and I was dogged and claimed she had no knowledge of it. Now, you know, do I just let it sit and wait for her to move again?

65 THERAPIST: Well, does she have to have knowledge if in your best judgment the plant is running in the way you. . . .

66 MR. P: Well, this is. . . .

67 THERAPIST: . . . see it?

68 MR. P: . . . a very specific job that she is involved in.

69 THERAPIST: Oh.

70 MR. P: This is one of the special projects that overlaps.

71 THERAPIST: I see.

72 MR. P: You know, it's . . . it's a special project that she's in charge of but part of it overlaps into the plant.

73 THERAPIST: You didn't take her into your confidence? . . .

74 MR. P: (voices overlap) Oh yes! Yes . . . yes. Oh yes! Oh yes! Oh yes!

75 THERAPIST: Oh.

76 MR. P: And this is what she's saying I didn't.

77 THERAPIST: Oh-h.

78 MR. P: This is what she's saying I didn't.

79 THERAPIST: That you did not take her into your confidence?

80 MR. P: Yeh. That she was not aware of what I was doing. You know and. . . .

81 THERAPIST: She had no response to your plan when you took her into your confidence?

82 MR. P: She did. She approved it.

145

83	THERAPIST:	(surprised) She approved it—oh!
84	MR. P:	And I have notations on this.
85	THERAPIST:	Oh.
86	MR. P:	I keep a little diary in my desk.
87	THERAPIST:	Yeh. So that you were *very* well protected.
88	MR. P:	Yeh.
89	THERAPIST:	So . . . but Sally says that you then go to the partners, which you've been doing right along?
90	MR. P:	(high pitch) Right!
91	THERAPIST:	Yeah.
92	MR. P:	And said (speaks rapidly) "Look, this situation came up, I want you to be aware of it, here are the facts . . ." (Therapist: Hmm.) This is all.
93	THERAPIST:	Well, why do you do it so there would be no . . . uh. . . .
94	MR. P:	(voice squeezes into high register, almost shouting) Well, so . . . so that they're aware of it. . . .
95	THERAPIST:	. . . you know, beef later on?
96	MR. P:	(speaks rapidly, conveys agitation) If this comes up, they are aware of what the situation is. Now as T. said to me at the time I spoke to him, I said, you know, I said to him, "All right. Do you understand?" you know, this and he said, "Yes, I do," you know, "No problem." He said, "Now I want to see what her problem is." And she very well may have and I said to him, "I-I have a feeling I know what her problem is. That this job is budgeted for so much money. And we're over the budget!" And she's realizing this. But she's not dealing straight with me. And I know it! When . . . come to me and say this, and say "Now, what can we do?" She suddenly pounces on something!
97	THERAPIST:	Well, is it possible since you realize that this is what is the hang-up. . . .
98	MR. P:	(interrupts) I think! I-I don't know this factually, you know this is a surmise on my part.
99	THERAPIST:	Is this something you can not air directly with her?
100	MR. P:	I tried to (Therapist: Oh.) . . . but, you know, it didn't come out. (short silence)
101	THERAPIST:	'Cause there may be several elements in there that. . . . One that Sally put her finger on, is, you know . . . I can understand that you'd want to certainly protect yourself with these bosses so that they wouldn't blame you for either the over-

	budgeting or the overspending. Neither one of you knew that there'd be this much additional cost to the. . . .
102 MR. P:	Oh yes. I was well aware of the cost and I had. . . .
103 THERAPIST:	You knew it. (voices overlap)
104 MR. P:	. . . outlined in a conference with her.
105 THERAPIST:	And you didn't tell it back to her? That it would cost more?
106 MR. P:	Yeh.
107 THERAPIST:	But she didn't take it in?
108 MR. P:	Yeh-yes. You know, claims . . . disclaims all knowledge of this thing.
109 THERAPIST:	So she' passing the buck.
110 MR. P:	Yeh! It's exactly what she's doing. (silence)
111 THERAPIST:	Well, under these circumstances what choice does Jack have, Sally? You did have a position there before.
112 MRS. P:	(softly) Yeah I still have it. I can't argue (fades and becomes inaudible).
113 THERAPIST:	But you can!
114 MRS. P:	(defensively) It's not my situation and I can't decide how it's to be handled!
115 THERAPIST:	But you're feeling (Mrs. P. overlaps) is that he goes running too much to the partners.
116 MRS. P:	Right, this is not the first time it's happened, it's not as if this is the only instance . . . and . . . and. . . .
117 MR. P:	(interrupts in high register) I'm not saying this is the only instance Sally, but it seems to me, and you know, I may have a . . . a *real* . . . ya know, ya know, this is why I'm talking about it. Because, my feeling is that one of the most important contributions that I as a plant person—now not only in terms of production—this is one thing, but in terms of personnel . . . people's problems, what people are saying. What they are thinking. All kinds of people!
	Ya know. I am their ears, eyes, and nose—if you want to call it that. In order that they may, uh . . . in a position to make value judgments and judgments at the top. . . . (pause) Now . . . if I, if I don't do this for them, then no one will.
118 THERAPIST:	But you're making a point here. Are you saying that—(self-interruption) yeh, but how is that connected with your going to. . . .
119 MR. P:	We-ll (raises voice) as I say, I'm talking about all k . . . ,

147

ya know, to them about all kinds of problems. This happened to be one specific that we're talking about. I mean I have another little . . . little bit with her tonight over a —— job which is our biggest account. Now, her way of running the plant was that she would go into every single department, and she would take every single order that the department had (Therapist: Hm.) and say, "All right, you do this one first, this one second," and so forth like this.

I have no intentions of operating that way. And I have discussed this openly with S. and T. (partners). I am not about to walk into the —— Department and say, "All right, Johnnie, bring the orders and let's line them up." And this is what she'd do. I have said to them that I take my cue of what I need to look into from the people in our production office. They are the ones that know if . . . if their jobs, their specific jobs aren't moving. They are the ones that are setting the schedules. All right? With me so far? All right. Sit down! Very much unbeknownst to me, she calls me up at ten minutes to five, "Run up here!" I go flying upstairs. And here's a real panic on the —— job. That quite frankly got started well over a month ago, but there was a hold-up on it, and one thing and another. Finally, we got to it.

120	THERAPIST:	Do you get wind of hold-ups when they occur?
121	MR. P:	Yah.
122	THERAPIST:	They let you know?
123	MR. P:	Yeh.
124	THERAPIST:	And you are aware of it?
125	MR. P:	Yeh . . . there was a hold-up on the job. (Describes specific work tasks in his factory. Identifying information deleted. Finally word came through from one of the department heads)—and I don't know how strongly he said it—"I've got to have a sample of one of these —— 'morrow for her to show ——."
126	THERAPIST:	For her to what?
127	MR. P:	To show —— to the woman in the plant.
128	THERAPIST:	Uh-huh.
129	MR. P:	Now, Johnnie didn't do it . . . I was not made aware of this specific promise on this specific job.
130	THERAPIST:	Should they have?
131	MR. P:	Yes, —— should have alerted me. So when she calls me

up . . . you know (voice rises) she blasts me about the job! And I said, "Now just a minute!" I knew the job was in —— department. I knew there was a —— job in ——. But there was no date! I was not made aware by R., you know, R. is there.

132 THERAPIST: Is R. responsible to you or to . . . her?

133 MR. P: Why he's the production person; he's-he's the account person. Now anything that's going on in the plant, he-he's the customer contact. Right? He . . . anything going on in the plant, it comes to me. It's up to me to see that it gets out.

134 THERAPIST: Well, whom did he go to?

135 MR. P: He didn't.

136 THERAPIST: Oh.

137 MR. P: He spoke to the —— department supervisor and then dropped it. He forgot to say something. And I said to her very clearly, "I knew the job was in there. R. did not speak to me, so I did not know there was a promise on this." Well, she just went right up to the ceiling! "What do you mean. You can't run a place like this. You've got to go in there and you've got to tell them this, this . . ." I said, "Uh-oh, stand still." I said, "I am not about to do that, and I'm not gonna do that!" I said to her, "I think Johnnie is too competent a supervisor for me to be going in there and laying out his work and if he isn't, then we ought to get one." Well, this really upset her! Now sh-she, ya know, she's real upset about this—and stormed out!

138 THERAPIST: Is this why she has been doing the other things, though, because people are likely to have these snags? And not report to the? . . .

139 MR. P: Well . . . all . . . ya know, we're developing a whole new technique. . . . (voices overlap)

140 THERAPIST: And you are giving them—going through a process of. . . .

141 MR. P: (sounds agitated) Yah. That's right! And there are going to be these rough edges (Therapist: Uh-huh.) And I expect them—I wasn't upset (Therapist: Uh-huh) about this! You know—and also I want to make clear what my position is. (Therapist: Hm.) And, ya know, ya know . . . people are too long in the company going along holding supervisors' hands. If a person is . . . if we're paying a person a competent salary and he is competent—damn it, he-he-he, it is his respons-

. . . . If he's in trouble, he comes to me, and says to me, "I'm in trouble. I can't do this" or "What do I do about it?" But don't go along merrily on his way.

And this is what's been happening . . . that, someone's been holding their hands—not giving them an opportunity to make decisions. At the same time, you know, putting all kinds of bounds on them in terms of overtime and the whole bit! Which isn't necessary. So that Johnnie didn't do it. Now there's a big panic, and, you know (almost inaudible) she comes to me and the conversations I had with her. So she storms out very . . . you know, very upset! "Well, you've got to get it to —— tonight." (Therapist: Oh . . . the—) Yeah. . . . So I said, "Okay, I'll get it —— tonight." And . . . uh . . . now, again, saw T.—not making a point but saw him— and I said, "Look, ya know, I just want to double check myself on something—am I right on this?" And, he, uh, *yes*, he agreed!

142 THERAPIST: Jack, is there . . . to get back to a point . . . because so far, your plan for (rise-fall intonation) letting people grow into their responsibilities, and taking responsibility, sounds wonderful, you know. I don't know how you feel about this, Sally, but it really sounds like the way people can grow into responsibility in their jobs. And, you know, I would agree with you that there will . . . well . . . until they get accustomed to really carrying this there's likely to be slip-ups, yeh?

143 MR. P: Yeh.

144 THERAPIST: So you have a very different theory and philosophy about responsibility than K. does.

145 MR. P: Yeh.

146 THERAPIST: Okay. But it's also understandable that this position that you have now means a hell of a lot to you. (Mr. P: Yeah.) You have finally been given the regard and respect of your worth.

147 MR. P: Yeh.

148 THERAPIST: Now, is it possible that—and I think this is what Sally put her finger on . . . is, you know—it may not have applied in this instance at all. You know the one where you had felt you put K. in a trap and you went to T. But, is it possible that you want to make doubly sure. . . .

149 MR. P: (high pitch) Sure I do!

150 THERAPIST: . . . that they know. . . .

151 MR. P: Sure!

152 THERAPIST: . . . that part of this is an anxiety.

153 MR. P: Sure I do!

154 THERAPIST: (to Mrs. P.) But you're saying this is a weakness and you
                   can't stand it. (Mrs. P.: Yes. [hissed].)

155 MR. P: Y-ya know, eh, I've been doing this . . . (interrupts and loses
                   fluency) you know, I've been doing this for ten days now!

156 THERAPIST: (continues to address Mrs. P.) But to a point where you then
                   rule out all the strength that . . . (Mrs. P.: [interrupts] No!
                   I haven't . . .) he's showing . . . and that. . . .

157 MRS. P: (shouts defensively) I didn't say anything about that he had
                   been wrong in what he had done or anything else! (Thera-
                   pist: But. . . .) All I said was, "You know this business of
                   running all of the time and covering yourself!" 'Cause you
                   didn't go there to . . . to inform that man of the situation in
                   labor relations in the plant. You said you "Gotta get up there
                   before she gets up there and starts talking." Ya know?

158 THERAPIST: So, let's see. Suppose he does? Suppose he feels anxious about
                   this? And his new position is . . . you know . . . pretty
                   new. . . . (Mrs. P.: Oh?) Well, why does this, you know,
                   somehow irritate you? Is it because. . . .

159 MRS. P: (interrupts, hardly audible) It's just not my way of doing
                   things. That's all.

160 THERAPIST: Ya . . . but I think that's another. . . .

161 MRS. P: Okay. You know and it is his . . . so . . . okay, you know!

162 THERAPIST: No, Sally. Let's not drop it. No, it isn't okay. Because, to you,
                   it is another . . . when he does this, I think for the moment
                   what gets wiped out is the position of strength, but the weak-
                   ness . . . anytime Jack is weak you get discouraged. You get
                   alarmed. To you it's the weakness. Since you expected him to
                   be so completely strong.

163 MRS. P: (animatedly and defensively) You know, if you don't exag-
                   gerate it, it's a flaw, you know (Mr. P.: Ah . . . all right
                   . . .) a beautiful mirror . . . it's some little (laughs) crack
                   in it. I didn't. . . .

164 MR. P: No. . . .

165 THERAPIST: No, Sally.

166 MRS. P: . . . it's no big thing.

167 THERAPIST: No, Sally.

168 MRS. P: . . . it's just that I don't think it's the way to operate . . .

		But! I can be wrong in . . . in your case. Maybe you have to operate that way.
169	THERAPIST:	Maybe he doesn't, maybe he. . . .
170	MR. P:	(interrupts) I . . . you know, six months from now I probably won't do this.
171	MRS. P:	(sotto voice) I don't know, you've been doing it a long time.
172	MR. P:	(barely audible) What do you mean I've been doing it a long time?
173	MRS. P:	(low register) You've just . . . have done it ever since . . . there . . . there to get your altogether. . . .
174	MR. P:	Sure I have, Sally! (Mrs. P.: Okay.) Sure . . . I wouldn't deny this.
175	THERAPIST:	Sally, there's another element there though.
176	MR. P:	(doesn't give way) But you know . . . look . . . you know . . . a-a-an . . . just . . . let me just point this out . . . uh, you know, I . . . I . . . too much is made of this one way and too much another way, too. . . . Look, for the first time —I've been working for this firm for six years. And for the first time in six years, for the past two months, I am beginning to work closely with two principals who I really never knew.
177	THERAPIST:	And you've wanted to know.
178	MR. P:	Yeh . . . and wanted to work with. Now . . . it seems to me, that the only way, one of the ways—not the only way— one of the ways, to best get their ideas, and so forth, is to— whatever the situation is involved—throw it out! And let's hear it. I've thrown things out and I've been batted right back down. It's all right. But, until I know—because regardless of what I want to do—until I know what would there be, their reaction to this, what will be their reaction if I do this? What will happen if I do this? Until I am sure, what these reactions are going to be.
179	THERAPIST:	These are your guidelines.
180	MR. P:	Yeh! I've got to . . . it seems to me I've got to do this! You know, nine times out of ten, I'll say to T., "Oh, a little situation came up today. We needed some help in one of the departments. Supervisor has thrown his hands up, can't get help." And I'm saying, you know . . . (becomes inaudible) ". . . ridiculous, we're going to get help." And I decided what I'm going to do and I-I didn't *have* to do this.

181	THERAPIST:	You didn't have to do what, Jack?
182	MR. P:	I didn't have to call him and say, but I . . . I did. I called him and said, "T., I'm hav . . . I'm having this situation come up. . . ."
183	THERAPIST:	(interrupts) Then why did you then if you didn't have to?
184	MR. P:	Again! Looking for his guid . . . you know, "What is going to be his reaction . . . uh . . . of this?"
185	THERAPIST:	You mean, whether he would. . . .
186	MR. P:	Yah!
187	THERAPIST:	You kind of use him as a check . . .
188	MR. P:	Yeah!
189	THERAPIST:	. . . for your own thinking.
190	MR. P:	Right! Right!
191	THERAPIST:	You don't feel quite certain yet.
192	MR. P:	Ya! And I-I don't want to. You know . . . if, if, if they've got an objection to this, then I'll find another way of solving it. But I'm learning each day. . . . you know I go a step each day and each day I learn something else and, you know, this no longer becomes an issue unless it comes up. You know, specifically.
193	THERAPIST:	What do you mean, "Unless it no longer comes up?"
194	MR. P:	Well, I said unless it comes up specifically. Well it . . . it . . .
195	THERAPIST:	Well, you mean if it comes up specifically, it still is the issue.
196	MR. P:	No . . . I'm not saying its' an issue, but, I mean . . . "Why?" . . . But you know, once I am sure that this is a-a-a basic pattern and a way of handling the situation . . . you know, all right. Then I go . . . I'll go ahead and say, "All right, this is what I'm gonna do." And I won't, you know, I won't ask. I will mention it. I won't ask. I'll mention it for many reasons. I mean, you know, money is involved and so forth. I mean (light laugh) to help you specifically to understand what I'm talking about, we are now tied up with a temporary employment agency. So what we're trying to do—whenever we've got gaps, where at all possible, they supply the personnel. All right? Now . . . this is not like hiring a person on the payroll, because in that, that . . . you know that direct labor is being charged. But at the end of the week we're going to get agency bills for, you know, X amount of people. Nobody knows about it. Jack

Porter is running around hiring people all over the place and nobody knows about it. So I mention it. You know, that there . . . there is a reason.

And also, if he had, you know, if he had an objection to my doing this, and saying, "Well, I don't think we should work it this way because. . . ." In-w-w-in reality, when we hire people from Task Force, a temporary agency it costs us about 10 percent more. (Therapist: Hm-m.) And that's all—when you add in payroll taxes, unemployment insurance, social security, and all that business, you know, and yet this is a money factor.

197 MRS. P: Well maybe it just takes a long time, Jack, for you to know just how much authority you have (Mr. P.: Eh . . .) in certain areas, and your . . . you know, and it just seems to me from what you've told that they've given you a lot of leeway. . . .

198 MR. P: That's right.

199 MRS. P: . . . and both have given you this responsibility. . . . And for you to have to check with them every time you make a decision or every other time you come to some point of crisis is a damn nuisance to them . . . and this is not what you're being paid for.

200 THERAPIST: (interrupts) Now wait. You're more . . . why are you so worried about them? Are you worried that they'll eventually say, "Jack is not the man for it. . . ."

201 MRS. P: Right.

202 THERAPIST: ". . . because he comes running?" Why is this so bothersome to you?

203 MRS. P: Because he's . . . been waiting for this opportunity to have real authority and they've given it to him.

204 MR. P: But honey, you don't operate in a vacuum.

205 THERAPIST: Suppose they—let's go along with Sally for a minute. Because, you know . . . let's i-it may give us some clues. Suppose you're right that, you know, they're ready to give Jack all the confidence. But suppose Jack does feel as he says, anxious about it? And he is. That's one side of it. His anxiety, however, creates a problem for you. Because it isn't so much a matter of a difference of opinion, because people can have differences of opinion and survive it quite well. But his lack

154

of sufficient confidence in his own authority, that is Jack's, worries you.

206	MRS. P:	Yeah!
207	THERAPIST:	It makes you . . . it makes him in your eyes less the strong person whom you can lean on.
208	MRS. P:	Yeah!
209	THERAPIST:	Now this has come up.
210	MRS. P:	(defensively) All right.
211	THERAPIST:	But, but . . . let's see why he has to be so all. . . .
212	MRS. P:	(interrupts) To me it sounds very logical, which is good.
213	THERAPIST:	It may be logical but let's see why it really has to be all that logical for you. Why does his need for some guidelines at this point, while he is growing into the job, somehow it takes away from the. . . .
214	MR. P:	(tries to inject comment) And don't forget the. . . .
215	THERAPIST:	(continues) . . . confidence that you can feel in him for yourself.
216	MR. P:	(to wife) And you see there are two of us going into it. You see, and this is the other thing that I think yo . . . you perhaps lose sight of. T. is going into this because basically scheduling now is under his control.
217	THERAPIST:	(interrupts) But there's an element here. . . .
218	MR. P:	You know there's a whole big change around.
219	MRS. P:	I don't know . . . I just would like Jack to be perfect. I just want you to be bigger . . . (becomes incomprehensible due to overlap).
220	THERAPIST:	(urgently) Well let's see why, Sally, you see there are two problems. One that Jack may have (turns to Mr. P.). And unlike . . . a-a-nd, you know you do, you've had some anxiety about it. . . . Because this is yours. (voices overlap)
221	MR. P:	(exclaims in high pitch) Y-a-a, all right, sure, sure! There's no question; it's no question!
222	THERAPIST:	And maybe we can pay some attention to that, too. But why, you know, the . . . the fact that he needs to be perfect for you to feel safe with him?
223	MRS. P:	(icily) I-this isn't so. You're making this into a whole . . . whole big thing.
224	THERAPIST:	Well, this isn't the first time it's happened, Sally, that's why. There have been threads of this, you know, in so many dif-

		ferent respects. And I think this is one of the core of your worries.
225	MRS. P:	I don't see anything wrong with it as it is, you know. (Therapist: On the other. . . .) I wish Jack could take my advice. I really do. I think it's good advice, and that's all, you know. And I don't see why I can't be free to give him good advice. . . . Always being asked . . . always being put on the spot. (husband's and wife's voices in strident overlap—comments not clear—Mr. P. finds it hard to intrude)
226	THERAPIST:	Yes, there are, there are these both. Both of these.
227	MR. P:	Ya, ya know. I am not. . . .
228	THERAPIST:	(to Mrs. P.) But you want to slip away from the thing that worries you so. And it's as if, you know, you're going to be attacked or criticized by me. (sigh) Sally, you've got to be perfect, too?
229	MRS. P:	(joshingly) I *am* near perfect and I'm trying every day to be perfect. . . .
230	THERAPIST:	You must be awfully hard to live with.
231	MRS. P:	. . . this is my whole life.
232	THERAPIST:	(pseudo-seriously) You must be damn hard to live with.
233	MRS. P:	It is very hard.
234	THERAPIST:	To live with a damn near perfect person. Makes everybody else feel so imperfect. (voices overlap)
235	MRS. P:	(laughingly) No, it's worse for somebody who's trying to be perfect. Perfection, I am sure, is easy to live with.
236	THERAPIST:	Oh, is it? Boy!
237	MRS. P:	(spoofing) I'm in there trying all the time! (squeals) I just want Jack to be fine, too, you know. (overlap) Why can't he be?
238	THERAPIST:	Look how fine he is being these days . . . (inaudible) . . . look how fine he is!
239	MRS. P:	I know!! And I didn't take any of that away from him. I'm just delighted! But I see. . . . (voices overlap)
240	THERAPIST:	Sally! I'm concerned about *your* need at this moment!
241	MRS. P:	(good naturedly) So seldom can I give him advice you know? (Therapist: Aw . . .)
242	MR. P:	Come on!
243	MRS. P:	And when I do then it's a big mish-mash (laughs) about my own insecurity, and. . . .
244	MR. P:	(in high register) Well, no! . . . (voices overlap)

245	THERAPIST:	His insecurity shows. Your insecurity shows. His doesn't show any less than yours. Hi . . . ya know. . . .
246	MRS. P:	All right.
247	THERAPIST:	. . . we're all agreed that, you know, what he's doing in part, is, you know, is fitting into the new position he's in and part of it is a real anxiety about, you know, having a position of authority. Who ever let him be in authority before in his life? His father? His mother?
248	MRS. P:	(giggles) His wife.
249	THERAPIST:	His sisters . . . his . . . well . . . I don't know. His wife wants him to be . . . (laughs with Mrs. P.) whe . . . whether she lets him be is another matter. Maybe you do at times more than he's . . . other people have permitted. So that, you know, this is, this is Jack's. Why should we, you know, why should you have to, uh, live with a sense of *danger*.
250	MRS. P:	I don't know. I . . . and I don't know what to say about it . . . so it's there.
251	THERAPIST:	So let's see if we can put our heads together. . . . So it's there. Are you so ready to let Jack's drop because it's there? No! (laughs with Mrs. P.).
252	MRS. P:	(laughs resignedly) All right . . . so now what do we . . . what do you want me to say? (overlap) (Therapist: What do I want you to say?) I have nothing to say about it. I know that, you know, you're right.
253	THERAPIST:	(softly modulated) No, it isn't a question of my being right, Sally. It's a question of our trying to find out what this does to you and why some of his imperfections rock the boat so for you.
254	MRS. P:	(sighs deeply)
255	THERAPIST:	. . . because they, you know, they do.
256	MRS. P:	(barely audible) I don't know why.
257	MR. P:	Now, I-let me just ask you about this because this is the other little thing that came up today. And I'd just be interested in your reaction to this.

    For three days, Peggy Adams has been out sick, supposedly; accounting department supervisors. She came in today—she was in for, till about 12 o'clock. Next time I came upon the floor I looked around and said, "Where's Peggy?" I came up to talk to her specifically about something, and she'd gone home. Well, I started checking around and find out that a couple of people in the production office knew about it. Uh, I checked with K. to see if she'd gone directly to her. And she said she knew nothing about it. So then I, again, when I talked to T., this was all of fifteen minutes during the day when I saw him, first time during the day, I said, "Were you aware that she was going home?" And he said, "No." I said, "Well, you know," I said, "I'm a little *upset* with her walking out of here at 12 o'clock and not saying anything." And, you know, not saying, "I'm leaving and Mrs. Brigham is coming in to take over," and you know, "I've got things pretty well s-set up."

258 THERAPIST: Who is Mrs. Brigham, is she one of the more. . . .

259 MR. P: Oh, she's the department supervisor (Therapist: Oh.) and Mrs. Brigham is the night supervisor who normally comes in at 4:30 and stays till 10. But . . . now, I said to T., I said . . . I said, "My initial reaction is to speak to her tomorrow about it, but, on the other hand, I want to talk to you first before I speak to her. I said because, you know, I may really upset this woman if I go to her tomorrow and say. . . ." Now, this is one of the old-timers, you know, who everybody is tiptoeing around. Uh. . . .

260 THERAPIST: Why would you upset her? Were you very angry?

261 MR. P: Well . . . I-I, ya know . . . no. But I, you know, I certainly would say to her, "Look Peggy, if you're, you know, gonna leave, and you're not feeling well, I want to know about it, and, uh . . . I want to know" . . . you know . . . "exactly what the, you know, disposition of work is (Therapist: Uh-huh) and so forth, and how these things are going to get done. And not just sheer walking out of here!" And, you know, and as I said to T., I wouldn't have stopped her if she really said she was sick and didn't feel she could stay all day. I wouldn't attempt to. But, on the other hand, I certainly want to know about it.

262 THERAPIST: But, let's examine why you're telling this to T., among other things.

263 MR. P: Well, I'll tell you why.

What . . . what my real conscious thought is, and real conscious thought is: That this woman is one of the nastiest women and everybody knows it. (Therapist: Uh-huh.) And, you know, she's just apt to say, you know, and use a big four-letter word and walk right out. This has happened. (voices overlap)

264 THERAPIST: And you'd be blamed for her being out. (Mr. P.: That's right!) So really, in a sense, what some of the anxieties are is to be blamed.

265 MR. P.: Yeh, look! I'm dealing . . . I am dealing with. . . .

266 THERAPIST: (interrupts) Wait, Jack. Hear me out for a minute. I have . . . you've really helped me to have a good deal of appreciation for . . . the realities in that firm. You know?

267 MR. P.: Yeh.

268 THERAPIST: But I think there is an additional factor here of being blamed.

269 MR. P.: Oh yeh! 'Cause you know I'm blamed for Nancy K. leaving. You know, this is all over the place. And, you know, eh, you know I've been told. . . . (Therapist: But I wonder whether. . . .) This is K. you know, "So and so leaves . . . and then you will have that problem on your hands," and you know, I get this over and over and over again.

270 THERAPIST: Yea, well this goes on in business all the time; and I don't mean to imply by that that therefore you should take it lightly or that it, you know. . . .

271 MR. P.: (interrupts) Look . . . I . . . you know. . . .

272 THERAPIST: Wait, Jack.

273 MR. P.: Yeh, all right.

274 THERAPIST: Just as I pursue Sally and will continue to do so and get back to it, I think that the business of being blamed and your own feeling of it carries a good deal of feeling of self-blame for so much that has gone wrong in your life. It feeds into this reality. Doesn't it strike you as the . . . there is an enormous amount of anxiety about the *being* blamed? You know, you-you tell T. this . . . for this . . . good . . . you know . . . and all the reasons add up to having a good deal of logic in them . . . but there is an overarching need for him to know so that he won't blame you. And all I'm trying to get at is why the feeling of blame is so intense. Whether it does indeed flow from another reservoir, other than this (*company*), you know the —— Company, and everything that goes in there . . . that we might need to pay some attention to. This does not diminish in . . . by (Mr. P.: No. No) any iota, Sally's feeling of threat which she then passes on to you. . . .

275 MR. P:	(interrupts) All right . . . all right . . . but, all right. The second thing I just talked about . . . was a very distinct possibility in reality.
276 THERAPIST:	Yeh.
277 MR. P:	Now, my . . . do you want to know what my . . . my personal attitude is? (races) I wouldn't give a goddam if she walked out of there tomorrow. We'd be in one hell of a fix, but we'd be better off for it. (Therapist: [attempts to reply]) And I think everybody knows this. I mean, you know. . . .
278 THERAPIST:	So is the danger that this might come through in the way you talk to her? Is this what you're afraid of? (overlap)
279 MR. P:	Yeah . . . there . . . there's a possibility of this. This is something I've thought about (voices overlap) (Therapist: Because there's so many ways) . . . of saying this. This is right . . . (Therapist: So, in effect, you're trying to get it . . .) I'll have to couch this in very, very, you know, careful language when I talk to her. Uh . . . so . . . eh . . . I'm well aware of this.
280 THERAPIST:	So, in a way, going to T. is kind of putting a brake on yourself by having another . . . you know . . . another, another halfway step. Because if you went directly to her you might really let her have it. And maybe she deserves it, but this would not be the most diplomatic or practical way. At this point.
281 MR. P:	(overlap) Yeh. That's right.
282 THERAPIST:	Oh . . . so that's another aspect of your anxiety . . . in how far does . . . how destructive is your anger? And it gets kind of mixed up.
283 MR. P:	(starts to say something, laughs) I don't know. . . .
284 THERAPIST:	But what about this self-blame? Because there is that. There's a lot of reality but there is also this *additional* force which I think is also there pushing you. (silence)
285 MR. P:	(almost whispered) I don't know . . . I guess . . . (high pitched) I don't know! I mean what you say is probably true.
286 THERAPIST:	Why are you blaming yourself for so much, Jack? I mean, what is it that you have been blaming yourself for? I know you've talked here about you shouldn't have frittered your college away . . . what else . . . eh . . . you know? What about this or anything else? (silence)
287 MR. P:	(faltering) I don't . . . I don't know what the answer is.

288	THERAPIST:	(softly) Could we try to find out?
289	MR. P:	Sure . . . (voice descends to inaudible register).
290	THERAPIST:	'Cause life could be much simpler for you if you didn't have all that.
291	MR. P:	(sigh)
292	THERAPIST:	Or less pressure for you, let me put it that way.
293	MR. P:	(hesitantly) But . . . you know, I-I-I . . . What you say, may—you know—be very, very true . . . and uh . . . (lapses into silence).
294	THERAPIST:	But? . . .
295	MR. P:	But there are certain, you know, real realities (laughs with embarrassment) into it . . . (voice drifts off, becomes inaudible).
296	THERAPIST:	Yeh. Jack, I'm not under-you know . . . underestimating that. But all I'm saying is that, you know, it adds up to another. . . .
297	MR. P:	(interrupts) An-an-and, you know, I go back to something I said a little while ago. You know I've had five and a half years, almost six years, of conditioning of things one way . . . and you know . . . six months. . . .
298	THERAPIST:	Conditioning which way? Of being blamed?
299	MR. P:	You know, you know, ya know . . . working in a-a-a devious type of environment—you know, people . . . and so forth . . . and (laughs with embarrassment and shows uncertainty) the one thing that . . . and, you know, I . . . I . . . it comes back to what I said before, but the one thing . . . and it comes back I guess to something you said, ya . . . I don't want the blame! I want to . . . if-if-if-if my judgment on a particular situation isn't right, I am willing to take the chance of being said to be, uh, overcautious, or whatever . . . label you want to put on it, uh, than to take the chance of gettin' involved in a situation that is tenuous at this point in terms of work, tenuous in terms of retraining people, getting them turned around into a different way of thinking and all of this. And I-I would rather be cautious!
300	THERAPIST:	Yeah, you know, I'm not even. . . .
301	MR. P:	(voice is loud and strained) You know (Therapist: Look. Jack . . .), I would rather be cautious and I would rather be questioning than to, you know, to find myself with a real "magillah" on my hands.
302	THERAPIST:	Jack, I'm not concerned with the right and wrong in this. Be-

161

cause, you know, it can be right in some instances—or right for some people and wrong. . . . But, it is very clear that underneath it is the continuing theme, just like for Sally there is the continuing theme: if you are not altogether perfect somewhere, your imperfection—particularly in certain areas —make her feel quite unsafe. And I don't think it has all to do with you, you feed into this for her. So there are realities at your firm and you're gonna have to find your own way of doing it, but we can't . . . that is, I don't think it'd be a good idea to ignore this business of self-blame. We've all of us gotten to know that there's been a lot of self-blame, a lot of feeling of guilt (Mr. P.: Yeh, that's right) for having done . . . said the wrong thing, done the wrong thing. A feeling that you kind of missed your chance, missed the boat—and here is one wonderful opportunity—you don't want to throw it! You don't want to . . . anything to go really wrong! Because you really feel this has been the opportunity you've been *waiting* for. And I can understand—can you, Sally?— that he'd be even more anxious about this and more likely to go and get, you know, the guidelines . . . the approval. And it's very tough for him not to. . . . But our concern *here* at least . . . we can afford to at least look at it!

303 MR. P:	Yeh . . . no, I'm not saying. . . .
304 THERAPIST:	We're not under the pressure of your firm when we're here.
305 MR. P:	No . . . no . . . I would . . . I would agree with that . . . (sustained silence). . . . (laughing lightly) What are you grinning about?
306 MRS. P:	(utters inaudible comment of few words)
307 MR. P:	(with animation) That mean ya love me, baby?
308 MRS. P:	No—(laughs good-naturedly)—I love you but . . . (laughingly fades out).
309 THERAPIST:	Ya . . . but she does love you. (to Mrs. P.) Why did you smile at him?
310 MRS. P:	I don't know.
311 THERAPIST:	Let's stay with you.
312 MR. P:	Hu-h?
313 THERAPIST:	Does she worry you when she begins talking that way that she might not love you?
314 MR. P:	No.

315	THERAPIST:	No? When she is not. . . .
316	MR. P:	No.
317	THERAPIST:	I don't mean tonight, but when she . . . found. . . .
318	MR. P:	No—she just cuts me—you know, I feel so good about it! (laughs)
319	THERAPIST:	(sympathetically) Ah.
320	MR. P:	You know and then . . . (laughs and slaps hands) bing, you know, there's a knife across your back, you know. I don't mean that literally.
321	MRS. P:	You know, but I wasn't very nice when I said it 'cause I was. . . .
322	THERAPIST:	You do know that?
323	MRS. P:	Yeh. I mean it—yeah, it's just—I remember all these other times when I never said anything . . . you know . . . ah . . . you know. . . .
324	THERAPIST:	So finally you dared to say it, which is good. (Mr. P.: Yeah.) But on the other hand . . . what we're discovering is. . . . (voices overlap)
325	MRS. P:	Yeh . . . you know, the way I say it was, you know . . . (not clear).
326	THERAPIST:	. . . well I think the way you said it has something to do with your own anxiety and your anger, for his failing you.
327	MRS. P:	There . . . there are a lot of things that Jack does that, that I don't approve of, and, they're not because they're wrong . . . or jus', you know, because I don't . . . you know, I don't trust as much as he does sometimes, I don't trust people. And I don't . . . you know, I hedge a lot more . . . kind of, you know, playing my cards close to my chest or something. (Therapist: Hm-hm.) And he's much more open and much more vulnerable (Therapist: Hm-hm.) than I am. And. . . .
328	MR. P:	Yeh, but you see, I-i-it, you can say I'm working for an ideal. I guess I am 'cause I guess in a sense of reality very often I'm very idealistic. You take in terms of this work situation . . . so many things are opening up. So many different ideas in terms of that firm are being stressed. For instance, T. has a book on his desk. He has had it there for years. . . . I've known what it is. Never really seen it. And the other day . . . I don't know what we were talking about . . . but, you know, he said, "By the way, I want you to sit down and study this." It happens to be the sales figures. . . .

163

(Therapist: Of your firm?) Yeah. . . . Year by year, client by client, department by department. Now, I am, in terms of my dealing with people . . . and in my dealings, trying to give out the same kind of freedom of expression of thoughts and of ideas. . . .

329	THERAPIST:	As what?
330	MR. P:	As they are being with me.
331	THERAPIST:	As the bosses?

332 MR. P: Yeh. Right. In other words . . . you know, I'll go back to my conversation with H.—"You've got a gripe? Don't do like you've done for 26 years. . . ." Not that I'm going to change every department. I, you know . . . don't misunderstand me. I've got no ideas of . . . that. . . . Uh . . . but that . . . at least he is aware that I am aware of this hedging and this one thing and another in situations. You know, "You got something to say? Let's say it! You know we're all big boys, we're all grown people and there's no reason why we can't have a conversation or a disagreement about something . . . and still go on and get a job done." And there can't be a give and take. And there can't . . . (corrects self) There . . . and there *can* be a give and take! There should be a give and take.

333 THERAPIST: Maybe there can't always be it though.

334 MR. P: But maybe there can't always be but . . . eh. . . .

335 MRS. P: (interrupts) What happened with Charley Bradley? . . . you know.

336 MR. P: I don't look upon that as bad.

337 MRS. P: (barely audible comment) Yeah . . . you see it's just a different way of looking at it.

338 THERAPIST: Wait. . . .

339 MRS. P: Jack was . . . was—had a few drinks with them and they were very confidential, I guess (husband and wife overlap).

340 MR. P: No, not only . . . no. . . . See, you-u-u put, you put . . . you put . . . you put a—I had a couple of drinks with them. We talked about work. You know, I explained to them what my philosophy was and—and in terms of how I hope to run things, this is all . . . all right?

341 MRS. P: And the next . . . and the next day he didn't want you telling him what to do.

342 MR. P: No, two days later (voices overlap) or a week later—a week

later (Mrs. P. injects comment) . . . he blasts me about something—when I was trying to give him some information. And, I let him get it off his chest and I went (laughs softly) right back to him and . . . (inaudible).

343 THERAPIST: And what?

344 MR. P.: And told him! I said, "Look. You know, we can disagree," and I-I said, "But you know you don't go off half angry about something. Say it. . . . You know, fine . . . and we'll discuss it."

345 THERAPIST: So you say what your feeling is, you feel capable of saying to a guy, "Now look, what's it all about?" (Mr. P.: Yeah.) And Sally, what you're saying is that if you've left—this is what you said a few minutes ago, too, when you talked about keeping the cards close to your chest, is that: "You mustn't lay yourself open. You mustn't be too free with people." Because they're going to hurt you. And somewhere the hurt that you've had. . . .

346 MRS. P.: People usually use this, and I can't, like Jack, if this happens, I can't say, "Wait a minute," you know, "Do this." I can't respond like that.

347 THERAPIST: Well what is it for you? Do you get completely devastated?

348 MR. P.: (attempts to interrupt and overlaps with Mrs. P.) For instance, we . . . and we talked. . . .

(Mr. P. overlaps as Therapist and Mrs. P. try to respond to each other.)

349 THERAPIST: (responding to Mrs. P.) No, but we ought to find out.

350 MR. P.: (to wife) See, for instance, we talked about exactly this same thing in terms of your work situation.

351 MRS. P.: Yeh. Yeh.

352 MR. P.: An-an-and, the gals who really are under your control, as the personnel manual is written, and who will procrastinate and 'crastinate, and you won't go to 'em and say, "Now look! Stop it and let's get it done!"

353 MRS. P.: H-m. (agrees)

354 THERAPIST: Well, what is it that gets in your way, Sally, here about this?

355 MRS. P.: Well, I'm just not. . . .

356 MR. P.: (interrupts) As you said, you put it very eloquent the other night: you want everybody to like you.

357 MRS. P.: Yes—and I really find it hard to . . . ya know—I want to have a good relationship with everyone. And I do. This is one

165

of my values. But on the other hand when it comes to a point where I have to say, "Look—you're not doing what you're supposed to do," you know . . . uh, uh . . . I can't, uh . . . I can't do it.

358 THERAPIST: Well, you know you both have something of the same problem and it expresses itself in somewhat different ways. Jack, you know, you want people to approve of you and have confidence in you. Because one of your great pains in life has been just that. And I think it started way back—in being slapped down. And it got embroidered in ways which are not yet completely understandable. But you want them to approve of you. I think Sally, the not being liked, must have started it—the feeling of not being liked also had its origins. Whether it perhaps started . . . even before your mother died. This, I . . . you know, I don't know. But, it must have . . . it might very well have felt to you that if your father—as indeed he was not being so responsible—you know, he had money enough for real estate, he had money enough for other things, but he did not. He was not being so very. . . . He might have had other charming qualities, but he did not act responsibly toward you. As a little child . . . what does a little child do with this? "My father doesn't *like* me enough." "My mother doesn't *like* me enough!" "Something is *wrong* with me." And so you spend all of your efforts in not creating any friction, any dust to fly. And you know, it's understandable . . . whether . . . and you really in a sense live out the present as if you were way back there. And you really feel peop . . . you know, people are not going to behave any differently towards you now than people behaved diff—behaved toward you when you were little. This is your . . . you know . . . you're both in a similar boat! . . . And I think it's wonderful when you finally take a chance and say to. . . . "Jack, you know, I don't—I disagree with you." but there is so much wrapped up in it that it comes out in the fury of the past life, Sally, you know.

359 MRS. P: (agreeing, barely audible) Yeh, that's right . . . it's not just an objective kind of thing.

360 MR. P: Yes . . . for instance . . . I-I-I (fails to make statement).

361 THERAPIST: It's just a what?

362	MRS. P:	It's not just an objective kind of thing.
363	THERAPIST:	Of course not. Yah.
364	MRS. P:	(inaudible comment) It's something that I do. . . .
365	MR. P:	And, ya know, and, I mean, for instance, I have said . . . and I would still like to do this . . . I would like—I said to Sally—Tim Kraft happens to be single . . . a fellow thirty-five or so . . . and I said to Sally, "Gee. I'd like to have him out to dinner one night." I do basically like the man! Yeah . . . okay. And, uh, I said, you know, "Let me know when I can invite him out," and ya know, sh-she's 'crastinating. She won't tell me 'cause she doesn't think it's a good idea.
366	THERAPIST:	Why is she so afraid of anything going wrong?

(*tape ends*)

Treatment issues in session five

out his decisions with his superiors? To what extent does it represent good ego functioning? To what extent, if at all, is it pathologically based behavior?

205   What are the dynamics of Mrs. Porter's anxiety when her husband shows uncertainty in his work situation?

223   What is happening at this point to make Mrs. Porter defensive?

228–239   What underlies the bantering between the therapist and Mrs. Porter at this juncture in the session?

248   Does Mrs. Porter's giggling comment indicate that she comprehends how she has undermined her husband's self-confidence?

256   Did you get the impression that in the past few minutes, the whole atmosphere of the interview changed from tension, anger, and denial to one of softness, warmth, and good humor? What brought this about?

268–274   What is the validity of the therapist's interpretation that Mr. Porter is caught with a sense of feeling blame which is rooted in his past experience? What does his reaction to this interpretation indicate?

297   What "conditioning" is Mr. Porter referring to?

321   Does Mrs. Porter's remark indicate she has gained insight about her own behavior in regard to her husband's work anxiety?

326   Did you feel that Mrs. Porter needed reasurrance at this point?

347   The therapist has managed to turn the attention to Mrs. Porter again. Do you consider she was correct in doing this?

358   What is the therapist attempting to accomplish here?

General questions

1. What was the major theme of this session?

2. What was the affective message Mr. Porter was sending throughout?

3. How would you describe the effect this had on Mrs. Porter?

4. How do you assess the therapist's handling of Mr. Porter's

tendency to dominate discussion in this session? What is going on for him?

5. What are the dynamics of Mr. Porter's work anxiety? Do you feel the session has enabled him to gain additional insight into its source?

6. In what way does the content of this session resemble vocational guidance? In what way is it different?

7. Would you say that the communication between the spouses was functional, i.e., a) Did they communicate clearly and directly? b) Did they listen to each other's messages with openness? c) Was there empathy between them?

8. What has Mrs. Porter learned from this session about her way of dealing with her husband's work problems?

SESSION SIX

It's a long time coming

out into the open

THIS SESSION,* *the last to be presented, deals with a single theme that has been frequently alluded to in prior sessions, but has never fully been disclosed as openly as it has here. Painfully, and with great resistance, the theme of their sexual disharmony is explored with the Porters. From the beginning of their marriage, they have not been "making it" satisfactorily in bed. It is a condition that has poisoned their relationship and has been allowed to fester. Even this late in treatment, it requires of Mrs. Porter that she take courage in hand to raise the issue of their sexual failure. The therapist uses the occasion to help the Porters air their grievances, offer their explanations of the sources of difficulty and to expose their respective reluctances around lovemaking. While it is clear that each is sabotaging the other in their role relations while also being undermined by their own past histories in this area, an element of mystery and some confusion surround the way husband and wife allocate blame for this failure in their marriage. Mrs. Porter admits to serious inhibitions in their past sex life, but states she has changed and is now capable of full responsiveness if properly approached. But the picture remains mixed. Mr. Porter indicates he has given up on the idea of a happy sex life and is willing to settle for less. Yet he shows interest in sex from time to time, and there is evidence his interest is not as dormant as he avers. The session is highly dramatic and the poignant feelings expressed by the Porters makes visible the depth of their suffering in this realm.*

* Session of October 26, 1967.

(*Settling in sounds; moving things around, getting ashtrays, etc., followed by prolonged silence*)

1 MR. P: (almost whispered) So where do we begin? . . . (silence).

2 THERAPIST: (softly) Is there a place where you want to begin, Jack?

3 MR. P: (barely audible) No. I'm just sitting here . . . (silence).

4 THERAPIST: Wish I could understand, or we could understand, the meaning of your usual—not always—but predominantly usual way of, you know, kind of waiting to kind of get th . . . I don't know whether it's for (slight rise-fall intonation) Sally to set the tone, or kind of collect yourself so you know what way you're going. But, I don't know, are you aware, or is it only that I think that, you know, this is usually the . . . the pattern.

5 MR. P: (slightly laughing with embarrassment) Usually if I've got something to say I say it. If I don't, I have nothing particular to say. . . . So . . . no point in just sitting here and having an hour of silence on a tape.

6 THERAPIST: No. But I'm wondering, you know, what this means. If there's nothing to say, there's . . . you know, been a lot of feeling about yourself and Sally. Um . . . about your disappointments, about your angers, even about your good feelings, you know. You've sai . . . we've been talking. And I'm wondering what it means if you have nothing to say.

7 MR. P: (low register) It probably means that I don't connect from one week to another.

8 THERAPIST: Um-hm.

9 MR. P: I rea . . . really don't give very little thought to it, from one week to another . . . (fades out). (silence)

10 THERAPIST: Well, do you think it's part of your feeling that, you know, still some doubt about whether there's anything that treatment can offer that would be of great use that you don't con-

173

nect, or is this generally the way you . . . operate, you know, that you don't connect? 'Cause there used to be sometimes when you'd come and you'd say, "Now look, you know, what do you think you were up to when you did thus and so."

11 MR. P: Well, I . . . I, you know, just . . . I don't see any great problems at this point. I have nothing to talk about.

12 THERAPIST: Oh! . . . Oh, then I can understand, if there are no great problems but that leaves me very curious too, because when we reached a kind of crucial point some weeks ago, while you were ready to settle for what seemed to be one way of life, there was still a great part of a problem like a, you know, the iceberg, that was making you quite unhappy. Are you saying this is changed? That you and Sally . . .

13 MR. P: Uh, Sally hasn't seen this as any great problem. . . .

14 THERAPIST: Oh. Oh . . . (silence) You were awfully, mighty angry because the part of the problem that you now designate as no great problem was the thing that really bugged you when you let yourself really connect with how you felt, in that respect. Uh . . . Sally, you felt made you feel like dirt because she was dissatisfied with your drinking, she then humiliated you, she . . . you had to feel tha . . . ya had to ki . . . feel . . . it felt as if you had to go crawling and you were damned if you would do it. Um . . . you know, you had a lot of feeling about it!

15 MR. P: (softly) Probably still do . . . it's. . . .

16 THERAPIST: So what about this . . . pattern, you know, kind of letting it go . . . be the . . . intense feelings going underground and being left just with a kind of hollow feeling that this is okay. Do you feel like it's okay, Sally? . . . (silence, 17 seconds)

17 MRS. P: We're living rather pe . . . peacefully, let me put it that way. (speaks very softly) Not arguing very much.

18 THERAPIST: You mean a kind of real peace or a uh, kind of a pact not to let old feelings and angers get at you? Or . . . what sort of peace? On the face of it, it can be very good. I don't understand. . . . (silence, 10 seconds)

19 MRS. P: I don't know, sometimes it's good and sometimes it's not. . . . (very prolonged silence, 48 seconds)

20 THERAPIST: What's made for the peacefulness of this recent—I don't know whether you mean week or weeks? You have any idea? You feel peaceful, too, Jack?

21 MR. P:	(mumbles, hardly audible) No problems.
22 THERAPIST:	Hum?
23 MR. P:	I said I've got no problems. (He laughs and therapist joins in.)
24 THERAPIST:	A halcyon state! What are we here for then?
25 MR. P:	Hm? (rapid delivery) A question I've been raising for six weeks.

(deep sigh from one of the women)

26 THERAPIST: (with sudden vehemence) I'm puzzled. You know, I really am! 'Cause it's like, you know, —— (refers to self by name) is sitting here and she's really looking for trouble and you're saying, "There ain't none. What do you want from me?" And boy, that-that would be a terrible state of affairs, you know. I'd be very critical of myself. And why you should be party to this when I'm the only one who sees a problem here, I wouldn't know. And I had the-the notion, which apparently in your eyes was a mistaken one, that, uh, there's a *deep* deposit of the kind of problems which really makes for the upper-level problems and this peace can be disrupted because periodically you feel, uh, like a second-class citizen in Sally's eyes (speaks with rise-fall intonation) and Sally—you feel at times that—not at times, but a . . . a very predominant feeling is that you better not touch Jack because you don't know when he's going to slap you down or reject you and you each take turns feeling this, and how there can be no problems with all this going on underneath . . . um . . . with. . . .

27 MR. P: Well, I-I-yeh. . . .

28 THERAPIST: . . . with feelings at times that, uh, Sally doesn't really unders . . . appreciate what it has meant and means to be a Negro . . . with Sally feeling, at times, uh, that you can't appreciate, you know, uh, what some of the things mean to her. How there can be no problems, I don't know. (to Mr. P.) But I'm sorry you were going to say something.

29 MR. P: Uh. Well, you know, probably about all you say is true.

30 THERAPIST: (slight surprise) Oh.

31 MR. P: You know, in reality, uh . . . (slight laugh). . . . I think we are each aware of these things now. You know, but what are you going to come up with?

32 THERAPIST: I don't know whether . . . you mean, you know, that it exists. . . .

175

33 MR. P:		Yeah, but when you gonna. . . . (mumbles) . . .
34 THERAPIST:		. . . but what's it about?
35 MR. P:		Well, I don't know. I-I-I-you know, I-I guess the question I raise in my mind is it necessary to know what it's all about, once you're aware of it.
36 THERAPIST:		Yeah. But does it get better because you're aware of it?
37 MR. P:		I think it does.
38 THERAPIST:		Oh. Oh, then maybe I'm cockeyed.
39 MR. P:		I . . . maybe. . . .
40 THERAPIST:		Do you think it gets better Sally?
41 MRS. P:		(in breathy voice) I don't know. (short silence)
42 THERAPIST:		I'm puzzled by . . . you look very sad and you say you don't know and I don't know whether this is the stage where you're afraid to be the one again to upset the applecart.
43 MRS. P:		(conveys resignation) No, I just don't know.
44 THERAPIST:		What don't you know?
45 MRS. P:		We have such . . . a . . . a much better life than we ever had before so that anything we've got now really seems very minor. You know, things go along, we argue once or twice a week, which is great for us, and none of it is very bitter, or . . . or very explosive and the children don't hear us, and . . . and so that's a lot better. So there's been a big improvement in us.
46 THERAPIST:		Um.
47 MRS. P:		And so the other things just go . . . you know, you learn to live with them.
48 THERAPIST:		(short silence) I also hear a kind of a "but" . . . (long silence—Mrs. P. crying in background). So why are you crying if everything is so good?
49 MRS. P:		(expresses self with anger) I'm just not going to be the one to say what's what! . . .
50 THERAPIST:		Um-hm.
51 MRS. P:		. . . this time! (voice quivers with emotion) I am *not* gonna say anything . . . (sniffs).
52 MR. P:		(squeezes voice into high register) Well, honey, if you've got a gripe, say it!
53 MRS. P:		(loudly with vehemence) I don't have a gripe! You do! And I wish you'd say it!
54 MR. P:		I don't . . . (in high register) Now, wait a minute! Now you can't speak for me!

55 MRS. P: Well, you should have, let me put it that way. . . .

56 MR. P: (voices overlap in rapid exchange) Well, all right. . . .

57 MRS. P: You should have.

58 MR. P: Now, maybe I . . . you know, you know, maybe this is what you're rag . . . I-I don't have a gripe. Now . . . (fades out).

59 THERAPIST: (to Mrs. P.) What makes you think he does; by something he does or says?

60 MRS. P: (determinedly) I'm not going to say. You know, if he doesn't think it's a problem, and he thinks he can live with it, that's great.

61 THERAPIST: Can you with it? Live with it? I mean. . . .

62 MRS. P: I don't know. Sometimes it's all right and sometimes it's not, you know. That maybe I can manage it, I don't know.

63 THERAPIST: I . . . what I hear you saying is that you don't want to be the prod again. (to Mr. P.) That's what I hear her saying th . . . she is saying why don't you really get on the ball and open up a little bit about your dissatisfactions which she knows exists.

64 MR. P: Who said I had any dissatisfactions?

65 THERAPIST: Hm?

66 MR. P: Who said I had any dissatisfactions?

67 THERAPIST: Sally is. Sally is saying, if I understand her. Am I understanding you?

68 MRS. P: (nods) Hm.

69 THERAPIST: Yeah.

70 MR. P: She's also saying I should if I don't, isn't she?

71 MRS. P: Um-hm.

72 THERAPIST: She should if you don't what?

73 MR. P: She's saying I should . . . (voices overlap).

74 THERAPIST: You should have problems if you don't.

75 MR. P: Yeah.

76 THERAPIST: Well, I don't hear you asking her . . . what it's about. Are you not curious?

77 MR. P: Well, I think I know what she's talking about, I (laughs lightly) you know, I. . . .

78 THERAPIST: You do think you know what she's talking about?

79 MR. P: Yeh. . . .

80 THERAPIST: Oh.

81 MR. P: I don't (fire engine sounds from street overlap) see there's any great problem.

177

82	THERAPIST:	Can you share it with me at least? 'Cause I'm in the dark.
83	MR. P:	(in low register—with depressed effect) I don't know. One night last week, I guess (sighs) I don't . . . uh, when we were about to have intimate relationship and for some reason suddenly my wife—I repulsed her! I don't remember the circumstance—I don't think it's very important, or maybe it is. So now she's feeling all bad about this, and you know. . . .
84	THERAPIST:	(interrupts) She repul . . . repelled you? I mean she sent you off?
85	MR. P:	Yeah.
86	THERAPIST:	She repulsed you? How did you feel?
87	MR. P:	I rolled over and went to sleep.
88	THERAPIST:	You didn't care?
89	MR. P:	No, it didn't disturb me, let me put it to you that way.
90	THERAPIST:	Um-hm.
91	MR. P:	And, uh, I guess this is what she's referring to. (to Mrs. P.) Is this what you're referring to?
92	MRS. P:	(hollow voiced) Yeah. (silence, 10 seconds)
93	THERAPIST:	Well, I don't understand this . . . feeling of not being disturbed by it. Is it that you've had such good rel . . . sexual relations of late, so, you know, the fact that she wasn't ready one night didn't bother you? Or is it that. . . . (voices overlap)
94	MR. P:	Well, I. . . .
95	THERAPIST:	. . . you're feeling depressed and your feeling is, "Well, the hell with it!"? (Therapist overlaps with Mr. P.)
96	MR. P:	(unclear) . . . apparently I was disappointing her in some sense, I don't know . . . (fades out).
97	THERAPIST:	Disappointed by not being more. . . .
98	MR. P:	I don't know.
99	THERAPIST:	. . . alarmed or disturbed or angry or what?
100	MR. P:	No, or at the . . . you know, in our intimacy, uh, you know, and she got mad at me and I rolled over and went to sleep.
101	THERAPIST:	Oh, you mean she wouldn't tell you in what way. . . .
102	MR. P:	Yeh.
103	THERAPIST:	(animatedly) Well, weren't you kind of annoyed with her for not even letting ya know what's wrong?
104	MR. P:	Well, this has happened before eh . . . (fades out).
105	THERAPIST:	(challengingly) But doesn't that distress you? You've often said, "Say, why don't you tell me."

106	MR. P:	(in depressed tone) I figured she'd tell me someday.
107	THERAPIST:	(incredulous) Well, h-how can you make your peace with this?
108	MR. P:	(in high register) Well, you know, I don't see anything to get excited about. (pause)
109	THERAPIST:	You know, Jack, I have a sneaking suspicion, and I don't know whether I'm right or not, but that when you react, overtly at least, react in this way, somewhere it isn't really so all right, but a kind of—the feeling joins a deeper feeling of your not being . . . first-rate. Well, you've. . . . (voices overlap)
110	MR. P:	(high voice) Yeah, well. . . .
111	THERAPIST:	. . . reacted this way in other instances (voices of Therapist and Mr. P. in strident overlap) not in sexual, in other ways. How come it's (unclear) now?
112	MR. P:	(loses fluency and sounds agitated) Yeah . . . look . . . look, it's . . . it's, you know (nervous laugh) you can attach any meaning to it you want . . . uh-h, you know, but-bu-you know, my real feelings is that, all right, it was one of those things, an-and, you know, i-it doesn't always happen and it won't happen, you know. . . .
113	THERAPIST:	You were mighty furious with her in Martha's Vineyard when she wouldn't have you once, twice, and she kept pushing you away. How come it was different this time?
114	MR. P:	I don't know. . . . (silence)
115	THERAPIST:	(to Mrs. P.) Is Jack correct in assuming that there was something that he did that displeased you sexually in his approach to you?
116	MRS. P:	Yeah.
117	THERAPIST:	He was right?
118	MRS. P:	Yeah. He was angry and he said (voice almost tearful) he was sick and tired of being compared to other men.
119	THERAPIST:	Oh! He was angry!
120	MRS. P:	Of course he was angry.
121	THERAPIST:	(to Mr. P.) Oh! You're pretending as if . . . uh . . . you were not angry?
122	MR. P:	(tone is low and hissing; unclear) shows . . . I was angry . . . shows you how much. . . . (voices overlap)
123	THERAPIST:	Why didn't. . . .
124	MR. P:	(voice in angry whisper; unclear) shows you how much these things really mean to me!

179

125 THERAPIST: No. What it does—what it might show us is how you push it down so far. . . .

126 MR. P: (controlled anger and sarcasm) Okay, so I push it down (voice in hollow whisper) Mrs. ——, so what, uh, you know? Really (exasperated sigh).

127 THERAPIST: Jack! I feel as if I have an unwilling victim here; as (Mr. P. attempts to interrupt) if I'm victimizing you.

128 MR. P: (voice in high register, almost shouting) Ya! . . . You don't have an unwilling victim! (shows strain) I'm so sorry. I'm tired and everything else, but, you know, I really, I don't see the great significance of it, you know, it's not any . . . big . . . part out of my life (Therapist: Hm-m.) an-and, uh, you know (fades out and takes a deep breath). (silence, 24 seconds)

129 THERAPIST I could understand it if you say it, you know, it makes— there's a discomfort discussing sex but when you. . . .

130 MR. P: (interrupts) I, uh, you know, Sally's making more out of it than-than, uh. . . .

131 MRS. P: (controlled anger, ringing tones) Okay, then, if that's really how you feel it simplifies life tremendously, you know. I thought maybe you were dissatisfied and that you didn't miss certain things, but if that's the case . . . and you don't really give a damn one way or the other, that makes life very, very clear, and we are going to waste a lot of time here try- ing to do . . . *change that.* . . .

132 THERAPIST: Apparently you're not satisfied (voices overlapping).

133 MRS. P: . . . you really don't care. No! I'd like a whole lot more out of life (mixture of tearfulness and anger) but I'd like to know (unclear). If it's not to be with Jack, I'd like to know that and I can stop trying (voice suddenly becomes soft) and, and forget it. You know, but I'd like to know it. If it really doesn't matter that much—and maybe I'm just over—you know (tearful) assuming that you feel the way I do and if you don't, it's a big help to know it.

134 THERAPIST: It's quite a proclamation that Sally just made, Jack. Do you have any reaction to it? (pause, 8 seconds)

135 MR. P: (suppressed uncertain tone) No . . . I-I, you know, I don't know what she's looking for you know, so . . . eh . . . eh . . . I cannot (fades out).

136 THERAPIST: You don't know what she's looking for? Can you tell him, Jack, Sally? (silence, 24 seconds)

137 MRS. P: (tearful with controlled anger) I'm a relatively young person . . . and I would like a relatively regular, enjoyable sex life with you or (explosively angry) *anybody* else that I would like it. (tearful) And I would rather it be you . . . for many reasons. But if you're-you're not interested, okay, then I'll adjust to that. An' I'll stop breakin' my butt and worrying about it! (silence, 28 seconds)

138 THERAPIST: (to Mr. P.) You seem to be having some private reaction to it with that kind of smile. I don't know whether you're feeling—what it is that you're feeling at this point, Jack? (pause)

139 MR. P: (low register) I don't either . . . (fades out and becomes unclear).

140 THERAPIST: What . . . what was happening to you while Jack, Sally was was elaborating on this and spelling it out?

141 MR. P: Well this is the second time. . . . (voices overlap)

142 THERAPIST: 'Cause you had a kind of knowing. . . .

143 MR. P: . . . she's said (embarrassed laugh) something like this to me and I just don't understand it and rather not comment on it.

144 THERAPIST: Jack, but how can we really talk if you'd rather not comment, you know? (26 seconds of silence) Were you thinking that she means it or not, doesn't mean it? (delivery becomes rapid) When you said it's the second time. You don't know, you'd rather not comment? There must be some feeling. Can you say why you don't want to comment on it?

145 MR. P: (takes breath) Well, I just think my comment, probably . . . too harsh.

146 THERAPIST: (animatedly) So what?! She's saying some pretty harsh things! They may be or they may not be true, but they're-they're hardly, kin . . . you know, uh, gentle. She's feeling very strongly about it! So why should you be. . . .

147 MR. P: (interrupts in high register) No, I just . . . I just don't like the overtones of it. And the overtones are, you know, "Take it or," you know, some. . . .

148 THERAPIST: Or you "go someplace else?"

149 MR. P: Or, she'll go someplace else.

150 THERAPIST: Well, what about that?

151 MR. P: (barely audible) I don't know if that's what she's saying.

152 THERAPIST: But . . . what about it? How do you feel about that? There's one possibility. I don't know whether she will or she won't, but there's always that possibility. How do you feel about that?

181

153 MR. P: I think it would be very sad if she did it, it's just . . . (fades out).

154 THERAPIST: Yeah, but. . . . She's saying that you know, you know, you have no reaction to this. You're . . . you're angry but you won't talk about it. Uhm, what's the . . . there's no chance of really . . . the problem continues even though there are lulls, uh, and there isn't—if I understand Sally correctly—that there isn't much hope for it being better or different. Uhm. And what do you mean . . . she's . . . you feel sad if that's the implication?

155 MR. P: (high register but without anger) I do! I just feel sad . . . that's it . . . (becomes inaudible).

156 THERAPIST: Well, wait, wait, Jack. Are you sayng that you wish that she would accommodate herself to your lesser (moves into rise-fall intonation) *need* or your satisfaction with less *sex* or with—you know, I don't . . . I don't understand.

157 MR. P: (laughs in staccato fashion) I just think it would be sad. . . .

158 THERAPIST: Well, she apparent . . . Sally apparently also feels it would . . . she would prefer not to . . . not that it go that way. But you're saying, you know, it would be sad. (voices overlap) At the same time that you. . . .

159 MR. P: (tensely) Well, I-I just don't like the implication that, you know, in all of this. Okay.

160 THERAPIST: Well, does it feel like a *threat* to you?

161 MR. P: Yeah. Sure. . . .

162 THERAPIST: But you're not giving her much choice, since you. . . . There's something that holds you back from going into the problem. The problem there is, obviously. I don't know whether this is a problem that you'd feel more comfortable in discussing alone (Mr. P. makes several attempts to interrupt) because a man may feel that it's not. . . .

163 MR. P: Well. . . .

164 THERAPIST: (loses fluency) . . . man, you know (to Mrs. P.) this involves some, you know, his manhood is involved.

165 MR. P: Nothing like that. Just, uh (rapidly) think it would be a mistake, let's jus' put it that way.

166 THERAPIST: What would be a mistake? Which part are you referring to there? To go into it? Or for Sally to go to somebody—to pick up in a relationship with somebody else. Which are you talking about?

167 MR. P:	The. . . . (voice in somewhat high register) Yeah the threat, that's all. (unclear) Whatever she said.
168 THERAPIST:	But what about the actual existing trouble? I don't know whether you're saying to her, in a sense, "Sally, no matter what the trouble is I wish you would be satisfied with what we have." (picks up speed) Even you're not satisfied, because you do get angry, except you don't remember. But I don't know what you're really trying to communicate to Sally when you say that it would be sad if she did. What are you trying to tell her? Can you help us know this? (silence, 12 seconds)
169 MR. P:	(barely audible) No. Just leave it.
170 THERAPIST:	Why, Jack, why shall I leave it?
171 MR. P:	'Cause I think it would be better not to. . . .
172 THERAPIST:	Without talking about the problem can you at least help me understand why it's worse to examine. . . . (voices overlap)
173 MR. P:	(firmly in high register) Yeah! I-I-I-you want to know the truth? I wouldn't tolerate it!
174 THERAPIST:	You wouldn't tolerate her going?
175 MR. P:	Uh-m. She, you know, she-she-she (nervous laugh) decides to do something like that, you know . . . goodbye!
176 THERAPIST:	All right. So that . . . you both give yourself an *ultimatum.*
177 MR. P:	I'm not giving any ultimatums, you (voices in strident overlap). . . .
178 THERAPIST:	Yeah. *Both* of you!
179 MR. P:	. . . (unclear) . . . you've asked.
180 THERAPIST:	No. Yeah. Sure. But you both—Sally's given you one ultimatum and you also . . . (voices overlap)
181 MR. P:	I don't deal that way and I'm not, I'm not using it as any threat or anything else . . . I'm . . . (interrupted).
182 THERAPIST:	Do you experience that as an ultimatum, Sally?
183 MRS. P:	I know what he means, yeah.
184 THERAPIST:	What does he mean?
185 MRS. P:	He means that if I do, he-he just won't approve of it and he won't sit idly by, I guess. He'd throw me out or something, I don't know.
186 THERAPIST:	All right. So this is, you know . . . what . . . (interrupted).
187 MRS. P:	(unclear)
188 THERAPIST:	All right. But the question is why it has to reach—(to Mr. P.)

183

Sally says it doesn't have to reach that extremity (sound of pipe hitting ash tray?—sigh from Mr. P.).

189 MR. P: (suppressed anger) I don't think it does either, but I just . . . I just (tensely) don't like, you know, having to operate under a threat and this is what *this is.*

190 THERAPIST: Oh.

191 MRS. P: You don't want to talk about. . . .

192 MR. P: No! No, no.

193 MRS. P: . . . why things aren't ideal; or why they're not . . . (voices in strident overlap)

194 MR. P: Look, Sally, nobody knows better than I do that they're not ideal, but I can live with it.

195 MRS. P: Well, *I* don't want to live with it!

196 MR. P: Well, then, if you don't want to live with it, honey, that's . . . (unclear and interrupted).

197 THERAPIST: Why do you want to live with it, Jack? How come?

198 MR. P: You know, I'd like to begin to (light laugh) direct my energies in some other f-fashion, you know, try to make a success out of myself instead of having to always worry about this kind of crap.

199 THERAPIST: I want to tell you something, Jack. That, for as long as this continues, there is so much energy expended in keeping it in low key, in keeping your anger down, that there isn't as much energy free really for your being a success in other things. It doesn't work that way. And the question would be why— I mean, there's a special discomfort—and I can appreciate that—in getting to the problem involved.

200 MR. P: I . . . (high register, rapid, loss of fluency) you know, I really don't know what the problem is. So, uh, you know, *you* talk about the problem. My wife is the one who's got the problem! I don't have the problem!

201 THERAPIST: You don't have a sexual problem . . . (voices overlap).

202 MR. P: No! No.

203 THERAPIST: . . . with Sally? She rebuffs you.

204 MR. P: (in high register) Well, then, you know, obviously, you know, I don't please her. Okay?

205 THERAPIST: Well, why not? And, you-you don't mind not pleasing her?

206 MRS. P: (utters inaudible comment)

207 MR. P: Uh-h. . . . I'm saying about it, you know. I do the best I can.

208 THERAPIST: (softly modulated) Well then actually are you saying, Jack,

184

		that in talking about it, your feeling is that what would get revealed would be in what way you don't please her?
209	MR. P:	All right.
210	THERAPIST:	And you feel humiliated about that.
211	MR. P:	(in high register) No. No, I'm not saying that at all!
212	THERAPIST:	What are you saying then? You sa-you say there is a problem but you don't want to spend your energies on it. (voices overlap) You're saying. . . .
213	MR. P:	(in ringing tones) I'm saying . . . I'm saying that I am not the one with the problem!
214	THERAPIST:	(softly and thoughtfully) Oh . . . Maybe you're not. But your . . . discomfort about discussing. . . .
215	MR. P:	There's no discomfort. . . .
216	THERAPIST:	. . . it reveals some kind of a problem because you don't say to her, "Now look, Sally, what in hell are you displeased about? Where are my—what am I—what is it that I'm doing that, you know, that gets you so miffed or so pissed off," or you know, whatever. Uh, you're not saying *that.* You're saying, "Okay, I don't please you kid," quiet, "I don't care. I'll be angry for a minute. I'll turn over." You know—your compromise there is kind of peculiar. Why should you want to, you know, make it okay with her when she's the one who's rebuffing you? When she has the problem, so to speak, accord- to you? . . . (39 seconds of silence) You don't even know how sh'. . . you displease her . . . is what you're saying, too, Jack, no?
217	MR. P:	Mmm.
218	THERAPIST:	It seems to me that's a pretty impossible situation to be in. (to Mrs. P.) You never tell him, Sally? (pause)
219	MRS. P:	(softly) Yeah, I do, sometimes . . . (deep sigh). (26 seconds of silence)
220	THERAPIST:	Can you help us? Can you at least help me understand in what way he displeases . . . Jack displeases you? No? You're going to hold out too.
221	MRS. P:	(pause) You know, when we were first married, I was kind of, you know naïve and I didn't know much about . . . I hadn't slept with that many people. I just didn't know very much. And Jack just knew everything according to the way I felt.

185

222	THERAPIST:	Hm-m.
223	MRS. P:	And I used to read books, you know, so I would please him, and know what to do (tearful) and everything.
224	THERAPIST:	He would tell you he'd teach you?
225	MRS. P:	Yeah.
226	THERAPIST:	Hmm.
227	MRS. P:	And then we, you know, just had this awful time, you know? And now . . . I tell Jack that I don't want him to do certain things, and this would please me more. He couldn't care less (tearful). He-he's . . . isn't interested in-in finding out how it could be better or different. . . . It's as if it wou . . . it . . . I know all of the implications of not pleasing somebody. I know how it feels not to please somebody (crying). But it isn't so shameful to have to find out and to . . . (crying) and to admit maybe you're not perfect! And Jack just won't admit this. And maybe he can't and I . . . maybe I shouldn't expect him to.
228	THERAPIST:	(softly) Well, some men feel *very* touchy.
229	MRS. P:	I know.
230	THERAPIST:	And feel as if they . . . their whole manhood is at stake in finding out. . . .
231	MR. P:	(interrupts) Look, look . . . now. . . .
232	THERAPIST:	. . . something about this (voices overlap).
233	MR. P:	. . . look, wait.
234	THERAPIST:	Hmm-m?
235	MR. P:	(annoyed tone) Just a minute. Just a minute (muttered).
236	THERAPIST:	Okay.
237	MR. P:	(laughs ironically) You know, ever since we have been married, you have been responsive in terms of touch and certain things, for instance, around your breasts, and (becomes animated) I think this was what you were getting upset with me about the other night. I don't know what the hell I did wrong!
238	THERAPIST:	Can you tell him, Sally?
239	MRS. P:	He's just mechanical! Just . . . it's (moves into nursery rhyme tempo) bing, bing, same old thing, in we go and that's the end of it. Roll over and go to sleep.
240	THERAPIST:	Um.
241	MRS. P:	As if I could be anybody! I could just be Sally Nobody there; it wouldn't make any difference.

242	THERAPIST:	(softly) So you felt washed out and . . . unloved as a woman.
243	MRS. P:	It's just a function with Jack. It's not really very much fun for him . . . (fades out weepily).
244	THERAPIST:	(to Mr. P.) Does she characterize that accurately?
245	MR. P:	It's just a function? I didn't get the last. . . .
246	MRS. P:	(hollow monotone) Just every once in awhile you need it and that's it, and then forget about it. Put it away in the drawer.
247	THERAPIST:	What you're saying even the once in awhile is very mechanical.
248	MRS. P:	Yeah.
249	THERAPIST:	. . . as if you don't count . . . for him as a woman? Just to get a release, sexual discharge. (to Mr. P.) That's what she is saying.
250	MR. P:	(high voice) True.
251	THERAPIST:	It is true?
252	MR. P:	Sure.
253	THERAPIST:	Oh.
254	MR. P:	It's been true for twenty years, so what's the—what difference does it make?
255	THERAPIST:	You're not curious to know why that is?
256	MR. P:	Who, with me?
257	THERAPIST:	Yeah. Why. . . .
258	MR. P:	Not really.
259	THERAPIST:	How come?
260	MR. P:	I don't know. I'm just . . . just not that curious about it.
261	THERAPIST:	Somewhere . . . I can't force curiosity.
262	MR. P:	(pause) Ahh, you know, one time I was curious about it. I was curious about it with my wife.
263	THERAPIST:	Yeah-h.
264	MR. P:	I guess.
265	THERAPIST:	And?
266	MR. P:	She was non-re-receptive an-and so, you know forget about it.
267	THERAPIST:	Well, *wait*. Are you saying that once you've been disappointed, you can't really forgive?
268	MR. P:	No. It's not a matter of forgiving! I mean, you know. . . .
269	THERAPIST:	Well, were you this matter-of-fact about your relationship with other women? With Nancy K.?* I mean was it . . . or is it only with your wife, that "forget it?"

* Woman with whom Mr. Porter was emotionally involved during the period of separation from his wife.

187

270 MR. P: (barely audible) People are different.

271 THERAPIST: Well, who's different? Were *you* different with her? or was Nancy K., different? or, what's the difference, Jack? (pause)

272 MR. P: (slight embarrassed laugh) I guess in approach. I don't know what the difference is. Different people react different ways now.

273 THERAPIST: You mean you're no different with Sally than you are . . . had been before with Nancy K. or anybody else? It's just that your wife re-reacts differently? Is that what you're saying? I'm not clear what you're saying.

274 MR. P: Yeah. Yeah. That's what I'm saying.

275 THERAPIST: (surprised) Oh. But you've also said another thing. You've said that there was a time when you were different. And then . . . .

276 MR. P: No.

277 THERAPIST: . . . Sally was not receptive and then "forget it" and became mechanical is what you're saying. Your whole interest, your whole expectation, your whole approach then changed, is what you're saying.

278 MR. P: (high pitch with low volume) Yeah . . . Yeah. . . .

279 THERAPIST: (to Mrs. P.) Was Jack different at one time?

280 MRS. P: (in soft, almost depressed tone) Not very much. It's just that at one time he wanted certain things that I didn't like to do.

281 THERAPIST: What sort of things are you talking about?

282 MRS. P: The only thing I ever objected to was having his penis in my mouth. I just wouldn't let him come in my mouth. (tearful) Just couldn't.

283 THERAPIST: You couldn't do that.

284 MRS. P: And I (laughs nervously) can't now, and I, you know, I just never could.

285 THERAPIST: Was that your preferred way of having sex, Jack?

286 MR. P: (almost inaudible) No. . . . (slight laugh) Sexual fun. (pause)

287 MRS. P: (tearful) So that was the big thing. That made me just a "cold fish!" (sniffle) . . . And no interest in-in what might get me to do what you want, you know? None of that! Just get into bed and be ready to do whatever he wants to do!

288 THERAPIST: Oh, you mean (overlaps with Mrs. P.) in fact he could help you overcome your aversion.

289 MRS. P: No.

290 THERAPIST: You mean you might even be helped to overcome your aversion. . . .

291 MRS. P: Yeah.

292 THERAPIST: . . . is what you're saying?

293 MRS. P: There are a lot of things I've learned to do that I never, you know, in the beginning, I didn't know . . . I-I didn't feel *warm* enough to. It's different, you know, and I can do a (laughs) a lot of things now that I couldn't do then.

But Jack isn't even interested in waiting for that. If you don't pan out, that's it. And there's no question of his trying to-to . . . for ex . . . he never reads a book. He doesn't know anything about women; it's just supposed to be—I don't mean that broadly speaking, but none of the psychology at least. (loudly) And about *me* particularly! After all of these years, to know what I will respond to and what I won't. And even when I *tell* him it doesn't register! And it seems like I'm *demanding* something of him when I try and tell him.

294 THERAPIST: (to Mrs. P.) Is that what put you off to begin with?

295 MR. P: (mumbles very softly) Did what put me off?

296 THERAPIST: That she . . . would have none of this practice? . . . Of oral intercourse?

297 MR. P: I don't know. You know (voice of Therapist and Mr. P. and fire engine overlap). . . .

298 THERAPIST: Was that—was it the anger with . . . with her that kind of set you. . . .

299 MR. P: (suppressed tone, hardly audible) No-no. . . . It seems to me, you know, I'm probably all wet but uh . . . but uh . . . you know (light embarrassed laugh) when you get married, you tr . . . you experiment and you try to find, uh . . . what is each other's meunière, if you want to call it that, and, uh, other than, you know, normal intercourse, I-we-we-we never seemed to have found anything.

300 THERAPIST: Well is it that you gave up on Sally in feeling that you never could find anything? (voices overlap).

301 MR. P: Well, I-I-I had thought I had tried everything. You-you know, maybe I-I haven't, you know.

302 THERAPIST: But Sally is saying that you don't realize that she may have changed. And I'm asking is whether the initial, initially that whatever the problems were that you both had in sex in the early years, made you so angry that you only kept one image

189

in front of you. Be . . . Sally, being the old Sally. And Sally was saying, "For pity's sakes, I have—I'm capable of—of a difference now, but you won't, you know, you won't wait and you won't try and give me credit for wanting more with you." And I'm trying to find out what there was for you. 'Cause there must have been something which, um, tuned you out.

303 MR. P: (high register, low volume) No, I guess in a sense after many attempts at something then, you know . . . (interrupted).

304 THERAPIST: Recently? or The old days?

305 MR. P: No, old days.

306 THERAPIST: How come it's (unclear) you know, after all the—you made many attempts in the old days that failed in other than sexual communication between you, and you made another try. So there must be some-something here that we can understand that this was something you gave up in sex. (silence)

(307–322 in muted, low register)

307 MR. P: (voice very low, sounds depressed) At this point, I really . . . just really doesn't mean that much to me.

308 THERAPIST: What doesn't, sex as a whole?

309 MR. P: Sex.

310 THERAPIST: (softly) You speak like an old man; an old, tired man.

311 MR. P: I am that.

312 THERAPIST: You are?

313 MR. P: Mm.

314 THERAPIST: (mock sympathy) That's a shame . . . That's a damned shame! How old are you in actuality? Not your feeling, but in age.

315 MR. P: Forty-two.

316 THERAPIST: Oh.

317 MR. P: (to Mrs. P.) Forty-one?

318 MRS. P: (inaudible)

319 THERAPIST: What's contributing to this aging—quick aging?

320 MR. P: (low and inaudible) I'm not really up for it.

321 THERAPIST: Hm?

322 MR. P: I just don't, you know, have the drives or the needs that I used to have (deep sigh).

323 THERAPIST: You have, apparently have some needs but there must be something else involved in . . . your not pursuing them because from time to time, you know, you apparently want some sex. So there must be something else.

324	MR. P:	(suppressed tone) From time to time, I have some sex.
325	THERAPIST:	But the kind of, you know, just a . . . a release of some fa . . . some sexual tension and then you're through.
326	MR. P:	Yeh. (silence, 20 seconds)
327	THERAPIST:	I would hazard a suggestion, Jack, that there's more involved in this feeling so old, and, uh, not being interested, uh, that may tie in with the problem even in the, uh, days when you thought, you know, you had no problems. There's something here that's . . . at forty-one for you to be so finished. (17 seconds of silence) Are you so spent at the end of a day's work you have no energy left for anything?
328	MR. P:	(suppressed tone) You know that's always been true.
329	THERAPIST:	Yeah, but there seems to've been even . . . I don't know, you know, you haven't been talking much about work, so I don't know whether it's still an enormous struggle for you to keep going there.
330	MR. P:	I don't know. Just basically tired at the end of the day. (silence, 16 seconds)
331	THERAPIST:	I think there's been maybe an old, long-time chronic problem. Sally says that she used to have one. . . . For all I know she still has them. She may have hang-ups from before, too. But we can't even find out whether you, you know, yours . . . this is the continuation of an old problem or not. You're an old man, you're not particularly interested. . . . And just a couple of years ago, not too much younger, you were, you know, interested apparently. Not with Sally, but outside of the marriage. So what does that mean? (32 seconds of silence) Is this what made for trouble last week in sex?
332	MRS. P:	What?
333	THERAPIST:	That Jack wanted you to, uh, mouth his penis?
334	MRS. P:	No. No.
335	THERAPIST:	And you didn't want and he turned away?
336	MRS. P:	(hardly audible) No. Just his feeling that . . . (fades out).
337	THERAPIST:	Had you felt like having sex with M . . . with Sally that night, Jack?
338	MR. P:	Hm?
339	THERAPIST:	Had you felt like having sex with Sally that night?
340	MR. P:	(not clear) Sure (?)
341	THERAPIST:	Do you enjoy her body?
342	MR. P:	Hm?

191

343 THERAPIST: Do you enjoy her body?

344 MR. P: Um-hm? Yes.

345 THERAPIST: I don't know whether you're asking or saying yes.

346 MR. P: Yes. Yes.

347 THERAPIST: Do you enjoy Sa . . . Jack's body—touching him? Playing with him? Exciting him? (Mrs. P. makes gesture.) You don't?

348 MRS. P: (almost whispered) Not very much. He doesn't enjoy me either.

349 THERAPIST: Yeah. But wait a minute. Is it repulsive to you to. . . .

350 MRS. P: (high register) No.

351 THERAPIST: . . . do foreplay?

352 MRS. P: No. Then there isn't that much of it.

353 THERAPIST: Would you like to? I'm trying to see how your respective. . . .

354 MRS. P: Yeah. Yeah . . . (rest of utterance not audible).

355 THERAPIST: . . . voluptances, you know (voices overlap) kind of dovetail. Well do you try arousing him?

356 MRS. P: Yeah.

357 THERAPIST: You do? And he doesn't respond or he doesn't let you? He rebuffs you? What happens?

358 MRS. P: No! He just lays there and anything I want to do is fine, and Jack lays on his back and won't even (laughs tearfully) you know, come to me!

359 THERAPIST: Uh-m.

360 MRS. P: . . . you know, it's a matter of *my* going to *him* every, almost every single time! (laughter and tearfulness) He's too damned lazy to even move. That's how much he wants me.

361 THERAPIST: You call it laziness.

362 MRS. P: Well, whatever . . . indifference, laziness, arrogance, you can call it that. I don't know what it is. Whatever it is, he wants me to come to him.

363 THERAPIST: I don't know whether it's any of them or maybe it's a combination.

364 MRS. P: Well you find whatever word fits. . . .

365 THERAPIST: (interrupts) Well, wait. Let's see. Is that . . . (to Mr. P.) does it give you more pleasure when Sally is active? . . .

366 MR. P: (interrupts angrily) I don't know what she's talking about because, uh, you know (to Mrs. P.) I can't think of a time you've come to me recently.

367 MRS. P: Jack, practically *every* time.

192

368 MR. P: (mutters) Sally, I don't know what you're talking about.

369 MRS. P: Every time. Lay back on your back. . . . And maybe you're more comfortable that way. It may just be that. I don't know. I used to think—you used to do this a long time ago—and I used to think "Oh, he wants me to be more aggressive," which is great because I thought—that's what I get from reading the books and so I'm (laughs lightly) more aggressive, but I'll be goddamned if I'm going to just be the *aggressive* one and force this thing on you!

370 THERAPIST: Could it be that he actually enjoys not being assertive himself? (to Mr. P.) Could be that you enjoy her playing with you . . . and. . . .

371 MR. P: That's not what she's talking about.

372 THERAPIST: Oh!

373 MR. P: It really isn't. (10 seconds of silence) It's. . . .

374 MRS. P: What am I talking about? . . .

375 (someone sighs)

376 MR. P: Honey . . . (fades out).

377 THERAPIST: (softly) Honey what? Why do you give up? Unless it's embarrassing and you'd rather not talk about it.

378 MR. P: No. I . . . eh . . . I-I really, you know, you all are losing me . . . I don't understand what you're saying 'cause, uh (sighs) I don't know what you mean by your coming to me or my coming to you, and I don't understand that, okay?

379 THERAPIST: Well ask her to explain it some more.

380 MR. P: (mumbles unclearly) . . . If you're talking about my getting in bed and layin' there and (sighs) as very often will happen, we'll start playing with toes and things like that and then finally I will move over towards you. Is this what you're talking about?

381 MRS. P: (softly) Yeah.

382 MR. P: Now what would you have me do? . . . (laughs) I'm serious. What would you have me? . . .

383 MRS. P: (interrupts angrily) You could get up and look at me at least.

384 MR. P: In a dark room?

385 MRS. P: Yeah.

386 MR. P: (expels air)

387 THERAPIST: Are you saying, Jack, that you don't feel when Sally is playing toesy with you, that this is an overture?

193

388 MR. P: (voice goes into high register) Sure I feel it's an overture. All right.

389 MRS. P: And it's a sign for me to get up and come over.

390 MR. P: (squeezes voice) I-I-h-h—It's not a sign for anything!

391 MRS. P: (very controlled) Well, that's the way it always turns out, Jack —or nine times out of ten. (voices overlap)

392 MR. P: (very high voice) Sally, I don't understand that! Ho-How can it be when we're both doing it?

393 MRS. P: Somebody's got to be on top and it's usually always me.

394 MR. P: (shouts) You mean that I will reach over and pull you towards me?

395 MRS. P: That's right.

396 MR. P: (shouts) And this you object to?

397 MRS. P: Yes. I do.

398 THERAPIST: You object to Jack's. . . .

399 MR. P: (interrupts) All right, okay (very fast speech).

400 THERAPIST: . . . pulling you over? Wait a minute. Wait. Pulling you over. . . .

401 MRS. P: He pulls me over on top of *him* as if *I* am supposed to do the loving, which is (exaggerated intonation) great sometimes. . . .

402 MR. P: No, I'm-no. . . .

403 MRS. P: . . . 'cause I know it's a reciprocal thing but not all the time!

404 MR. P: 'Cause I'm holding you in my arms, I'm holding you. . . .

405 MRS. P: Yeh.

406 MR. P: . . . and I'm kissing you.

407 MRS. P: (softly) Yeah.

408 THERAPIST: Is he?

409 MRS. P: (softly) Yeah.

410 THERAPIST: But your feeling is that because you're on top that he doesn't care?

411 MRS. P: And then he's ready for intercourse and tha-that is it!

412 THERAPIST: Well maybe he comes very fast. . . .

413 MRS. P: Yeah.

414 THERAPIST: Do you come very fast, Jack? Hm?

415 MR. P: Yeah. Hmp, 90-second wonder (slight laugh).

416 THERAPIST: Well, wait. Has this been a problem? (voices overlap) That you come so fast?

417 MRS. P: No, he doesn't come exceptionally fast.

418 MR. P: (very low and unclear)

419	THERAPIST:	You . . . (interrupted).
420	MRS. P:	He just doesn't spend much time on me and *my* gratification, which is what I'm looking for at this point, too. (to Mr. P.) I'm not (slight laugh) really there just to please you. (voices overlap) I know it is a (unclear—possibility?). . . .
421	MR. P:	(stammers) Yo-you-you think this is a . . . you think that's some particular pleasure. . . . Is this what you denote out of that? That is some particular pleasure?
422	MRS. P:	Yeah.
423	MR. P:	(unclear and very low) Oh, forget it!
424	THERAPIST:	Oh, Jack, you're (voices overlap) so quick. . . .
425	MR. P:	(loudly) I don't mean forget it, but it, you know, it-it-you know, it means nothing to me. (half laugh—exclamation) It does nothing for me!
426	THERAPIST:	What does nothing for you? That she's on top of you?
427	MR. P:	(high voice) Yeh! Well, you know (becomes incoherent) I-I-I-I-I-I-I-you-you. . . .
428	MRS. P:	Well I don't know what *does* give you pleasure then. I really don't.
429	THERAPIST:	Can you tell her?
430	MR. P:	(mumbles inaudibly) . . . I-I don't know. You know, but that's a long story.
431	THERAPIST:	Well, so what? We've got *this* time and *next* time. . . .
432	MR. P:	Yeah. . . .
433	THERAPIST:	. . . and if it's a *long* story, it's a *long time* getting out into the open. And maybe that's the only, you know, so . . . up to you. You have the choice, but it's the only way I know.
434	MR. P:	(interrupts in low rapid speech) I just don't-I just don't, you know, I don't understand what she's saying. I don't understand what kicks she thinks I get out of that.
435	MRS. P:	Well, Jack, the thing is that what I-I thought all this time I'm doing something that you want to do and I'm *waiting* for you to do something, I would like to do. . . . (voices overlap)
436	MR. P:	If I'm going to. . . .
437	MRS. P:	. . . if I specifically tell you to do something which does take some of the romance out of it—you've gotta admit that. If I specifically say, "Jack, will you please do this"—and you'll do it, dutifully and the-then you'll stop and the . . . if . . . if there's no curiosity about me!
438	THERAPIST:	What is your pleasure?

195

439 MRS. P: (animatedly) I love for him to touch me just all over, and I just love. . . . .

440 THERAPIST: (interrupts) Vaginally as well? . . . Or?

441 MRS. P: . . . to be held and touched. Yes. Yes.

442 THERAPIST: Um-hm.

443 MR. P: And I don't do this?

444 MRS. P: No. Not very much. You don't.

445 THERAPIST: Wait. You know you're throwing up your hands Jack. . . .

446 MR. P: (agitatedly) I-I-I just don't understand 'cause this is what I do all the time.

447 MRS. P: Or at least not enough. If you do it not enough to get me—I think . . . Oh! Why do I . . . do I have to say all these things?

448 THERAPIST: Because they're so.

449 MRS. P: All right! I say to you, you know, "Please do such and such," and—I'd give you anything, Jack . . . an-anything, I'd do anything that you want and you just stop short all the time and there I *lay* (tearfully). (silence, 16 seconds)

450 THERAPIST: So, you apparently experience this very differently, both of you. You're not aware—to . . . you know, this seems kind of strange to you, doesn't it?

451 MR. P: (in high register) No! No! No, you know, I'm sorry, I don't understand.

452 THERAPIST: You don't understand how she can feel this way? You don't understand that this is how you behave?

453 MR. P: What she is saying is true.

454 THERAPIST: You mean you get a lot of pleasure out of touching her and stimulating her?

455 MR. P: (high voice) I enjoy touching her and stimulating her. Sure.

456 THERAPIST: And yet she has the feeling that you don't. How. . . . Maybe her, you know, maybe it's something in her perception of you. So let's . . . (interrupted).

457 MR. P: You know I can't even kiss my wife half the time. Half the time she won't kiss me. . . .

458 THERAPIST: Oh. So you're wondering what it is that she just wants from you.

459 MR. P: Ye . . . eh.

460 THERAPIST: . . . well, I suggest that we (sighs) try to find out more about this next week, but it's going to be *rough going*. If . . . all I can promise, you know, suggest is that it may be less rough

196

going eventually. But it's the only way we can ever get at it in finding out what she wants, and Sally finding out what you want. And getting to some of the hang-ups underneath. 'Cause if your marriage—I don't think your marriage really stands a chance or the peace doesn't stand a chance to remain at peace. . . . So I'll see you folks next week.

461 MRS. P: Okay.

(sound of couple departing)

Treatment issues in session six

1-6   What does the prolonged silence at the beginning of the session signify? How would you assess the therapist's manner of dealing with this?

7   What meaning would you attach to Mr. Porter's statement that he does not connect from one week to another?

14   What is the therapist attempting to do here?

19   This is a long silence. Should the therapist have broken it sooner?

26   If the therapist were to criticize herself for this utterance, what might she identify?

47   What do you make of Mrs. Porter's reference to "other things"?

48-60   Did the couple come to this session caught up with a specific problem or is it a matter of chance that an issue is presented for consideration?

63-76   The therapist confronts Mr. Porter with the fact that his wife knows he is dissatisfied about something, as yet unspecified, in their marriage. Does it appear that Mr. Porter would prefer she drop the subject? If yes, what is your attitude about the therapist's persistence?

82   Would you say that in the last few minutes the focus was on the couple's communication with one another? Do you remember this as a frequently used technique in the interviews you have heard?

83   Was the recent unhappy sexual encounter disturbing the couple when they came for this session?

109   Mr. Porter is given the interpretation that he experiences

his wife's rebuff by feeling he is not first-rate. How do you think he experiences this interpretation? As a threat? As a reflection of support and concern for him?

112   How do you account for Mr. Porter's loss of fluency?

125   What do you think was the reason why Mr. Porter became so angry at this point?

133   How do you understand the message Mrs. Porter is sending? Is there a metamessage?

137   Is Mrs. Porter the partner who is pushing for a happier sex life?

168   What is the therapist attempting here?

200–213   How should the therapist respond to Mr. Porter's argument that his wife has the sexual problem, not he? Is the therapist tuned in to Mr. Porter?

220   Why does the therapist turn to Mrs. Porter at this point? What does her tone of voice convey?

223   How would you assess Mrs. Porter's report of her effort to learn about sex through reading books?

227   What are the implications of Mrs. Porter's tearful assertion that she knows what it feels like not to please somebody?

230   Would you say that the therapist's response here is supportive? To Mrs. Porter? To Mr. Porter?

235   Does Mr. Porter sound annoyed to you?

261   How would you interpret the therapist's statement: "I can't force curiosity"?

266   What impact did the nonreceptivity of Mrs. Porter early in the marriage seem to have upon her husband?

287   What is the source of Mrs. Porter's reluctance to comply with her husband's desires?

293   Does Mrs. Porter's comment indicate she has grown in her capacity to experience sex on a more adult level?

296   Is the therapist's reference to fellatio affectively neutral?

306   How do you understand the discrepancy, referred to by the therapist, that Mr. Porter has tried to improve his marital relationship in general, but not his sexual relations?

330   What is your impression of Mr. Porter's assessment of his reason for his sexual behavior? What does his "feeling old" signify?

355   What might be the therapist's intention when she explores both spouses' feelings about sexual foreplay?

358–360   What is the psychodynamic meaning of Mr. Porter's preferring to "just lay there" when a sexual encounter takes place? Why is this so irritating to his wife?

427   How would you describe the vocalization you just heard? What did it tell you?

457   What is the significance of Mr. Porter's comment that he can't kiss his wife half of the time?

460   What "hang-ups underneath" is the therapist referring to?

General questions

1. Was the therapist on sound ground when she persisted in staying with the sexual problem despite heavy resistance from Mr. Porter?

2. How would you describe the sexual difficulties the couple is reporting?

a) From the *interactional* point of view: Is their behavior complementary or symmetrical? Is it a "one-upmanship" on the part of one partner? Do the spouses communicate their dislikes and likes of each other's sexual behavior only when angry and frustrated? Why is their communication so dysfunctional?

b) From *Mrs. Porter's* point of view: How do you assess Mrs. Porter's revulsion to fellatio? What about her wish to be "touched all over"? Do you think she is frigid? Does her sexual behavior reflect other psychopathology, revealed in earlier interviews?

c) From *Mr. Porter's* point of view: What is your impression of his reluctance to discuss sex and his discomfort when pushed to do so? Does it seem reasonable to you that his wife's rejection of his sexual approaches has made him lose his "sexual curiosity"? or the pleasure in foreplay? What is your thinking about his sexuality? Would you make any link with his psychopathology?

d) What might be some of the historical antecedents for the dysfunctional behavior of each partner?

3. How is each spouse contributing to the sexual disharmony?

4. What impression did you get of the therapist's attitude toward sex and different sexual practices? Did she seem

uncomfortable or embarrassed? Did she pursue the subject unnecessarily?

5. Would you say that such open discussion regarding sexual behavior appears frequently in clinical interviews? Do you believe that most clinicians can deal comfortably with this matter? Do you think they are knowledgeable about sexual dysfunctioning? Have any of the lectures you have been exposed to in your training dealt with sexual problems and their treatment? Do any of your reading lists include references to this topic?

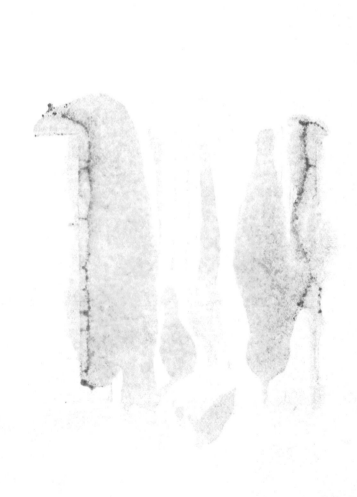

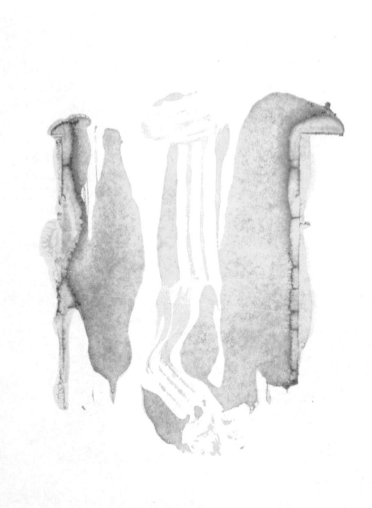